The Communist Party of Western Ukraine
1919–1929

THE COMMUNIST PARTY OF WESTERN UKRAINE 1919–1929

by

Janusz Radziejowski

Translated by Alan Rutkowski

Canadian Institute of Ukrainian Studies
University of Alberta
Edmonton 1983

Canadian Cataloguing in Publication Data
Radziejowski, Janusz, 1925–
The Communist Party of Western Ukraine, 1919–1929

(The Canadian library in Ukrainian studies)
Translation of: Komunistyczna Partia Zachodniej Ukrainy, 1919–1929.
Includes index.
Bibliography: p.
ISBN 0-920862-25-X (bound).
ISBN 0-920862-24-1 (pbk.)

1. Komunistychna partiia Zakhidnoï Ukraïny—History.
I. Canadian Institute of Ukrainian Studies. II. Title. III. Series.
JN6769.A562R313 324.243802 C83–091109–X

Cover design: Keith Kobylka

Printed in Canada by D. W. Friesen & Sons Ltd.
Distributed by the University of Toronto Press
5201 Dufferin St.
Downsview, Ontario
Canada M3H 5T8

Dedication page

Contents

List of Abbreviations

AAN	Archiwum Akt Nowych (Central Archives of Modern Records), Warsaw
CA KC PZPR	Centralne Archiwum KC PZPR (Central Archives of the CC PUWP), Warsaw
CC	Central Committee
ECCI	Executive Committee of the Communist International
CP(B)U	Communist Party (Bolsheviks) of Ukraine (Komunistychna partiia [bilshovykiv] Ukrainy, KPbU)
CPEG	Communist Party of Eastern Galicia (Komunistychna partiia Skhidnoi Halychyny, KPSH)
CPG	Communist Party of Germany (Kommunistische Partei Deutschlands, KPD)
CPP	Communist Party of Poland (Komunistyczna Partia Polski, KPP)
CPSU	Communist Party of the Soviet Union (Kommunisticheskaia partiia Sovetskogo Soiuza, KPSS)
CPU	Communist Party of Ukraine (Komunistychna partiia Ukrainy, KPU)
CPWB	Communist Party of Western Belorussia (Kamunistychnaia partyia Zakhodniai Belarusi, KPZB)
CPWU	Communist Party of Western Ukraine (Komunistychna partiia Zakhidnoi Ukrainy, KPZU)
CWPP	Communist Workers' Party of Poland (Komunistyczna Partia Robotnicza Polski, KPRP)
FCP	French Communist Party (Party Communiste Français, PCF)

IRSD	International Revolutionary Social Democracy (Internatsionalna revoliutsiina sotsiialdemokratiia, IRSD)
NBCG	Non-Party Bloc for Co-operation with the Government (Bezpartyjny Blok Współpracy z Rządem, BBWR)
OUN	Organization of Ukrainian Nationalists (Orhanizatsiia ukrainskykh natsionalistiv, OUN)
PA IIP TsK KPU	Partarkhiv Instytutu istorii partii TsK KPU (Party Archives of the Institute of the History of the Party [attached to the Kiev] CC CPU), Kiev
PPP	Polish Peasant Party (Polskie Stronnictwo Ludowe—PSL)
PSP	Polish Socialist Party (Polska Partia Sosjalistyczna, PPS)
PUWP	Polish United Workers' Party (Polska Zjednoczona Partia Robotnicza, PZPR)
PWP	People's Will Party (Partiia Voli naroda, PVN)
RCP(B)	Russian Communist Party (Bolsheviks) (Rossiiskaia kommunisticheskaia parti [bolshevikov], RKPb)
SDKPL	Social Democracy of the Kingdom of Poland and Lithuania (Socjaldemokracja Królestwa Polskiego i Litwy, SDKPiL)
SR	Socialist Revolutionary
UCP	Ukrainian Communist Party (Ukrainska komunistychna partiia, UKP)
UCP(B)	Ukrainian Communist Party (Borotbists) (Ukrainska komunistychna partiia [borotbistiv], UKPb)
UCY WU	Union of Communist Youth of Western Ukraine (Związek Młodzieży Komunistycznej Ukrainy Zachodniej, ZMK UZ)
ULP	Ukrainian Labour Party (Ukrainska Partiia Pratsi, UPP)
UMO	Ukrainian Military Organization (Ukrainska viiskova orhanizatsiia, UVO)
UNDU	Ukrainian National Democratic Union (Ukrainske narodno-demokratychne obiednannia, UNDO)
UNLP	Ukrainian National Labour Party (Ukrainska narodno-trudova partiia, UNTP)
UPCC	Union of the Proletariat of City and Countryside

	(Związek Proletariatu Miast i Wsi, ZPMiW)
URP	Ukrainian Radical Party (Ukrainska radykalna partiia, URP)
USDP	Ukrainian Social Democratic Party (Ukrainska sotsiialdemokratychna partiia, USDP)
USRP	Ukrainian Socialist Radical Party (Ukrainska sotsiialistychna radykalna partiia, USRP)
WAP im. F. Dzierzynskiego	Wojskowa Akademia Polityczna im. Feliksa Dzierzynskiego (Feliks Dzierzynski Military Political Academy), Warsaw
WUPR	West Ukrainian People's Republic (Zakhidno-ukrainska narodnia respublyka, ZUNR)

Introduction

At the end of the First World War Ukrainians were divided among the new states forming in East Central Europe: Poland, Czechoslovakia and an enlarged Romania. To varying degrees in each of these states, the Ukrainians were caught up in a revolutionary ferment, which, engendered by the powerful impact of events in Dnieper Ukraine, expressed deep-seated, and often conflicting, national and social aspirations. On both their ethnic territory and abroad, Ukrainians began to demand their rights. With the February Revolution in Russia, the Ukrainian question became an increasingly important issue in international politics, debated at the time of bilateral treaties (e.g., Brest Litovsk), during the negotiations of the Versailles treaty, on numerous occasions in the League of Nations, and in both the Communist International and Socialist Workers' International.

Outside Soviet territory, the Ukrainian problem was most salient in Poland. In the interwar period it was the subject of heated controversy. Contemporary historians, however, have given little attention to this subject. There has been hardly any work on the significance of the Ukrainian question and the Ukrainian Communist movement for the history of the Polish revolutionary left. Yet, unless one is familiar with the problems of the Communist Party of Western Ukraine (CPWU) and its early history, it is impossible to understand many aspects of the Polish Communist movement. It is especially difficult to appreciate fully the positions taken by the Polish party on a number of fundamental political problems of interwar Poland, particularly the national question. The CPWU was in the beginning a strong, relatively independent formative influence on Communist political thought in Poland.

Historians deliberately stayed clear of the CPWU. The rehabilitation accorded the Communist Party of Poland (CPP) and its affiliated organizations in 1956 was not extended to the West Ukrainian party because of the openly oppositionist stance of its leadership toward the Comintern in the late 1920s. Full rehabilitation came only in 1963 with the publication of an article in the central organ of the Communist Party of the Soviet Union (CPSU) entitled "Za pravilnoe osveshchenie istorii Kommunisticheskoi partii Zapadnoi Ukrainy," *Kommunist*, no. 10 (1963).

Before 1963, Soviet historical works on West Ukrainian Communism were characterized by "depersonification"; they were chronicles of events rather than party history. One interesting work, however, was Mykola Kravets' *Narysy robitnychoho rukhu v Zakhidnii Ukraini v 1921–1939* (Kiev, 1959). Kravets described both the working-class movement (strikes, mass demonstrations) and the party (dates of conferences and congresses, excerpts from some resolutions). He omitted, however, not only the disputes and conflicts, but the internal life of the party as a whole. Several other works on the revolutionary movement in Western Ukraine dealt with the party minimally, neglecting its relations with the CPP, and failing to mention that the CPWU was an affiliate organization of the Polish party.

After the appearance of the rehabilitating articles in *Kommunist*, the Soviet scholar Ievhen Halushko published *Narysy ideolohichnoi ta orhanizatsiinoi diialnosti KPZU, 1918–1928* (Lviv, 1965), for its time one of the best monographs on the CPWU. I discussed it at length in the quarterly *Z pola walki*, no. 4 (1966): 169–74, and later in the Ukrainian periodical *Nasha kultura* (Warsaw), no. 1 (1978): 12–14.

O. Karpenko's work on the precursors of the Communist movement in Western Ukraine, "Do pytannia pro vynyknennia i orhanizatsiine oformlennia Komunistychnoi partii Skhidnoi Halychyny," in *Z istorii zakhidnoukrainskykh zemel*, vol. 2 (Kiev, 1957), also revealed new information. Roman Rosdolsky, an ideologue of the Communist movement in Western Ukraine during its formative period, elaborated on this theme in his article, "Do istorii ukrainskoho livo-sotsiialistychnoho rukhu v Halychyni (Pidchasvoienni 'drahomanivky' 1916–18)," *Vpered. Ukrainska robitnycha hazeta*, no. 3–4 (1951). The American scholar Roman Solchanyk wrote on the same theme in "Revolutionary Marxism in Galicia before 1918," *East European Quarterly*, no. 1 (1976): 35–41. Solchanyk has also drawn on published sources in many languages to write an accurate and penetrating article on "The Foundations of the Communist Movement in Eastern Galicia 1919–1921," *Slavic Review*, no. 4 (1977): 774–94, and a doctoral dissertation that surveys the history of the CPWU from its inception to its dissolution: "The Communist Party of Western Ukraine, 1919–1938" (The University of Michigan, 1973). Mention should also be made of G. Iwański's "Z dziejów Komunistycznej Partii Galicji Wschodniej," *Z pola walki*, no. 4 (1967): 25–52. Iwański was the first to write about activities of the Communist Party of Eastern Galicia (CPEG) such as the strong insurrectionist tendency that characterized the early period of Communist activity in Western Ukraine. One of the best scholarly memoirs is that of Mykhailo Tesliuk, a veteran of the party leadership: "Na shliakhu bilshovizatsii KPZU (II zizd KPZU)," in *Na choli vyzvolnoi borotby. Spohady kolyshnikh aktyvnykh diiachiv KPZU* (Kiev, 1963). His memoirs concern the Second Congress of the CPWU, an important moment in the history of the party.

Archival materials, however, are still the basic source of information on this little-researched topic. The present monograph is based primarily on the archives of the CPWU and CPP, which are kept in the Central Archives of the Central Committee of the Polish United Workers' Party (PUWP) and the Kiev Institute of Party History of the Central Committee of the Communist Party of Ukraine (CPU). Also useful were the archives of the Communist Party (Bolsheviks) of Ukraine (CP[B]U), specifically materials dealing with the West Ukrainian movement, stenographic reports of CP(B)U central committee sessions and correspondence between the CPWU and CP(B)U.

The resources of the Central Archives of the Ministry of Internal Affairs and the Central Archives of Modern Records (Archiwum Akt Nowych) yielded supplementary material, especially on the activity of legal political groups affiliated with the CPWU. This was indispensable for piecing together accounts of mass actions and the elections. I have also made use of archival materials and reprints published by the state archives of Lviv and Lutsk.

The main theme of this book is the ideological evolution of the Communist Party of Western Ukraine from 1924 to 1928. It was necessary, however, to devote some attention to the years 1919–23 since they influenced the later period. The historical background is dealt with only insofar as it illuminates external processes affecting the party. The minorities policy of the Polish government, its motivations and evolutions, is outlined to explain the feelings of the Ukrainian people.

In geopolitical terminology I have followed the usage of the revolutionary left. Thus Eastern Galicia is that area comprised of the *województwa* of Lviv, Stanyslaviv and Ternopil. Eastern Galicia together with Volhynia is Western Ukraine. I have also used the term "Eastern *Kresy*" for the combined territory of Western Ukraine and Western Belorussia, keeping in mind that this term has extra-geographical connotations.

This work was originally written as a doctoral dissertation under the direction of Professor Jerzy Tomaszewski and defended in 1970 at the University of Warsaw. To him and to the other members of my doctoral committee, Professors Janusz Gołębiowski and Janusz Żarnowski, I express my sincerest thanks. I am also grateful to former members of the CPWU who offered advice and information, especially on the large number of pseudonyms.

The original Polish edition of this book was published in 1976 in Cracow by Wydawnictwo Literackie. In preparing the English version of this work it was necessary to add some explanations for the reader unfamiliar with Polish history. Additional research published by the author in Polish journals has been included (chapter five), biographical notes have been expanded, references to recent publications of other authors have been added and the last part of the book has been slightly revised. This edition appears at the initiative of the Canadian Institute of Ukrainian Studies, University of Alberta. The author extends his sincere thanks: to CIUS staff, in particular to Dr. John-Paul Himka; to the translator, Alan Rutkowski; and to the many professors of the university whose friendly interest and advice have helped in the preparation of this book.

Janusz Radziejowski
Edmonton

Chapter One

The Formation of the Communist Movement in Western Ukraine, 1918–1923

The conclusion of the Treaty of Riga left Poland with many millions of non-Polish inhabitants. The exact population of the national minorities in interwar Poland has never been established because the only authoritative sources, population censuses, were falsified (and not by the statisticians). The first Polish census, moreover, was carried out under unfavourable conditions, since postwar migrations were still in progress and Galician Ukrainians boycotted the census. The data from the 1921 census, as all specialists on the subject agree, are useless for establishing the national composition of the country. The data on nationality from the 1931 census were distorted by the census takers and therefore are also unreliable. The 1931 data on religious affiliation, however, do permit a limited reconstruction of the national structure.

Two noted historians of the Polish economy, Zbigniew Landau and Jerzy Tomaszewski, estimated Poland's national composition on the basis of the 1931 census and obtained the following results: Poles—20,644,000; Ukrainians—5,114,000; Jews—3,114,000; Belorussians—1,954,000; Germans—780,000; Russians—130,000; Lithuanians—83,000; Czechs—38,000; others—50,000.[1] At 16 per cent the Ukrainians were the largest minority, inhabiting Eastern Galicia and Volhynia where they made up a clear majority,[2] as well as the eastern regions of Lublin, Chełm and the southern districts (*powiaty*) of Polissia. The overwhelming majority of the Ukrainian population (90 per cent) lived in the countryside.[3] Of the Ukrainians in Volhynia and Polissia, approximately 6 per cent were workers, whereas in Eastern Galicia the number varied from 17 per cent in Stanyslaviv *województwo* to 14 per cent in Lviv *województwo*, and in the city of Lviv itself 65 per cent.[4] Thus, the Ukrainians living within the borders of the Polish state at that time made up a predominantly peasant society. As such they did not possess a large bourgeoisie, and the Ukrainian large landowners made up only 1.3 per cent of that class in Poland.[5]

The small Ukrainian middle bourgeoisie, middle class and intelligentsia were concentrated in Eastern Galicia, while in Volhynia, Chełm and Polissia the young, newly emerging indigenous intelligentsia was generally composed of teachers and clergy. Ukrainians were a relative minority in the towns, behind Poles and Jews (in Volhynia).[6] Of the region's working class employed in industry and mining, the Poles made up 43.5 per cent, Ukrainians 33.5 per cent and Jews 20.9 per cent.[7] Ukrainians, however, formed the majority of the agricultural workers.

The peasantry of the Eastern *Kresy* (i.e., Western Ukraine and Western Belorussia) suffered from an unrelenting land hunger. In Eastern Galicia this was the result of the advanced fragmentation of peasant holdings and enormous overpopulation, while in Volhynia and Polissia it was caused by the economic backwardness of the region, a large portion of which (in some areas up to 80 per cent) was marshland and otherwise barren. Thus the population was faced with constant poverty and sometimes starvation. The towns, which in Volhynia were mainly crafting and commercial centres, could not absorb the unemployed. Industry was either completely stagnant or minimally developed.

Ukrainians and Belorussians in the *Kresy* were employed in industry as unskilled labour and as a rule were the most poorly paid of all workers. It was more profitable for industry to import skilled Polish workers from the more developed regions of the country than to train locals. Thus the average wage of a Ukrainian worker in the eastern and southeastern regions was lower than that of a Polish worker. In time this disparity probably increased, since, independently of economic factors, the political authorities fostered a "tendency to eliminate Ukrainian and Jewish workers from autonomous and state enterprises and institutions."[8]

Divided between Austria and Russia before 1918, Western Ukraine did not attain political and cultural homogeneity in the interwar era. In Volhynia, Chełm and Polissia political parties had been illegal since tsarist times, and there was no organized national movement. But the October Revolution, the civil war and the national upheaval in Ukraine greatly bolstered national feelings in this area. The masses' approval of the social transformation taking place in the East was bound up with feelings of national pride and a passionate sympathy for the newly established Ukrainian Soviet republic.

The situation was different in Eastern Galicia. The Ukrainian national movement had begun to develop there in the second half of the nineteenth century. The Ukrainians had taken advantage of the relative freedom under Austria and transformed Lviv into an important centre of cultural and political life for all Ukraine. A number of legal Ukrainian parties were formed there in the 1890s and a parliamentary life developed in which for several decades Ukrainian deputies took an active part. A rich and highly developed Ukrainian press, a school system and independent organizations were established and Ukrainian humanistic culture flourished thanks to the eight Ukrainian chairs at Lviv University. Because Poles occupied a privileged position in the economy (as large landowners), and hence also in the political system (the police, courts and administration, including the vice-royalty), the budding Ukrainian movement came to view Polish nationalism as its chief opponent. The authorities in Vienna fostered this conflict and turned it to their own advantage.

Toward the end of the First World War, when the final disintegration of Austria-Hungary was only weeks away, the Ukrainian parties of the Vienna parliament, acting as the Ukrainian national Rada (with Ievhen Petrushevych as president), with the support of the Ukrainian Sich Riflemen,[9] took power in almost all of Eastern Galicia after a coup d'état on 31 October 1918 and proclaimed the establishment of the West Ukrainian People's Republic (WRUP).[10] The counteraction of Polish military organizations in Lviv, supported several days later by regular divisions of the Polish army, soon turned the conflict into a Polish-Ukrainian war. After an unsuccessful attempt to mediate and fearing the approaching Red Army, the Entente, on 25 June 1919, authorized the Polish side to carry out military operations up to the river Zbruch, with the understanding that the future political status of Eastern Galicia had still to be settled. The Polish forces took advantage of this decision and in July 1919 drove the remaining Ukrainian divisions out of Western Ukraine.[11] Though the West Ukrainian state had existed for barely six months, its legislative and administrative activity, the creation of its own army and the enthusiasm accompanying its patriotic efforts left a deep mark on the consciousness of Galician Ukrainians. The police terror of the new Polish regime increased Polish-Ukrainian antagonism, which was exacerbated by the Entente's failure to decide the fate of this region.

This antagonism was also fostered by the policies of the Polish government, which up to 1926 was strongly influenced by the Popular National Union (*Zwiazek Ludowo-Narodowy*), otherwise known as National Democracy (*Narodowa Demokracja*). The programme of this party called for political, economic and cultural domination by the Poles. The Ukrainians and Belorussians were to be assimilated. Moreover, Polish national democracy was aided in this programme by the Christian

Democrats and the conservative Piast peasant party.[12] The emigre historian and Piłsudskiite, Władysław Pobóg-Malinowski, describes the situation as follows:

> The Polish right, preaching absolute Polish supremacy in this area [Eastern Galicia] ... contributed to the deepening and sharpening of these anti-Polish feelings.... They were able to stir up trouble all over Poland by crying "national treason" at the appointment to a government post not only of a native Ukrainian, but even of a Pole of mixed blood. The ministers in Warsaw, the *wojewody*, the *starosty* and police in Little Poland were all terrorized by this terrible demagoguery both in the press and in the Diet.[13]

This policy of the right wing and state authorities dominated by the right was not confined to demagoguery, but also took other, more tangible forms.[14]

From the beginning of its existence the Polish administration set out to deprive the Ukrainians of all they had attained under Austrian rule. The Ukrainian chairs at Lviv University were abolished and Ukrainian professors dismissed on the pretext that they refused to swear allegiance to the Polish state—though at this time world opinion and the Council of Ambassadors of the Entente had not recognized de jure the annexation of Eastern Galicia to Poland.[15] Ukrainian youth was denied admission to institutions of higher learning: applicants were required not only to make a declaration of loyalty, but, in the wake of the Polish-Ukrainian war,[16] to give proof of service in the Polish army. Professors and students of the underground Ukrainian university and polytechnical institute, which had begun operation in 1921, were persecuted and all instructional materials found were burned.[17] In 1925 after most of the Ukrainian professors had been arrested and convicted, these underground centres of higher learning were dissolved.[18] A significant number of Ukrainian young people, in spite of measures to discourage them, went abroad to study, usually to Czechoslovakia. On their return to Poland, with no possibility of obtaining government employment, they reinforced the ranks of the opposition and helped to create a network of well-organized co-operatives or dedicated themselves to work in the extra-official educational societies, Ridna shkola and Prosvita.[19] The co-operatives, Ridna shkola and Prosvita were themselves constantly harassed by the authorities, which furthered intensified the Ukrainians' antagonism toward the Polish state.

The Polish administration restricted the use of the Ukrainian language, which before the war had enjoyed equal rights with Polish in Galicia. By 1919 it was illegal to address letters or packages in Ukrainian, and those mailed were returned to the sender with the note "addresses in Ruthenian are not permitted."[20] People were sometimes brutally attacked for speaking Ukrainian in the street.[21] In July 1924 the use of the "Ruthenian" language was restricted in government agencies to "external" correspondence.[22] The use of the designation "Ruthenian" was enforced in an attempt to ban the use of the term "Ukrainian."[23]

The introduction of the name "Eastern Little Poland" for Galicia also provoked the Ukrainians' resentment. The change of name was viewed not only as an additional Polonizing measure, but also as an attempt to obliterate the memory of the autonomy Galicia had enjoyed under the Habsburgs. The Council of Ambassadors had ordered Poland to give the region autonomy, but this was successfully thwarted by the Polish right.[24]

Polish historians have written exhaustively on the assimilationist role of the so-called *lex Grabski* (July 1924): school legislation for the Slavic minorities that introduced bilingual schools in the Eastern *Kresy*.[25] This legislation established a Polish advantage in choosing the language of instruction (twenty votes were sufficient to make it Polish, while Ukrainian required forty) and at the same time served as a pretext for the mass liquidation of the Ukrainian school system, including that of Prosvita.[26] The new school system became, as Ignacy Daszyński[27] foresaw, an unequal partnership. In the bilingual schools only drawing, gymnastics and occasionally singing (in gymnasia—Ukrainian literature) were taught in Ukrainian. In the early period, with which we are especially concerned, many schools did not teach the Ukrainian language (or in the gymnasia, Ukrainian literature);[28] Ukrainian history and geography, contrary to the law, were never introduced. Sometimes this was due to a lack of qualified teachers, but at the same time many Ukrainian teachers were transferred to ethnically Polish areas. Ukrainian public opinion held the education minister, Stanisław Grabski, and his general "Ukrainophobia" responsible for some of the thoughtless and provocative actions that occurred (banning the use of the name "Ukrainian" and insisting that Ukrainian students take part in school festivals celebrating the victory over the Ukrainians in Lviv).[29] Indeed, a few years later Grabski openly argued the necessity of constitutionally unequal civil rights and discrimination in favour of the Polish population.[30] His views were echoed by other representatives of Polish national democracy. Yet there must have been strong anti-Ukrainian prejudice and intolerance at various levels of government. Some historians now think that the local administration yielded to pressure from the Poles living in these regions. Greatly influenced by national democracy, they "reacted hysterically to every effort on the part of the authorities to comply with the demands of other nationalities."[31]

In Volhynia the situation was aggravated by the persecution of the Orthodox church. Immediately after the war the process of "revindication" was begun, by which Orthodox churches were reconsecrated as Catholic churches. Theoretically, the intention was to eradicate the effect of the former tsarist attacks on Catholicism. In practice, however, in regions where there were no Catholics the Orthodox churches were simply burned or torn down. During the first decade after the war, in Chełm and Pidlissia alone, 195 Orthodox churches (not including those reconsecrated as Catholic churches) were burned down, demolished or closed.[32] Moreover, in accordance with the decree on agrarian reform, Orthodox parishes were divested of great quantities of land, which were then turned over either to the state or to the Catholic church, whose landholdings not only were not expropriated but even increased.[33] The Orthodox clergy skilfully used these issues to increase the already strong feelings of resentment among the Orthodox populace.

Also resented was the government's attempt to limit the Volhynians' contacts with their co-nationals in Eastern Galicia by maintaining the so-called Sokal Cordon (the former border between Austria and Russia). It was difficult for Galician Ukrainians to settle in Volhynia, theatrical groups from Lviv were not permitted to cross the border and Volhynians could not subscribe to Galician Ukrainian journals.[34]

The agrarian-reform legislation and resulting colonization caused especially bitter feelings in the *Kresy*. If agrarian reform in Poland proper represented some advance for the peasants and satisfied their demands in part, in the *Kresy* it was used exclusively against their national and economic interests. There the large estates were divided among colonists made up of former Polish soldiers, officials and others trusted by the authorities. The aim was the creation of something analogous to the Russian Cossacks, a privileged peasantry devoted to the regime and ready to help control Ukrainian and Belorussian areas and weaken their ethnic homogeneity.[35] Polish historians have given much attention to the question of colonization. Suffice it to say that the reform's colonizing intent was clearly stated in the Lanckorona pact, the joint platform of Polish national democracy and the Piast peasant party in 1923.[36]

A further grievance of the Ukrainian minority in Poland was the removal of Ukrainians from posts in government agencies (such as the railway, post office and courts) in Eastern Galicia. Those dismissed were also expelled from the consumer co-operatives for civil servants (*konsumy*), even if they had paid up their memberships; during this period of postwar scarcity, exclusion from the *konsumy* could seriously undermine a family's material situation.[37] The pretext for the dismissals was the failure to make declarations of loyalty. Over six thousand persons lost their jobs in this small area, although after all had made the required declarations some were rehired. None of the two thousand Ukrainian railway workers were re-employed, however, and the same held true for more than a thousand former government clerks.[38] Later the dismissal of Ukrainians continued, but more cautiously and less obviously. In Volhynia, where "the wantonness of the administration knew no bounds,"[39] the situation was similar. Ukrainian civil servants and workers were not as numerous in Volhynia, but most of the Ukrainians elected to office in the self-governing administration were removed. In fact, in spite of intermittently held elections, self-government never really existed. In a country where national minorities accounted for more than a third of the population, no non-Pole ever held the position of minister, *wojewoda* or even district *starosta*.

In the 1920s, the situation of the Ukrainian and Belorussian minorities was generally worse in Poland than in neighbouring countries; in terms of employment and wages, Ukrainians and Belorussians were even worse off than they had been under tsarist Russia. For comparison it is worth citing the following data on education. In Transcarpathian Ukraine the first Ukrainian school system was only established in 1918, when this area was incorporated by the new Czechoslovak state. But already by 1921–2, 89 per cent of Ukrainian children were attending Ukrainian schools, and Ukrainian secondary schools accounted for 42 per cent of all secondary schools in the area.[40] The Ukrainian Free University and Ukrainian Pedagogical Institute were opened in Prague in 1923. At the same time, agricultural engineers were being trained at the Ukrainian Economic Academy in Poděbrady.[41] When Western Belorussia came under Polish administration in 1919, there were, according to Konstanty Srokowski, 350 Belorussian elementary schools. By 1923 all but 23 (for a population of one and a half million) had been liquidated. By contrast, for the 66,000 Belorussians living in Latvia there were fifty elementary schools, two gymnasia and one teachers' college, all with Belorussian as the language of instruction and all subsidized by the government.[42] Only in Romania was the situation of the Ukrainian minority similar to that in Poland, but there the Ukrainian movement was somewhat weaker and less organized than in Polish-controlled Eastern Galicia.

Unlike their compatriots in Soviet Ukraine, the Ukrainians in Poland were unable to obtain even a minimal form of state organization as the basis of their social life. When Ukrainian representatives reminded the Polish authorities of the autonomy promised for Eastern Galicia they were ignored. To complete this gloomy picture, Polish national democratic propaganda promoted the view that the Slavic minorities—"having an almost primitive culture"[43]—could hardly aspire to the role of co-managers of the country.[44]

All this of course was not without its influence on the posture of Ukrainian political parties. The largest Ukrainian political party in Galicia was the Ukrainian National Labour Party (UNLP), later called the Ukrainian National Democratic Union (UNDU). The labour party was a national, middle-class party, but, like all Ukrainian parties, some elements were ideologically opposed to the large landowners. Like the more left-wing peasant Ukrainian Radical Party (URP),[45] the UNLP opposed the Polish government and sympathized with the fledgling Ukrainian state in the east. At first the Communists ignored this partially pro-Soviet orientation of the centre and even centre-right parties, and acknowledged its existence only after 1926 when it began to wane.[46] Non-Communist sources are more candid in their description of pro-Soviet sympathies among the Ukrainian political parties.[47]

Extreme reactionary Ukrainian groups were at that time small and weak. The small group around Dmytro Dontsov, which was then entering its reactionary phase, is perhaps the only one worth mentioning. The Ukrainian Military Organization (UMO), precursor of the integral nationalist Organization of Ukrainian Nationalists (OUN), did not have its own political programme, but considered itself the military arm of the Petrushevych exile government in Vienna and under the authority of the Inter-Party Rada, which included the UNLP and the URP.[48] It used armed actions to defend the decisions of the Rada and make them binding for all Ukrainians.

Because of the generally progressive colouration of West Ukrainian politics in the twenties, the newly emerging Ukrainian Communist movement minimized the importance of the Ukrainian right wing, a fact that influenced the movement's character.

The latter half of 1918 saw the emergence of small and scattered Communist groups in Eastern Galicia. In Drohobych, Boryslav and Stryi, the memberships, especially in the latter two cities, were drawn in part from the Jewish Social Democratic Party and Poalei Zion.[49] Mojżesz Mandel, Natan Shapiro (Sukhy), Leon Pasternak and others came from these parties. While Polish Communists were to play an important role in the development of the Communist movement in Western Ukraine, emissaries of the Communist Workers' Party of Poland (CWPP) began their activity in this area only after 1920. This is understandable since up to the middle of 1919 Eastern Galicia made up a large portion of the West Ukrainian People's Republic where Ukrainian leftist groups played the leading role. It is these groups that interest us here.

In 1918 an organization of "socialist communists" led by Vasyl Kotsko, Hryhorii Mykhats and Ivan Kushnir was created in Drohobych, and probably had connections with Communist military circles from Soviet Ukraine. In February 1919 the organization attempted an armed insurrection against the WUPR in order to integrate its territory into the Soviet Union. The attempt, however, lacked mass support and collapsed in a matter of hours. The organizers were arrested (but subsequently released) and Kushnir was killed in the conflict.

The Borotbists provided another important source for the recruitment of future leaders of the Communist party in Eastern Galicia. The Ninth Conference of the CPWU (1928) names the Borotbists, as well as

International Revolutionary Social Democracy (IRSD), as organizational precursors of the party.

The Borotbists were a left-wing faction of the Ukrainian Socialist Revolutionaries (SRs) active in Dnieper Ukraine. They took their name from their official newspaper, *Borotba* (Struggle). In May 1918 the Borotbists broke with the right-wing of the SRs and formed a separate party. In 1919, after joining with a faction of Ukrainian left social democrats (the so-called "independentists"), they took the name Ukrainian Communist Party (Borotbists) (UCP[B]). They opposed the Central Rada, fought against Petliura's Directorate, and joined forces with the Bolsheviks in the partisan movement. In May 1919 they became part of the Soviet government in Ukraine. Initially, the Borotbists differed from the Bolsheviks in their demand for a completely independent Ukraine and later in their constant emphasis on the Ukrainian question and their demands for a looser federation, redivision of the armed forces along national lines and other such issues. This led to a series of conflicts with the Bolsheviks, during which the Borotbists characteristically sought support from other Communist parties. In late-January 1920 the central committee of the UCP(B) sent a letter to the leadership of the CWPP proposing the establishment of contacts. The letter points out the similar conditions under which both parties were operating and states that "Poland and Ukraine had in the past suffered not only bourgeois oppression, but the national oppression of the old Russian centre," and that "the historical inertia of the centre gives the Communist revolutions in Ukraine and Poland many common features."[50]

In 1920, after unsuccessful attempts to join the Comintern as a separate party, a considerable number of Borotbists followed the advice of the Comintern's executive and joined the CP(B)U. Many Borotbists (such as Oleksander Shumsky, Vasyl Blakytny, Panas Liubchenko, Andrii Khvylia and Hryhorii Hrynko) were prominent figures in the early days of Soviet Ukraine, occupying key positions in the party and state apparatus.[51]

The existence of independent Borotbist organizations in Eastern Galicia is evident from resolutions and statements of the Vasylkivists during the second party schism in 1928:

1) "a group of the IRSD as the original core of the CPWU and the UCP(B)—Maksymovych and others—joined forces to lay the foundation of the Communist Party [of Eastern Galicia]."[52]
2) "In the years 1918 to 1919 Bolshevik ideas penetrated Western Ukraine via two channels: through the Borotbists . . . and directly through the Bolsheviks . . . but it is important to remember that in the Galician context . . . CP(B)U and UCP(B) influence converged programmatically and tactically into a single current."[53]
3) "A revolutionary . . . underground Borotbist organization (that of

Maksymovych, Ialovy and Khrystovy) was active in Western Ukraine during the Ukrainian-Polish war."[54]

All reports of Borotbist origin known to us come from the later period. Of the numerous CPWU questionnaires handed out to congress delegates only Maksymovych's declares former affiliation with the Borotbists. One must remember, however, that among Communists, Borotbist affiliation was not something of which to be particularly proud. Things were different in 1928 when it was common to be reproached with an exclusively "national" or "petty-bourgeois" past. By then kinship with the Borotbists, who once struggled against the Petliurite version of Ukrainian nationalism, was regarded more favourably.

Expressions such as "a Borotbist organization" may be exaggerated. The "organization" was probably no more than a loose grouping around Communist party organizers sent into Eastern Galicia by the UCP(B). One of the founders of Borotbism, Hnat Mykhailychenko, even attempted to infiltrate the area in December 1919, but was killed by Denikin's forces while crossing the front line.[55]

The founding conference of the Communist Party of Eastern Galicia was held in Stanyslaviv in February 1919. Although its participants were soon arrested, the conference was significant for the development of the movement. Three Borotbists—Mykola Khrystovy, Mykhailo Ialovy and Karlo Savrych—played a leading role in calling and preparing this conference.[56] The first two were well-known Borotbist activists in Eastern Ukraine, emissaries of their party.[57] Savrych (Maksymovych), who was elected to the leadership of the new party, had also been living in the East, but was a native Galician. Born in 1892 in Rohatyn district, he had studied law at Lviv University. During the war he was located in the East, where he joined the Borotbist party in February 1917. According to some sources Maksymovych was already a card-carrying member of the CP(B)U at the Stanyslaviv conference.[58] But even if by this time he had already left the Borotbists (which is contradicted by other evidence),[59] he never lost contact with them. We should remember that from 1922 to 1924, as secretary of the Ukrainian embassy in Warsaw (Shumsky was ambassador), he remained active in the Western party. Later as the CPWU's representative to the CP(B)U and secretary of the Foreign Bureau to Aid the Revolutionary Movement in Western Ukraine, he continued to work closely with Shumsky.

Prior to the split of 1928 the leaders of the CPEG never criticized Borotbism, though they had justification for doing so. They were critical, however, of the Ukrainian Communist Party (UCP), another leftist group that was resolutely opposed to the CP(B)U.[60] It is likely that the Borotbist version of communism, as a "purely Ukrainian" and recently peasant (socialist revolutionary) phenomenon, was more suited to the mentality of the leftist Galician Ukrainians.

A more important precursor of the CPEG-CPWU was International Revolutionary Social Democracy.[61] There is also more information about it since it was a native Galician group active in the region for several years. It originated in youth circles, called *drahomanivky*, whose ideal was the socialism of Mykhailo Drahomanov. In 1913 a split occurred when the left wing, inclined toward radical socialism, accused its former comrades of nationalism. In 1916, after an interruption caused by the outbreak of the First World War, the left resumed its activity. The leadership was composed of Osyp Krilyk (later pseudonym: Vasylkiv), Roman Kuzma (later pseudonym: Turiansky), V. Syroizh, Roman Rosdolsky (later pseudonym: Prokopovych), Ivan Khlon (later pseudonym: Iko) and Maria Giżowska, later one of the defendants in the St. George trial.[62] All except Syroizh became prominent activists and founders of the CPEG and CPWU.[63] According to Rosdolsky's estimate, the organization had about five hundred members, almost exclusively from the young Ukrainian intelligentsia (gymnasium and university students, and even young officers of the Sich Riflemen). Besides Lviv, the left-wing *drahomanivky* had circles in Drohobych, Stryi, Przemyśl, Stanyslaviv and Ternopil. In the spring of 1918 the group took the name "International Revolutionary Social Democracy." The omission of "Ukrainian" in its name underscored its internationalism. The youthful revolutionaries, however, had no connection with organizations of other nationalities. They could have no common language with the Polish Galician Promienist group which, in addition to having a more moderate programme, stood for the reconstruction of an independent Poland within the prepartition boundaries.[64] Therefore the organization's influence was limited to the Ukrainian intelligentsia, and its contacts with the masses were minimal. Later assertions of the multinational composition of the IRSD (for example, Vasylkiv's speech at the St. George trial and statements made by Turiansky to the press in 1928) were dictated, in Rosdolsky's opinion, by factional considerations and did not correspond to reality.[65] The organization was primarily involved in self-education and propaganda. In its early period, 1916–17, it published *Vistnyk drahomanivskoi organizatsii* (Herald of the Drahomanov Organization), with Rosdolsky as editor and chief contributor. Later it published the papers *Klychi* (Watchwords) and *Vilna shkola* (Free School) successively. These papers criticized the pro-Austrian orientation of the USDP, propagated the views of Rosa Luxemburg and Karl Liebknecht on the war, hailed the October Revolution in Russia, and reported Lenin's early speeches and decrees. At the same time they published and circulated Otto Bauer's pamphlet, *The Russian Revolution*, and condemned the Red Army's march on Kiev in 1917 to overthrow the

Central Rada government in Ukraine.[66] In Rosdolsky's opinion, this was evidence of a certain theoretical immaturity in the views of the young Galician Marxists.

The existence of a radical internationalist strain in the views of the left-wing *drahomanivky* is confirmed in a collection of excerpts from *Vistnyk* reprinted in 1928 by Turiansky. These excerpts reveal that he expected the Ukrainian question to be solved by a worldwide socialist revolution that would produce a European Federation of Republics unifying the peoples of Europe. Turiansky did not quote anything that confirms Rosdolsky's view about the ideological immaturity of the organization.[67] Contemporary Soviet historians also emphasize that the IRSD's internationalism was accompanied by a national narrowness, glorification of Drahomanov and a positive attitude toward the Central Rada's policies.[68] Before the October Revolution and until 1918, however, relations between the Russian Communist party and the Central Rada were not yet hostile. The Kiev Bolshevik organization (the CP[B]U did not yet exist) recognized the Central Rada as a partner in the struggle against the right during the Kornilov putsch. Later it maintained contact with the Central Rada and intended to take power peacefully through elections to the workers' soviets.[69] Therefore in 1917 the situation was not yet as clear as it appears from hindsight.

In December 1918 an IRSD conference considered the proposed creation of a Communist Party of Eastern Galicia.[70] The majority decided that the establishment of the Communist Party which would by its nature be opposed to the Petrushevych government, would weaken the position of the West Ukrainian republic (at that time fighting for its life against the Polish army) and was therefore inadvisable. This decision shows the discrepancy between the theory and political practice of the IRSD on the national question.

The other centre of the West Ukrainian movement was Soviet Ukraine. The movement here was initiated by organizations of Galician Communists in the CP(B)U composed of former prisoners of war captured by the tsarist army. They had received their revolutionary baptism either in the ranks of the militant Bolshevik party or in the Galician army in the East.[71] These activists created various Galician committees within the leadership organs of the CP(B)U.[72] The committees, whose ideological and organizational patron was Volodymyr Zatonsky, sent emissaries and propaganda literature to Lviv, and were more involved with the region under Polish administration than with the WUPR. They won support among the leading circles of the Communist International and the Russian Communist Party, and their representatives, Arnold Baral and Mykhailo Levytsky, spoke for the emerging Communist movement of Eastern Galicia at Comintern congresses.[73] In July-August 1920, when the Galician Soviet

Republic was established in Ternopil, the government and higher party authorities, with Zatonsky at the head, were appointed from this group. After the withdrawal of Soviet forces at the end of 1920, decisive influence among pro-Communists in Galicia passed to the group headed by Osyp Krilyk[74] and Karlo Savrych (Maksymovych). The latter was then in Vienna, the location of a party agency and the party organ *Nasha pravda* (Our Truth), but he maintained close contacts with Galicia. This group, as mentioned, was initially aided and supported by the Borotbist party and later by former Borotbists within the CP(B)U, including Skrypnyk. Zatonsky, however, remained distrustful of the Vasylkivists.[75]

A third source of inspiration for the establishment of a Galician Communist party was the Communist Workers' Party of Poland. Immediately after Polish forces took Galicia, CWPP emissaries began work there, creating their organizations primarily in the towns. In 1921 a bitter factional dispute erupted between the Vasylkivists and the CWPP organizers and their followers. On 15 February 1921 the recently formed joint four-man central committee of the CPEG split into CWPP loyalists and "secessionists."[76] Among the more prominent secessionists were Krilyk-Vasylkiv, Savrych-Maksymovych, Roman Rosdolsky-Prokopovych, Mykhailo Tesliuk, Pavlo Ladan, Petro Lyshega, Panteleimon Kraikivsky, Vasyl Korbutiak (returned from the United States, where he had been a member of the Socialist Party), Volodymyr Popel, Sydir Senyk, Fedir Bei and Liudvik Rozenberg (Lvivsky). The CWPP loyalists (excluding local CWPP representatives, such as Czesława Grosserowa, Kazimierz Cichowski and Stefan Królikowski),[77] were Ukrainian Communists sympathetic to Zatonsky: Nestor Khomyn, Hryhorii Mykhats, Hryhorii Ivanenko, Ivan Maienta, Ivan Vantukh and Natan Shapiro. Adolf Langer-Dłuski, Leon Pasternak, Adolf Ursaki and several others were connected with the Polish revolutionary tradition but did not officially represent the CWPP.

The secessionists were almost exclusively Ukrainians. There were only two Jews—Liudvik Rozenberg, mentioned above, and Iung-Shanin, a defendant in the St. George trial who was later removed from active party work. The CWPP's membership, on the other hand, included the three main nationalities, Ukrainians, Poles and Jews, but in Eastern Galicia, in contrast to Volhynia, it was composed primarily of the urban working class and students, few of whom were Ukrainians. CWPP followers were concentrated in the Union of the Proletariat of City and Countryside (UPCC), a legal Communist organization created in 1922 for participation in elections to the Diet and Senate.

The Vasylkivists (secessionists) had connections with the insurgent Ukrainian peasantry and the radical Ukrainian intelligentsia of the national liberation organizations. The Ukrainian Social Democratic Party (USDP), the organizational base of the Vasylkivists, came more and more under the latter's control. Rosdolsky, the main speaker at meetings of the Ukrainian socialist youth, won many sympathizers for the Vasylkivists; and Shumsky, Skrypnyk and Ukrainian Communists in Canada gave substantial help to the Vasylkivists.

After the formation of the West Ukrainian People's Republic in 1918 and its war with Poland, national feeling in Eastern Galicia was particularly tense. Many of the Ukrainian youth, including the future activists of the CPEG—Vasylkiv, Rosdolsky, Korbutiak, Rozenberg, Osyp Bukshovany[78] and others—had fought against the Poles. The Ukrainian countryside was in a state of ferment, as peasants carried out acts of sabotage and arson, and attacked state institutions. The government answered with punitive expeditions, pacifications and executions.[79] Polish right-wing militants organized bombings of Ukrainian cultural institutions.[80] The Entente made its decision on the fate of Eastern Galicia only in 1923 and its indecisiveness fostered uncertainty and opposition. The CP(B)U gave substantial aid to Galician and Volhynian partisans in their fight against Polish rule. It is important to remember that the original Communist circles of 1918–19 had established contact with the CP(B)U, either directly or via the Borotbists, received aid from it and considered themselves to be components of the party. In early 1920 representatives of the CPEG applied to the Comintern as an autonomous section of the CP(B)U. Later in the same year, when the Soviet republic was established in the Ternopil region, the legal Communist party (the Communist Party of Galicia) saw itself as a component of the CP(B)U.[81]

Thus in addition to the anti-Polish bias of the masses and ideological differences there was also a precedent in this area for a Communist party independent of Warsaw. Equally important, the Vasylkivists had strong ideological ties with circles in the CP(B)U leadership, which differed from the CWPP's central committee in its views on the national question.

The partisan movement extended across the entire Western Ukraine at this time. National populist elements led the movement in Eastern Galicia, but Communists also joined and created separate sections under their own leadership. In Volhynia the movement was dominated by Communists and was aided by the so-called Zakordot (*Zakordonnyi otdel* or Foreign Division) of the CP(B)U central committee. The Zakordot was established in 1920[82] primarily for organizational and military work. Many of its workers were military personnel such as Stepan Melnychuk, Petro Sheremeta, Ivan Tsepko and other Communist partisan leaders in Eastern Galicia.[83]

In Volhynia the Zakordot directed the entire partisan movement. Among the organizations active in Volhynia at that time were the Ukrainian Red Insurgent Organization, the Ukrainian Revolutionary Insurgent Organization and the Ukrainian Popular Insurgent

Organization.[84] Probably all three originated in the Volhynian Ukrainian Military Organization, which was controlled by the Zakordot. Though the Communist party did not organize the partisan movement, most party members and the core leadership were drawn into it. The Communist movement in Volhynia was not at that time formally subordinate to or even connected with the CPEG-Vasylkivists. On the political level it was directly subordinate to the CP(B)U and militarily to the Zakordot. Ideologically, the so-called Volhynians (Khomyn and Ivanenko) were much closer to the CWPP than to the Vasylkivists.

The partisan movement used harassment tactics—arson, armed attacks on landed estates and police patrols—and was thus referred to as a sabotage movement. The chief aim of the partisans was the conquest of Western Ukraine, or at least Volhynia, and its annexation to Soviet Ukraine. Toward this end they counted on a Polish-Soviet war.

The Vasylkivists in Eastern Galicia became progressively more insurrectionist in spirit. The CWPP, on the other hand, with its ties in the primarily Polish working class and urban intelligentsia, and under less pressure than the Vasylkivists, was more concerned with an all-Polish revolution than local issues. Conflict was inevitable. An important source of information on the origin and nature of the differences is a letter from Sydir Senyk (Syrel) and Krilyk (Vasylkiv), members of the Lviv central committee to the CP(B)U central committee. The letter announced that a split had occurred in the Communist movement in Western Ukraine.[85] The conflict arose out of the differences between the authors of the letter and the other central committee members (Pasternak and Khomyn), who recognized the sovereignty of the CWPP and attempted to impose their viewpoint on the latter. The letter argued that the masses in Eastern Galicia were decidedly anti-Polish. Not only the insurgent Galician peasantry but even the Ukrainian proletariat, so passive before the war, had been caught up in these sentiments. This necessitated the creation of a party centre of local elements in touch with the mood of the masses. The influence of Petrushevych and Petliura had clearly declined, but "the bestial, bloody dance of the Polish *szlachta* is not over." For this reason Eastern Galicia was more revolutionary than the ethnically Polish regions and its pace of revolutionary development was much faster. Therefore the Polish central committee was not competent to direct the revolutionary movement in Eastern Galicia. The final decision on the fate of Eastern Galicia had not been made and a plebiscite was a real possibility. "The Soviets" were demanding the creation of a separate state in this region. In this situation, "the leadership should be located in Lviv and not in Warsaw." With uprisings in Germany, Czechoslovakia and Hungary, it was essential to maintain an irredentist policy in Eastern Galicia which could bring about "the isolation and destruction of bourgeois Poland." The letter concluded with a formal argument: the East Galician party, "being a section of the Third International, is subordinate to it and the form of this relationship can be altered only by a national party conference."[86]

The document shows that the Vasylkivists were extremely pessimistic about the revolutionary potential of the Polish proletariat and saw Poland as a bulwark of international reaction. In this they differed from the CWPP. The less experienced of the Vasylkivists at times expressed clearly nationalistic views. Thus, for example, their report to the Third Congress of the Comintern explained that Eastern Galicia was dominated by a "country with which it was connected only by a bloody tradition of mutual struggle," and "feelings of national animosity have penetrated deeply into the soul of the masses.... As for the Polish intelligentsia, the entire country [sic] is, to a man, nationalist and chauvinist and will see nothing beyond the sop of national independence." In such a situation, according to the document's anonymous authors, it was impossible to rally the masses under the CWPP banner. The authors suggested that it would be easy to start an uprising in Galicia ("the masses will follow anyone who says fight") and announced that the party already had a military organization with eight thousand troops.[87]

Many documents confirm that the Vasylkivists were planning an uprising in Eastern Galicia. The military command of the CPEG central committee began to create and train armed units and to stockpile arms. They relied on help from the Red Army.[88] Somewhat later, when most party leaders had been imprisoned after the St. George trial, the remaining members, including Maksymovych, issued an appeal for an armed insurrection throughout the Vienna-based Committee to Aid the Revolution in Eastern Galicia.[89] The majority of party organizations in the countryside were transformed into partisan units.[90] CWPP loyalists, however, were highly critical of the movement, especially when it became apparent that in Eastern Galicia it was led by elements who were far removed from Communist ideology. The 1922 elections to the Diet provided another area of dispute. Contrary to the decision of the CWPP, the Vasylkivists boycotted the elections.[91] First to proclaim the boycott was the Petrushevych emigre government in Vienna. Thus, the Polish left saw the decision of the Vasylkivists as a "united national front" with the Ukrainian right.

The most cogent defence of the Vasylkivist position was offered by Roman Rosdolsky, later a noted Marxist historian.[92] In his opinion the growing Galician partisan movement was characterized by its bitter antagonism to the owners of great estates; the movement was of a class nature and could not be considered exclusively national in character. The peasant masses radicalized the movement, forcing the leaders, sons of the "petty and middle Ukrainian bourgeoisie," to proclaim the slogan "To the

Landlords' Estates."[93] In this situation, according to Rosdolsky, Communists should support the movement, while criticizing its leaders for their weakness and inconsistency. He also justified boycotting the elections in Eastern Galicia since it was not de jure part of Polish territory. From the legal point of view, Rosdolsky recalled, Poland had no more right to hold elections in that area than it had to collect taxes or carry out military conscription.[94] Even the countries of the Entente, albeit weakly, protested the elections in Eastern Galicia. This was no accident: the existing state of affairs was the result of the Entente's partial recognition of the Galician Ukrainians' right to self-determination. According to Rosdolsky, the essence of the conflict over the elections was the Polish bourgeoisie's unwillingness to relinquish domination over the area and the Ukrainian bourgeoisie's refusal to accept this. The campaign to boycott the elections, appealing to all classes of Ukrainian society, was a democratic anti-imperialist action. Communists, therefore, if they were not empty doctrinarians, had to perceive that even these small limitations on the Polish imperialist drive were useful for the class struggle in all Poland and for the all-Polish revolution, in which Eastern Galicia would play a large role.[95]

But within the Vasylkivist leadership there were carefully concealed differences. Evidently, Rosdolsky had great hopes for the Polish revolution, recognized the necessity of a common party for the entire territory of the Polish state and even accused Vasylkiv of succumbing to the ideology of the Ukrainian Communist Party, which was opposed to that of the CP(B)U.[96] At the time, though, these differences (known only to a very small circle) were marginal. Unlike other young political groups, the Vasylkivists were characterized by a strong internal bond and a conscious factional discipline.

The CWPP position was most clearly stated at the factional conference in April 1921, although it was far from unanimous. Cichowski and Królikowski, representatives of the CWPP central committee in the Ukrainian party, sought a closer connection between the Ukrainian and Polish movements. Pasternak, on the other hand, emphasized the separateness of the East Galician lands in general and of the revolutionary movement in particular. He proposed that the separate demands of the people of the region be represented, for example, in the slogan "a Soviet Galician Republic." Pasternak's proposition was not accepted, however, and instead the conference adopted the slogan, "a Polish Republic of Soviets in closest union with Soviet Russia and Ukraine."[97] The slogan did not help the factions to overcome the dispute.

The CWPP loyalists favoured a single party for all Poland and differed only in their definitions of the Ukrainian party's autonomous rights. A sizable group of Ukrainian Communists from Volhynia, who considered themselves loyal to the CWPP, also criticized certain aspects of the CWPP position. Zatonsky himself, whose position may be authoritative, wrote in a letter of 28 October 1921 to Polish Communists in Moscow[98] that among Ukrainian activists in Eastern Galicia (the Vasylkivists) "nationalism is more or less clearly discernible," but "the unfortunate truth is that not all Polish Communists are free of a certain dose of this same sin." They are too preoccupied with maintaining "the purity of [their political] line,"[99] which in the Galician context "has a touch of, if not nationalism, then 'megalomania'." They must understand that "Eastern Galicia is not Masovia." But Zatonsky favoured the subordination of the CPEG to Warsaw because, beyond other considerations, "the Communists there [in Eastern Galicia] are too weak and green to be entrusted with tactics." In Zatonsky's opinion the intelligentsia of the CPEG leadership was due for a major "purge to eliminate those elements reminiscent of our own UCPism (Vynnychenkoism)."[100]

Zatonsky proposed the establishment of a relationship between the East Galician and Polish Communist parties such as the one that existed between the CP(B)U and the Russian Communist Party (Bolsheviks) (RCP[B]), and he categorically ordered the CWPP central committee not to emphasize its authority. An analogous relationship existed, Zatonsky recalled, between the Russian republic and Ukraine. For the latter, Russia is the centre and mainstay of socialism. He opposed the subordination of Communists in Polissia and Volhynia to the Galician Communist party and favoured their direct subordination to Warsaw since "there is no [*sic*] bond between Eastern Galicia and the rest of the Ukrainian lands in Poland." This confusing demand was probably rooted in Zatonsky's fears that since the people in those areas once connected with the Russian revolutionary movement were more pro-Soviet than the Ukrainian people of Eastern Galicia, these lands would be subordinated to Lviv. He trusted neither the region's Communists nor the revolutionary fervour of its peasants. From his own experience of the Soviet republic in Ternopil he was convinced of the passivity of the East Galician peasantry, which had taken no revolutionary initiative despite the encouragement of its new leaders.[101]

The Polish party's position on the national question at its first congress in 1918 sharpened the conflict with the Vasylkivists. The congress declared the national question irrelevant in a period of socialist revolution, and Poland was on the eve of such a revolution. For this reason the congress also rejected such intermediary forms of national liberation as autonomy, nor was it interested in the border problems.[102] Clearly it expected its Ukrainian comrades to adopt a similar position, but such was not the case. Moreover, according to the CWPP, the leadership of the young Communist movement was not sufficiently interested in the problems of the all-Polish revolution, but set itself aims that revealed separatist and even nationalist inclinations. Much had happened since 1918, but some viewpoints remained to form the background of the conflict in 1921.

The accusations of the Vasylkivists (particularly vocal at the Second CWPP Congress), that the CWPP never protested the occupation of Eastern Galicia or issued a protest appeal, were untrue,[103] as the following sections from such appeals demonstrate.

> 1) From the appeal "to the soldiers of Haller's army": Soldiers. It is a lie that you are going to Poland to protect its threatened borders. It is not in defence of the fatherland that the blood of Polish soldiers was shed for half a year in Eastern Galicia. The war with the Ruthenians is a war of the Polish lords with the Ruthenian peasants: the latter want the land they have worked for centuries for the parasite landlords.[104]
> 2) An appeal issued by the central committee of the Polish party stated: Soldiers and Poles, you will be shedding your blood to repress the peasants in Lviv, Belorussia and Eastern Galicia and save the Polish magnates.[105]

The Communist International had to settle the dispute. At first its leaders took a middle position. Many aspects of the criticism levelled at the Polish party on the national and agrarian questions (the latter did not arouse such passions) appealed to them, but they decisively rejected attempts to create a separate Galician party.

A special commission of the Comintern's executive made the final decision on 29 December 1922, in the form of a letter to party members in Eastern Galicia. It repeated the earlier decision on autonomy for the CPEG, condemned the attempt of the oppositionists (the Vasylkivists) to create an independent party, and gave the oppositionists until May 1920 to resolve the split. At the same time it advised the Polish party to act with more tact.[106]

Although the oppositionists achieved a formal union in the allotted time and elected a common executive committee,[107] ultimate agreement was reached only at the Second CWPP Congress. Fortunately for the Vasylkivists, their demands corresponded to changes on the national and peasant questions that the party leadership had prepared for adoption at the congress. Even former adversaries now accepted certain theses of the Vasylkivists. Typical in this regard was Królikowski. He still maintained that "nationalism celebrates its triumphs among the Ukrainian masses and has not been without its influence on certain Communist circles,"[108] but he attributed this to a reaction against oppression by the large landowners and Polish authorities in the *Kresy*. Also, he accepted that in Eastern Galicia, the Polish masses and even workers in the labour unions at times succumbed to chauvinism. Królikowski maintained that the Polish revolutionary left could eliminate mutual distrust and have normal relations with the Ukrainian masses only by meeting the demands of the oppressed Slavic minorities. This demanded not only a proclamation of the right to self-determination, but an outright declaration about the future union of the *Kresy* with the Soviet republics. Such a declaration would be expedited because the nationality question had become a revolutionary question in Poland since the war.[109]

Most delegates stressed the lack of consideration of some CWPP emissaries. Dłuski mentioned cases that affected the whole party and Vasylkiv talked of even greater offences,[110] but with regard to slogans, differences of opinion remained substantial. Dłuski and Jerzy Czeszejko-Sochacki considered the slogan "Polish Republic of Soviets" when applied to the Ukrainian lands unsuitable,[111] while Władysław Stein-Krajewski considered it apt.[112] Radek was opposed to the slogan of a "Galician Soviet Republic."[113] The congress agreed that reliance on the Red Army rather than on the revolution and separate uprisings amounted to an abandonment of internationalism.[114]

The congress resolution satisfied the demands of the Ukrainian delegation on two fundamental problems: by proclaiming the right of self-determination for the Slavic minorities and announcing that in practice this would mean joining the Soviet republics.[115] It also passed a resolution on the division of large landholdings among the local peasantry. Many minor differences were eliminated and Vasylkiv solemnly proclaimed the end of the dispute and solidarity with the Polish party and its resolutions.[116] The congress also carried out organizational changes advantageous to the Ukrainian party.

The Communist Party of Eastern Galicia was transformed into the Communist Party of Western Ukraine, with party organizations in Volhynia and Chełm subordinate to it. In turn, the entire party was subordinate to the CWPP. Thus all resolutions of its executive bodies, including congress resolutions and the composition of the elected leadership, were controlled by and required the approval of the Polish party. Also, unless special exceptions were made, all resolutions of the CWPP were binding on the CPWU.[117]

The most active members of the opposition at the congress, Julian Leński and Henryk Stein-Krajewski (L. Domski), pointed out the danger of playing on national feelings. Leński, recalling the negative experience of the Red Army in the war with Poland in 1920,[118] doubtless had in mind the appeals made by former tsarist generals, which influenced the national sentiments of the Russians. These appeals had left an unfavourable impression on Communists in Soviet Russia and, especially, in Poland.

Notes

1. Z. Landau and J. Tomaszewski, *Robotnicy przemysłowi w Polsce. Materialne warunki bytu, 1918–1939* (Warsaw, 1971), 95 (Table 37).
2. An exception was Lviv *województwo*, to which was added the present region of Rzeszów inhabited almost exclusively by Poles. These artificially formed boundaries resulted in a Polish majority in Lviv *województwo*.
3. *Mały Rocznik Statystyczny* (1939), 24. Greek Catholics in Eastern Galicia and the Orthodox in Volhynia were considered Ukrainians.
4. Landau and Tomaszewski, *Robotnicy przemysłowi*, 109 (Table 45).
5. Z. Landau and J. Tomaszewski, *Zarys historii gospodarczej Polski, 1918–1939* (Warsaw, 1962), 46.
6. *Mały Rocznik Statystyczny* (1939), 25.
7. Landau and Tomaszewski, *Robotnicy przemysłowi*, 110.
8. *Ibid.*, 111–13.
9. Ukrainian military formations originally organized under Austrian command during the First World War.
10. The West Ukrainian People's Republic later changed its name to the West Ukrainian Regional People's Republic to emphasize its willingness to join the Ukrainian state in the East.
11. For more details on this, see H. Jabłoński, "Druga Rzeczpospolita a Galicja Wschodnia," *Wiedza i życie*, no. 10 (1948), and M. Lozynsky, *Halychyna v 1918–1920* (Vienna, 1922).
12. See, for example, the text of the so-called Lanckorona pact concluded in 1923 between the Christian National Unity (Chrześcijańska Jedność Narodowa) and the Piast peasant party. Extremely chauvinistic toward the national minorities, the pact demanded the introduction of a *numerus clausus* for non-Poles in universities and more colonization via the agrarian reform in the Eastern *Kresy*. S. Głąbiński, *Wspomnienia polityczne*, part 1 (Pelplin, 1939), 526–7.
13. W. Pobóg-Malinowski, *Najnowsza historia polityczna Polski 1848–1945* (London, 1956), 2: 437.
14. We will not go into the theoretical dispute between advocates of incorporation and advocates of federation for the Eastern *Kresy*, since it has been discussed repeatedly by Polish historians. See A. Chojnowski, "Mniejszości narodowe w polityce rządów polskich w latach 1921–1926," *Przegląd Historyczny*, no. 4 (1976); J. Lewandowski, *Federalizm: Litwa i Białoruś w polityce obozu belwederskiego* (Warsaw, 1962) and S. Mikulicz. *Prometeizm w polityce II Rzeczypospolitej*, (Warsaw, 1971).
15. See the memorandum from Ukrainian scientific and cultural institutions to the academies, universities and other scientific institutions throughout the world 30 June 1920, in *Z istorii revoliutsiinoho rukhu u Lvovi. Dokumenty i materialy, 1917–1939* (Lviv, 1957), 49.
16. *Ibid.*, 50, and Pobóg-Malinowski, *Najnowsza historia*, 2: 437.
17. See the report of the Lviv police on a repressive action against the secret

Ukrainian university, 3 December 1927, in *Pid praporom Zhovtnia. Vplyv velykoi zhovtnevoi sotsialistychnoi revoliutsii na pidnesennia revoliutsiinoho rukhu v Zakhidnii Ukraini, 1921–28. Dokumenty i materialy* (Lviv, 1964), 76–80.

18. "Though no anti-state charges were proved against the university, the professors and students were still... sentenced to several years in prison for teaching without a licence." A. Bocheński, "Położyć kres szaleństwu," *Polityka* (formerly *Bunt Młodych*), no. 23 (1937): 1. Ukrainian sources do not mention the sentence of "several years imprisonment" for secret teaching. It is possible that Bocheński had in mind the sum total of various sentences.
19. Prosvita (Enlightenment) was founded in 1868 in Lviv and concentrated on organizing libraries, public reading rooms and community centres; it sometimes ran schools and vocational courses. In 1906–14 it was also active in Dnieper Ukraine. Some local Prosvita headquarters in the 1920s were dominated for a time by the Communists. Ridna shkola (Native School), called the Ukrainian Pedagogical Society until 1926, was founded in 1881 in Lviv to aid in organizing and running private Ukrainian elementary and secondary schools. It also held adult-education courses to eradicate illiteracy and defended the interests of the Ukrainian teaching profession.
20. This information was given by the organ of the Ukrainian Social Democratic Party, *Vpered*, no. 8–9 (1919), reprinted in *Pid praporom zhovtnia*, 178.
21. Such incidents are described in *Vpered*, no. 18 (1918), reprinted in *Z istorii revoliutsiinoho rukhu*, 25.
22. See "Ustawa z 31 VII 1924," *Dziennik Ustaw RP* (1924), 1301–2.
23. On 29 December 1923 the curator of the Lviv school district, Stanisław Sobiński, sent a letter to all schools—including private Ukrainian schools—instructing them to use the term "Ruthenian" rather than "Ukrainian"; his instructions included examples of the desired usage. He warned that documents sent to his office that did not observe this rule would be ignored. See the leaflet *Denkschrift der Ševčenko-Gesellschaft der Wissenschaften in Lemberg aus Anlass des Verbotes des nationalen Namens des ukrainischen Volksstammes durch das polnische Kuratorium des Lemberger Schulsprengels* (Lviv, 1923). The leaflet was signed by Dr. Kyrylo Studynsky, president of the Shevchenko Scientific Society and director of the Philology Section, and by Volodymyr Hnatiuk, secretary of the society and member of the Academy of Sciences in Petersburg [*sic*]. This memorandum contains the full text of Sobiński's letter. Ukrainian sources maintain that this action of the Polish authorities had a legal basis in a special order of the ministry of internal affairs, but I have not been successful in locating such a document. Probably there were only oral recommendations from the ministries.
24. Głąbiński, *Wspomnienia polityczne*, 520. See the quotation above from Pobóg-Malinowski's work. On 26 September 1922 the Diet passed the bill "O zasadach powszechnego samorządu wojewódzkiego, a w szczególności województwa lwowskiego, tarnopolskiego i stanisławowskiego"; this promised to found a Ukrainian university in Lviv. *Dziennik Ustaw RP*, no. 90 (1922)

poz 832, 1553–5. The university was never founded.

25. See S. Mauersberg, *Szkolnictwo powszechne dla mniejszości narodowych w Polsce w latach 1918–1939* (Warsaw, 1968), 60–102, and L. Sorochtej, *Sprawa ukraińska w Polsce a rząd Władysława Grabskiego* (Warsaw, 1961), 234–41. A mimeographed copy of the latter work is in the Wojskowa Akademia Polityczna (WAP) im. F. Dzierżyńskiego.
26. T. Hołówko, "Stosunki administracyjne na Wołyniu," *Robotnik*, no. 65 (1926): 1. The author, a former member of the Polish Socialist Party (PSP) who worked closely with Piłsudski, held office in this period.
27. Ignacy Daszyński (1866–1936) was co-founder and leader of the Polish Social Democratic Party of Galicia and Cieszyn Silesia, and, after independence, a member of the united PSP.
28. See motions made in the Diet on 25 November 1925 concerning the organization of the Ukrainian, Belorussian, Jewish, German and Lithuanian school systems and the abrogation of laws hindering the cultural development of these peoples, in *Posłowie rewolucyjni w Sejmie. Wybór przemowień, interpelacji i wniosków* (Warsaw, 1961), 583–5.
29. A. Chernetsky, *Spomyny z moho zhyttia* (London, 1964), 128. The author had belonged to the leadership of the Ukrainian Social Democratic Party in Lviv since 1909.
30. S. Grabski, *Państwo narodowe* (Lviv, 1929).
31. Chojnowski, "Mniejszości narodowe," 601.
32. W. Mysłek, *Kościół katolicki w Polsce w latach 1918–1939* (Warsaw, 1966), 115. According to other sources, in 1919 alone the government closed 250 orthodox churches. See *Parlament Rzeczypospolitej Polskiej, 1919–1927*, ed. H. Mościcki and W. Dzwonkowski (Warsaw, 1928), 332.
33. Pobóg-Malinowski, *Najnowsza historia*, 2: 439; Mysłek, *Kościół katolicki*, 110.
34. K. Srokowski, *Sprawa narodowościowa na Kresach Wschodnich* (Cracow, 1924), 40. In part this publication is a report of research on the Eastern *Kresy* done by Srokowski at the recommendation of Premier Władysław Sikorski.
35. Some influential persons in the goverment attempted to change *Kresy* policy. During Grabski's premiership and on his initiative, a "plan of a general policy in the *Kresy*, in districts threatened by bands in the winter 1924–25" was proposed to the government. The plan contained proposals for radical economic reforms in favour of the local peasantry. It was rejected.
36. Cz. Madajczyk, *Burżuazyjno-obszarnicza reforma rolna w Polsce, 1918–1939* (Warsaw, 1956), 173; Landau and Tomaszewski, *Zarys*, 71–7, and Głąbiński, *Wspomnienia polityczne*, 526–7.
37. A memorandum issued by officials of the Ukrainian Citizens' Committee in Lviv on 6 December 1920. *Z istorii revoliutsiinoho rukhu*, 69–70.
38. *Ukrainska Zahalna Entsyklopediia* (Lviv-Stanyslaviv-Kolomyia, n.d.), 3: 658–60.
39. Hołówko, "Stosunki administracyjne," 1.

40. M. Kuzmin, *Shkola i obrazovanie v Chekhoslovakii* (Moscow, 1971), 222–4.
41. *Ukrainska Zahalna Entsyklopediia*, 1: 836; 2: 1,007; 3: 1,018. For a more comprehensive comparison of the situation of Ukrainians in Poland and Czechoslovakia, see T. Hołówko, "Emigracja ukraińska w Czechach," *Robotnik*, no. 60 (1925).
42. Srokowski, *Sprawa narodowościowa*, 11, 15, 29. The author's conclusion (p. 56) is interesting. He considers Polish policy on the Slavic minorities, based on their national oppression and economic exploitation, to be similar to the nationalities policies of Prussia, tsarist Russia and Hungary.
43. J. Makarewicz, *Mniejszości narodowe* (Lviv, 1924), 19.
44. The nationalities policy of the Polish government in this period is considered chauvinistic by nearly all Polish and non-Polish historians today, regardless of political orientation.
45. In 1926, after joining the socialist revolutionary organization in Volhynia, this party took the name Ukrainian Socialist Radical Party (USRP).
46. Jerzy Sochacki, for instance, wrote: "Among the Ukrainian bourgeoisie and upper strata of the petty bourgeoisie there was a more or less clear orientation in favour of the Ukrainian Soviet Socialist Republic." J. Czeszejko-Sochacki [J. Bratkowski], *Na drogach nacjonalizmu, oportunizmu i zdrady* (Lviv, 1928), 34. This was affirmed even more unequivocally by the "majority" at the Fourth Conference of the Communist Party of Poland.
47. Chernetsky, *Spomyny*, 59–66. Chernetsky gives detailed information on how pro-Soviet feelings permeated all layers of Ukrainian society, from workers' organizations to bourgeois parties. In his opinion, only the USRP did not succumb to this (but here Chernetsky is not supported by the evidence).
48. R. Ilnytzkyj, *Deutschland und die Ukraine 1934–1935* (Munich, 1955), 74; *Entsyklopediia Ukrainoznavstva*, ed. V. Kubijovyč and Z. Kuzelia (Munich-New York, 1949), 1, part 2: 557.
49. The file of Leon Rozenman, former member of the Boryslav group. CA KC PZPR, 9580, and Halushko, *Narysy*, 20–1.
50. This document written by Mykhailo Poloz fell, along with the envoy, into the hands of the Polish police and was probably unknown to the CWPP.
51. The evaluation of this party has varied over the years and to this day is the object of lively controversy. The chief historical works on the subject are: M. Kulichenko, "Taktika bolshevistskoi partii v sviazi s osobennostiami razvitiia sotsialisticheskoi revoliutsii na Ukraine," *Voprosy istorii KPSS*, no. 10 (1967): 107, 109; *Ocherki istorii Kommunisticheskoi partii (bolshevikov) Ukrainy* (Kharkiv, 1929), 190–2, 217, 243; M. G. Rafes, *Dva goda revoliutsii na Ukraine (Evoliutsia i raskol Bunda* (Moscow, 1920), 11, 113–14, 120, 127; I. Majstrenko, *Borot'bism: A Chapter in the History of Ukrainian Communism* (New York, 1954), 315. The author made use of a typescript of the Ukrainian version of Majstrenko's book.
52. *Do vsikh chleniv KPZỤ* [Resolutions of the Ninth Conference] (Lviv, 1928), 8.

53. K. Maksymovych, "Istoriia KPZU v natsionalistychnomu osvitlenni M. Levytskoho," *Nasha pravda*, no. 1–2 (1928): 72.
54. R. Turiansky, "Do pytannia istorychnoi genezy KPZU," *Nasha pravda*, no 3–8 (1928).
55. A. Pryideshyn, "Hnat Mykhailychenko," *Nova kultura*, no. 7–8 (1923): 29–37.
56. Speech of Stepan Volynets (secretary of the CPWU central committee), *IV Konferencja Komunistycznej Partii Polski (24 XI-23 XII 25). Protokoły obrad i uchwały*, part 1 (Warsaw, 1972), 422.
57. Majstrenko, *Borot'bism*, 317.
58. A. Hoshovsky, "Pamiati zasnovnyka KPSH—Karla Maksymovycha," *Nasha kultura* (supplement to *Nashe slovo*), no. 1 (1967): 12–13.
59. P. Arsenych, "Savrych," *Ukrainskyi istorychnyi zhurnal*, no. 1 (1969): 126–8.
60. The Ukrainian Communist Party was formed from the left wing of the Ukrainian Social Democratic Workers' Party ("independentist" faction) in January 1920. In 1919 the independentists took part in an armed struggle against the Soviets, later toned down their hostility to the Bolsheviks, but always remained in opposition. The UCP was a legal party until 1924 when it was disbanded, part of the membership going to the CP(B)U. It had its organizations abroad and Volodymyr Vynnychenko, former premier of the Ukrainian Central Rada, belonged to one of them. The ideological precursor of the UCP was the CP(B)U activist and former Ukrainian social democrat, Vasyl Shakhrai (or Shakh-Rai). In a pamphlet co-authored with another less well-known activist, Shakhrai, turning to Lenin, posed the question: Can one be a Communist and at the same time desire the separation of Ukraine from Soviet Russia? A few months later, when Shakhrai was dead (shot by the White Guards), Lenin answered in the affirmative.

    Shakhrai had a strong influence on future members of the UCP and Borotbists. See S. Mazlakh and V. Shakhrai, *On the Current Situation in Ukraine* (Ann Arbor, 1970), and V. Iu. Ievdokymenko, *Krytyka ideinykh osnov ukrainskoho burzhuaznoho natsionalizmu*, 2d ed. (Kiev, 1968), 250. See also V. I. Lenin, "Letter to the Workers and Peasants of the Ukraine apropos of the Victories over Denikin," *Collected Works*, 45 vols. (Moscow, 1960–70), 30: 294–6.
61. The name International Revolutionary Social Democratic Youth was also used.
62. Roman Rosdolsky [V.S.], "Do istorii ukrainskoho livo-sotsiialistychnoho rukhu v Halychyni (Pidchasvoienni 'Drahomanivki' 1916–1918)," *Vpered. Ukrainska robitnycha gazeta*, no. 3–4 (1951).
63. According to Turiansky, the IRSD leadership also included Bilensky, Butynsky (pseudonym) and Sofiia (Kopertynska). Khlon was not a member, but a co-founder of the organization. See Turiansky, "Do pytannia," 147.
64. Rosdolsky, "Do istorii."
65. Liudvik Rozenberg, of Jewish origin, belonged to the IRSD, but Rosdolsky

writes that he was an exception. In 1918–19 Rozenberg was an officer in the Ukrainian Sich Riflemen in Western Ukraine; from 1920 he belonged to the Ukrainian Section of the Czech Communist Party, and in 1923 became a member of the CPEG central committee. He left the party in 1925. He spent the 1930s in an oppositionist Communist group and was imprisoned in the Bereza concentration camp. He was arrested by the Soviet authorities in Lviv in September 1939.

66. Rosdolsky, "Do istorii."
67. Turiansky, "Do pytannia," 145–66. According to Turiansky, the name IRSD was adopted in 1915, which contradicts both Rosdolsky and the name of the journal (*Vistnyk drahomanivskoi orhanizatsii* was retained until 1917).
68. O. Karpenko, "Do pytannia pro vynyknennia i orhanizatsiine oformlennia Komunistychnoi partii Skhidnoi Halychyny," *Z istorii zakhidnoukrainskykh zemel* (Kiev, 1957), 2: 189; Halushko, *Narysy*, 13.
69. A. Nagornaia, "Bolsheviki Ukrainy v period Oktiabria v svete sovremennoi falsifikatorskoi literatury," *Voprosy istorii KPSS*, no. 3 (1967): 80. S. Korolivsky, M. Rubach, N. Suprunenko, *Pobeda sovetskoi vlasti na Ukraine* (Moscow, 1967), 269. J. Radziejowski, "Ruch narodowy i rewolucyjny na Ukrainie w okresie działalności Centralnej Rady," *Studia z dziejôw ZSRR i Europy Srodkowej*, no. 9 (1973).
70. Maksymovych, "Istoriia KPZU," 72. According to other sources this was a conference of the IRSD, left-wing Radicals and other leftist groups. See Karpenko, "Do pytannia pro vynnyknennia," 173.
71. After losing the war with the Poles, the Ukrainian Galician Army joined forces with Petliura in Eastern Ukraine and after his fall went over to Denikin. They tried unsuccessfully to win Denikin over to the cause of an independent Ukrainian Galician Republic. Next they joined the ranks of the Red Army where they underwent re-education. The Red Army became a political school for many Western Ukrainians.
72. See Iwański, *Z dziejôw*, 30–1.
73. Baral, pseudonym Vladyslav Savko (1890–1957), was, up to 1917, an anarchist active in Lviv and Vienna. In 1919 he founded a Communist group in Lviv. Józef Kowalczyk and Ozjasz Szechter, later members of the CPEG and CPWU, belonged to the youth section of this group. In 1920 Baral was a member of the government of the Galician Soviet Republic and participated in the Second Congress of the Comintern. Later he was active in the Communist Party of Austria. From the 1930s he lived in the Soviet Union. Levytsky was born in Rohatyn in Stanyslaviv *wojewôdztwo*. During the First World War he was taken prisoner by the Russians. In Turkestan he joined the RCP(B). In 1919 he went to Lviv as the emissary of the Galician committee. In 1920 he was a member of the government of the Galician Soviet Republic and participated in the Comintern's Second Congress. In 1921 as Soviet ambassador in Vienna he worked closely with the CPEG and CWPP.
74. Krilyk, pseudonym Vasylkiv, was born in 1898 in Lviv. As a law student he joined a *drahomanivka* and was one of the founders and leaders of the

IRSD. During the Polish-Ukrainian war he fought in the forces of the West Ukrainian Peoples' Republic. He was wounded in the arm and partially disabled. He was interned in Czechoslovakia where, together with Rosdolsky and others, he organized Communist circles among Ukrainians in 1920. In 1921 he was secretary of the central committee of the CPEG ("Vasylkivist" faction, or, as it was also known, the "separatist" faction [*rozłamowcy*]). Next to Maksymovych, and later Turiansky, he was the most outstanding party leader and a very skilled organizer. He published in the party organs less frequently than Turiansky, but was often the inspiration behind the words of others. Direct and engaging as a comrade, he easily won the sympathy of his subordinates. He reportedly had one fault—stubbornness. Only with great difficulty could he be persuaded to change a decision. In sharp ideological disputes this fault became the virtue of principle.

75. On Skrypnyk's and Zatonsky's differences on the national question and in their assessment of the Vasylkivists, see M. Skrypnyk, "Natsionalistychnyi ukhyl v KPZU. Dopovid na plenumi TsK KPbU, 7 VI 1927," in *Dzherela ta prychyny rozlamu v KPZU* (Kharkiv, 1928), 72.
76. "To the Central Committee of the Communist Party of Ukraine in Kharkiv" (in Ukrainian), letter of Vasylkiv and Syrel (Senyk), 15 February 1921, AM CA KC PZPR, 1956/57, page 78; and Iwański, *Z dziejów*, 32.
77. Grosserowa (1883–1937) was a member of the PSP, a leader of the PSP-Left and member of the central committee of the CWPP. She was also known by her maiden name Jachimowicz. She died in a prison hospital in Moscow. Cichowski (1887–1940) was a member of the Social Democracy of the Kingdom of Poland and Lithuania from 1907. He participated in the revolution and civil war in Russia, belonged to the central committee of the CWPP and CPWU, and was co-organizer of the international brigades in Spain. He was executed in the Soviet Union. Like Grosserowa, Cichowski came from an aristocratic Polish family. Królikowski (1881–1937) was a worker, a member of the PSP and PSP-Left and the central committee of the CWPP and CPWU. He died in the Soviet purges.
78. Bukshovany (1888–1933) was a commissioned officer in the Ukrainian Sich Riflemen and leader of its First Brigade during the First World War. *Ukrainska Zahalna Entsyklopediia*, 414. Later he fought in the ranks of the Ukrainian Galician Army, and became an officer in the Red Brigades. In 1920–1 he served on the editorial board of *Nasha pravda* in Vienna. Somewhat later he became a paragon of the "nationalist deviation" known as sabotagism.
79. From the beginning of the Polish-Ukrainian conflict (November 1918) a network of prison camps was established in Eastern Galicia. An International Red Cross Commission visited these camps in October 1919 and estimated the number of prisoners at 23,500. Courts were set up within the camps; they sentenced prisoners for their "behaviour" during the war, during the "Bolshevik invasion" and later. Death sentences were also handed down. The mortality rate was high because of unhygienic conditions. The camps were liquidated in 1922. *Ukrainska Zahalna Entsyklopediia*, 659.

80. *Ibid.*
81. Halushko, *Narysy*, 44, 50.
82. Nazarenko et al., *Ocherki*, 295.
83. O. Vasylkiv, "Do dzherel i prychyn suchasnoho rozlamu KPZU," *Nasha pravda*, no. 3–8, (1928): 83.
84. Report of the Division of the Second Chief Command, CA KC PZPR, 296/II–20, and Information on the Zokordot trials and torture in Polish prisons, CA KC PZPR, 1356/8, rozdz 24, 147–8.
85. "To the Central Committee of the CPU in Kharkiv," 11.
86. *Ibid.*, 13.
87. "To the Third Comintern Congress" (unsigned, in Ukrainian), 18 June 1921, AM CA KC PZPR, 785, 1, 3–4.
88. Iwański, "Z dziejów," 34.
89. *Nasha pravda*, no. 7–8 (1923): 1.
90. Halushko, *Narysy*, 115.
91. In this matter they had the support of the organizational bureau of the CP(B)U central committee, but the decision taken by the CWPP central committee, to participate in the elections, was approved by the central committee of the RCP(B).
92. In 1926 Rosdolsky retired from political activity to devote himself to historical studies. He earned doctorates first in Vienna, and then in Lviv (in the 1930s). During the Second World War he was arrested by the Gestapo and placed in concentration camps. After the war he settled in the USA where he continued his research. He was the author of many works in Ukrainian, German and Polish. He is perhaps most famous in the West for *The Making of Marx's Capital* (which has been translated into several languages including Japanese) and *Zur nationalen Frage* [on Engels and the "non-historic peoples"], but he is also the author of several first-rank studies in social history such as *Stosunki poddańcze w dawnej Galicji*, 2 vols. (Warsaw, 1962). For more on Rosdolsky, see J. Radziejowski, "Roman Rosdolsky: Man, Activist and Scholar," *Science and Society*, no. 2 (1978).
93. R. Rosdolsky [A. Tenet], "Halytskyi vulkan," *Nash stiah*, no. 4 (1922): 9.
94. R. Rosdolsky [T. Prokopovych], "Halytskyi vyborchyi konflikt," 26.
95. *Ibid.*, 27.
96. R. Kuzma [Lazarkevych], "Vasylkizm iak zakhidnoukrainska modyfikatsiia ukapizmu," *Kultura*, no. 7–8 (1930): 11, and information from R. Rosdolsky. One should remember that Rosdolsky was the only writer in the CPEG who came out in the party's own press with criticisms of the UCP. R. Rosdolsky [T. Prokopovych], "Shakh-Rai contra Lienin," *Nash stiah*, no. 4 (1922): 13–17.
97. *Ibid.*, Iwański, "Z dziejów," 38.
98. See the letter of 10 October 1921 addressed to Marchlewski, Walecki and Bobiński and signed by Zatonsky. Partarkhiv Instytutu istorii partii TsK KP Ukrainy (PA IIP TsK KPU), f. 233, op. 1, od. zb. 11, 1–9.
99. Here Zatonsky had in mind the "twenty-one conditions" of acceptance into

the Comintern, which held that there should be only one Communist party in a country and that it should be subject to the principles of centralism.

100. UCPism (*ukapizm*) refers to the Ukrainian Communist Party; Vynnychenkoism to Volodymyr Vynnychenko. See above, p. 25, note 60.

101. V. P. Zatonsky, "Pershi kroky Radianskoi vlady Zakhidnoi Ukrainy," in *KPZU—orhanizator revoliutsiinoi borotby. Spohady kolyshnikh chleniv KPZU* (Lviv, 1958), 44–5.

102. *KPP. Ucwały i rezolucje* (Warsaw, 1959), 1: 42.

103. See Vasylkiv's speech in *II Zjazd Komunistycznej Partii Robotniczej Polski. Protokoły obrad i rezolucje* (Warsaw, 1968), 131.

104. The leaflet was signed: "Organization of Communist Soldiers of Warsaw, May 1919." Centralne Archiwum Wojskowe (CAW), 123/1/113, 27–8.

105. May Day, 5 IV 1919. CA KC PZPR, 1031/17–1031/18, 8–8a.

106. Iwański, "Z dziejów," 48.

107. A joint central committee was elected, composed of Krilyk (Vasylkiv), Rozenberg, Popel and, from the CWPP loyalists, Langer (Dłuski), Seweryn (Sewer), J. Wizenfeld and Mykhats.

108. *II Zjazd*, 358.

109. *Ibid.*, 221–2.

110. *Ibid.*, 363 (Dłuski), 130 (Vasylkiv).

111. *Ibid.*, 335, 363.

112. *Ibid.*, 69.

113. *Ibid.*, 325.

114. *Ibid.*, 366 (Wincenty Dmowski), 367 (Jan Paszyn), 67 (Krajewski).

115. *Ibid.*, 573.

116. *Ibid.*, 579.

117. *Ibid.*, 549–50.

118. *Ibid.*, 157.

Chapter Two

Internal Stabilization in the CPWU, 1923–5

The Search for New Tactics

The Second Congress of the CWPP was a victory for the Vasylkivists. Although their demand for organizational independence was not met, their proposition that Western Ukraine should join the Ukrainian Soviet Socialist Republic won broad recognition. Furthermore, the acceptance of this proposition nullified all previous arguments on strategy. Though the Vasylkivists' sabotage policy had come under criticism at the congress, they themselves had begun to recognize its harmfulness.

The strictures imposed by the autonomy statute also posed few problems for the Vasylkivists. In 1924 the Comintern's executive committee passed a special resolution permitting contacts between the CPWU and the CP(B)U for ideological consultation.[1] In practice, this legalized the already existing contacts of the CPWU leadership with Skrypnyk, Shumsky and others. In addition to receiving help from the CP(B)U and the financial aid which the Comintern funneled through the CPP Central Committee, the headquarters in Lviv was also aided by the Ukrainian left in Canada. Material and ideological support was never concentrated solely in the CPP, a fact which afforded the Ukrainians a large measure of freedom.

In 1924 the Foreign Bureau to Aid the Revolutionary Movement in Western Ukraine was moved from Vienna to Kharkiv.[2] This agency was again headed by Maksymovych who, in that capacity, was appointed deputy minister of the CP(B)U Central Committee. The Foreign Bureau was itself the official representative of the CPWU to the CP(B)U. The agency was used for such matters as quick consultation, training within the

Soviet Union, and as a source of material aid. From 1924 *Nasha pravda* was published in Vienna instead of Kharkiv, and changed from a newspaper into a sizable journal, which became the main theoretical organ of the party. These facts indicate that the ideological influence of the CP(B)U on the CPWU was considerably stronger than that of the CPP, despite the recommendation of the Comintern, and despite the fact that, organizationally, the CPP was in command.

After the dissolution of the USDP by the Polish authorities in December 1923–January 1924,[3] the entire USDP left joined the Communists and became the strongest group within the CPWU, as revealed from the questionnaire of the Second Congress. They at once began to play a major role, much to the dismay of CWPP members. On 23 February 1924, Vasyl Mokhniuk, Andrii Pashchuk, Osyp Skrypa, Toma Prystupa and Iakiv Voitiuk, members of the Ukrainian socialist club in the Diet, left and formed a USDP club under the total control of the CPWU. Later that year, on 7 November 1924, when any resumption of legal activity by Ukrainian socialists was out of the question, they joined the Communist faction.[4]

The first act of the CPWU executive after the Second Congress of the CWPP was to inform the membership of the victory and the stabilization of the leadership. In an article in the party organ,[5] Vasylkiv said that both the leaders and activists of the CPWU were "people who [before the war] had been far from the leading circles of the workers' movement."[6] In his opinion this enabled the young party to avoid past mistakes. Vasylkiv saw positive aspects in the CPWU–CWPP co-operation: for example, the party was strengthened by the Poles' greater experience in illegal work. On the other hand the CWPP was still burdened with the national indifferentism of the SDKPL, which prevented it from "drawing the majority of the Polish proletariat away from nationalist influences."

Vasylkiv believed that the CWPP had also adopted the SDKPL's purist revolutionary views, which alienated the peasants and made it impossible to counteract what he considered the unwarranted power of the "Piast" and "Liberation" peasant parties. For these reasons the CWPP could not understand the importance of "the separatist struggle of the Ukrainian and Belorussian masses."[7] The CPEG had had to fight for a change in this policy. Vasylkiv said that the CWPP considered the national movement of the Ukrainian and Belorussian peasants "objectively counter revolutionary," but he did not attempt to document this debatable thesis. thesis. Although he remarked on "certain mistakes," the CPWU leader rarely mentioned the sins of his own party. He even passed over those the Comintern had pointed out, which did not impress the CWPP. The only conciliatory note in the article was a statement that the conflicts between the two parties belonged to the past. Adolf Langer Dłuski, an editor of

Nasha pravda, tried to block publication of Vasylkiv's attacks, but could not get support from the Polish party.[8] The CWPP leadership was perhaps counting on Vasylkiv and decided to allow him to strengthen his own position, despite the latter's one-sided interpretation of both the former dispute and the recently held congress.

After this article, which clinched their victory, the Vasylkivists immediately devised a completely new strategy. The initial stimulus was not the arguments of the Polish Communists, but the situation within the party. Figures on the composition of the CPWU indicate that either the party had failed to attract the Polish workers, who made up a majority in the larger industries, or it had lost contact with them because of factional fighting. The party had nine divisions (Lviv proper, suburban Lviv, Stanyslaviv, Kolomyia, Sambir, Boryslav, Ternopil, Volhynia and Przemyśl) with 1,712 members (1,326 Ukrainians, 227 Jews and 149 Poles). The Polish members came mainly from Lviv (65), Kolomyia (24) and Stanyslaviv (56).[9] The workers were concentrated in refineries in Drohobych, large railway shops in Lviv and Przemyśl, and plants in Sanok.

Several months later Vasylkiv wrote: "Once we were a party of workers in general, that is, a party which, besides the proletariat, had gathered into itself (and not around itself) other working classes, or the kind of party the social democrats sometimes like to think they are."[10] The problem, however, was more complicated; the CPWU was in danger of becoming a proletarian party without the support of the proletariat. But the leadership appreciated the seriousness of the situation and decided on a massive rebuilding and re-education of the party, together with a revision of its political conceptions. As a result the leadership of the CPWU moved closer to the position of the CWPP, sometimes even repeating the CWPP's earlier criticisms.

Discussion began with the question of sabotage, an insurrectionist ideology which, sanctified by the blood of its martyrs, was strong within the party and became the chief problem to be solved. A special article in *Nasha pravda* explained the attitude of Communists toward terror as a method of struggle with the state.[11] A convinced defender of this tactic, Osyp Bukshovany, was invited to contribute an article.[12] A political activist with a professional military background, he argued that sabotage was a necessary first stage in a struggle leading to a general uprising in the *Kresy*. He invoked Lenin's remark that a revolutionary who waits for the outbreak of armed conflict in a pure class form will never see it. Bukshovany maintained that the party was at an impasse because, for doctrinaire reasons, it had not followed the "path of further struggle" indicated in October 1922 by Melnychuk and Sheremeta.[13] P. Kulykovsky (Rosdoslky?)[14] and Serhii Vikul[15] polemized with Bukshovany, claiming that there was no future in a peasant uprising without the support of the proletariat.

The CPWU leadership's position on the international Communist movement was close to that of the CWPP. The Ukrainians were perhaps less cautious in formulating opinions that coincided with those of the "three Ws."[16] CPWU Central Committee member Pavlo Ladan devoted a special article to the discussion within the Communist Party of Germany about the events of September-October 1923 in that country.[17] He criticized Zinoviev's thesis that Hans von Seeckt and Friedrich Ebert had a common goal and differed only slightly in their views. Ladan came close to August Thalheimer's view that these politicians did not represent personal differences but rather distinct social groups: the petty bourgeois and workers' aristocracy (Ebert and Gustav Noske), and big capital (Seeckt); and that, from the workers' point of view, these groups did not form a solid reactionary mass. Against Zinoviev and following Thalheimer, Ladan held that it was necessary to defend bourgeois democracy against predacious big capital and fascism. And although, as the article emphasized, the united front in Germany made mistakes, "avoiding these mistakes"—and here Ladan agrees with Thalheimer—"would not have changed the results of the October events" in Germany.[18]

A cautious sympathy for the Thalheimer-Brandler group shows through in Ladan's article; he avoided referring to them as "rightist." When the Comintern executive condemned this wing of the German Communist party, *Nasha pravda* confined itself to quoting the resolution, preceding it only with a note that the Comintern executive committee "came to the conclusion that it is now necessary for the left and centre to close ranks against the right and its errors."[19] That marked the end of the German question.

No less characteristic was the position of the CPWU on the internal dispute of the Russian Communists over inner-party democracy. This began in November 1923 after the workers' strikes in Kharkiv and Moscow which took the Soviet party completely by surprise. The party leadership suddenly realized the party had few links with the working masses. Grigorii Zinoviev, head of the Comintern, and second only to Stalin and Lev Kamenev in the RCP(B), wrote in *Pravda* that one could observe a certain intellectual "stagnation" in the party ranks. The worker in the USSR, he said, at the present moment did not want to associate with the party, because he saw less restrictions and greater intellectual and social possibilities outside it. Zinoviev cautiously suggested that this situation resulted from the party's handing down "important problems to the membership with solutions decided in advance," which fostered a passive attitude.[20] Zinoviev's article sparked a lively debate in which Trotsky, Ivan Smirnov and Evgenii Preobrazhensky led the opposition. They argued that the mistakes lay not in the method of transmitting information to the party membership, but rather in the party's powerful hierarchy, which relegated rank-and-file members to a passive role.[21] Unless this organizational structure were changed, they believed, it would lead to the degeneration of the leadership and the entire party.[22]

When criticism of the opposition became acute (especially with Zinoviev's attacks on Trotsky and Karl Radek), the CWPP Central Committee, at the urging of Maria Koszutska and Adolf Warski, sent a letter in December 1923 to the central committee of the RCP(B) and the executive of the Comintern, pointing out the uncomradely and dangerous manner of polemizing with the opposition. In a letter signed by Stalin, the central committee of the Russian party rejected the charges of the Polish party and accused it of factionalism. There were also differences of opinion on the affairs of the German Communists and Germany, which demonstrated, according to the Poles, that the Comintern was too arbitrary in its treatment of non-Russian Communist parties.[23] The dispute continued at the Comintern's Fifth Congress, held a few months later.

The CPWU also devoted a special article to the Russian affair in its central organ.[24] The views of both sides in the dispute were summarized in a calm and objective manner, free of the truculence which the CWPP had noted in the RCP(B) Central Committee. The most critical comment of the Ukrainian paper was that: "It goes without saying that in some areas the opposition has gone further in its criticism of inner-party policy than either reality or the good of the party demanded. On the other hand, much of what was healthy in the criticism has been approved by the majority of the party."[25]

In spite of the charges made against the opposition in *Pravda*, the CPWU organ stated that "there was evidently no tactical attempt on the part of individual members of the opposition to unite for a more effective struggle to change inner-party policy."[26] The article quoted the opposition's argument that not every oppositional thought should be considered factionalism and that it would be organizational fetishism to consider the resolution of the Tenth Congress of the RCP(B), which forbade factions, proof against serious divisions brought about by objective conditions.[27] The article also argued against an overly rigid interpretation of factionalism that would restrict freedom of discussion.[28] Thus, up to and including the Fifth Conference, the position of the CPWU on the situation in the RCP(B) was the same as that of the Polish party.

In realizing its nationalities policies, the CPWU appealed to the patriotic feelings of Ukrainian society. For example, Vasylkiv wrote an article on the prospects of the Ukrainian national movement.[29] The article was particularly well timed, since the centre and right Ukrainian parties were disturbed by the decision of the Council of Ambassadors in March 1923 to approve Poland's annexation of Eastern Galicia. This act marked the end of the Western orientation of the parties, which began to split and search for new programmes.[30]

Vasylkiv felt that the struggle for national independence had failed, because the attempt of the Ukrainian petty bourgeois to create a capitalist state without its own capital was utopian.[31] He argued that it was structurally impossible for Ukraine to exist as an independent capitalist state; it could achieve independence only as a revolutionary state of workers and peasants.[32] Somewhat earlier, the unofficial party organ, *Nova kultura*, had published an editorial in a similar vein.[33] One must assume that Vasylkiv was its author, since a few years later he alone was accused of propagating the theory of the "non-bourgeois nature of the Ukrainian people."

The periodical *Kultura*, founded in 1924 and financed by the party, was a legal Ukrainian monthly that replaced *Nova kultura* after the latter was banned by the authorities. It was edited by the Communist activist, Stepan Rudyk, who not only acquainted its readers with the intellectual life of socialist Ukraine, but skilfully introduced them to the multi-national European culture of the leftist tradition. Marx, Engels, Lenin, Plekhanov, Trotsky, Georges Sorel, Luxemburg, Gramsci, Maiakovsky, Ivan Franko, Anatole France, Henri Barbusse, Martin Mexö, Romain Rolland and many others appeared in the pages of *Kultura*, as authors or as subjects of critical discourse. CPWU members contributed, under pseudonyms—Kuzma-Turiansky as Lazarkevych, and Rosdolsky as Prokopovych or P. Suk. Stepan Volynets occasionally contributed, under his own name, reflections on French literature, of which he was a great admirer. *Kultura* tried to serve the interests of all Ukrainian society by discussing subjects such as the failure of the Ukrainian independence struggle or polemizing with the "fatherlandish" concepts of the right or with Russophilism. It discussed Marxist philosophy and was careful to present opposing views.

The Fifth Conference of the CPWU

The final battle over the future ideological basis of the CPWU took place at its Fifth Conference. Originally the party planned to hold a congress, but because only twenty-one out of thirty-six delegates could attend,[34] it decided instead to hold a conference empowered to elect a central committee. The conference met in Kharkiv, probably toward the end of April 1924. Most of the absent delegates were CWPP loyalists, and members of the CWPP who did attend the conference interpreted their limited representation as a factional move on the part of the Vasylkivists. A dispute erupted over the authority of the remaining delegates, but eventually they were all recognized. Only Maksymovych, as the head of the Foreign Bureau, had his privileges to a vote of counsel revoked. The representatives of the CWPP were Koszutska and Edward Próchniak; Oleksander Shumsky, Mykola Skrypnyk and probably Emmanuil Kviring represented the CP(B)U. Vasylkiv gave the political report.[35] After describing the party's achievements (winning over the USDP, the creation of a club in the Diet, the extension of party work to Volhynia, Chełm and Polissia), he appraised the political situation and the party's fortunes. He believed that a national struggle with a strong social base was taking place in Western Ukraine, and that this movement should be turned to the party's advantage. The party had influence among the Ukrainian masses, who were very pro-Soviet, in contrast to the Polish working class, which in Western Ukraine was a workers' aristocracy and had succumbed to national chauvinism.[36] Jewish workers, on the other hand, tended toward the political left and were generally friendly toward Ukrainian workers.[37] But the most revolutionary class in Western Ukraine was the peasantry.

The main point of the report, however, concerned the situation in the party. According to Vasylkiv the factional fight and prolonged dispute with the CWPP had resulted in "our being sidetracked from work among the working class."[38] "In order to stay afloat the party sought its base among that part [of the masses] to whom it was close, it sought its base in the countryside and this has distorted our ideology."[39] It was this distortion and an overestimation of the revolutionary mood that led to the erroneous decision to boycott the elections to the Diet in 1922,[40] and finally to the view, which was widespread in the party, that the peasants could make the revolution without the aid of the proletariat.

Vasylkiv charged that the party had been overly "primitive" in its slogans, which demanded the secession of Western Ukraine from Poland, and he admitted that supporting the nationalists' boycott of Polish schools was a mistake.

In the discussion following the report, the conference agreed that the party had to establish closer ties with the working class. The only practical way to do this was to gain influence in the trade unions by creating "red" factions, although this would be more difficult to achieve in Western Ukraine than in the former Congress Poland. With certain exceptions, like the union of leather workers, union leadership in Western Ukraine was controlled entirely by the Polish Socialist Party. There was nowhere for the Communists to gain a foothold. Most Ukrainian workers did not belong to trade unions,[41] regarding them as instruments of Polonization or, at best, assimilation. The workers accused the unions of failing to defend Ukrainians who were dismissed and failing to protest mass layoffs of Ukrainians.[42] Organizations from the "camp of Ukrainian nationalism" called for the creation of separate Ukrainian trade unions.[43] The Fifth Conference attempted for the first time to change this situation by adopting the slogans "Workers of all nationalities to the general unions" and "Ukrainian workers: join the general unions"[44] On the basis of the conference resolutions, the party formed trade union and railway divisions and began systematic work in the union movement.

Much of the conference was devoted to the sabotage ideology, which had several adherents within the party. Bukshovany defended sabotage as a revolutionary means of struggle, but was not supported by the majority of the delegates.[45] The conference recognized that the sabotage movement, which had peaked in 1922, continued to enjoy sympathy among certain classes of the peasantry, and was influencing the party in the guise of the so-called "bombism" theory. A resolution was passed that "the sabotage deviation has threatened the party from the moment of its appearance as a serious movement in Eastern Galicia" (i.e., since 1921).[46] The delegates also felt that the nationalists and national-Bolsheviks within the party who supported the sabotage ideology would be forced out once the party was solidly based on the industrial proletariat. The conference resolution asserted that "the party counters nationalism by calling for a united front of the working class to fight for the dictatorship of the proletariat in Poland and for Soviet Western Ukraine to join the USSR."[47]

"The Russian affair," that is, the conflict between the CWPP and the Comintern over the Polish party's attitude toward the opposition in the RCP(B), was more complex than has sometimes been claimed.[48] Reports on this question were given by a representative of the CP(B)U (probably Kviring) and Koszutska. The latter defended the position taken by the Central Committee of the CWPP in December of the previous year; in her opinion, the issues put forward by the opposition for discussion in the Russian party could not be dismissed lightly.[49] After hearing her arguments, Vasylkiv declined to vote on the matter, although, like many of his followers, he was aware that this might be an opportune moment to criticize the CWPP and thereby strengthen his own position.[50]

Before the vote on the Russian question, Shumsky had persuaded Vasylkiv to support Kviring's resolution,[51] which condemned the CWPP's posture, while in the corridors the Vasylkivists were told that a majority of the Central Committee of the RCP(B) now favoured the Ukrainianization of the USSR, which would shortly be accomplished.[52] Finally a resolution was passed condemning the Trotskyist opposition and noting the "vagueness" of the Central Committee of the CWPP on the matter. This point of the resolution was passed by Vasylkivist votes, with the few CWPP members abstaining.[53]

Another important resolution called for the creation of a legal party with a revolutionary programme, to be called the Workers'-Peasants' Union or some other name indicative of its internationalist character. The conference also decided to try to re-activate the Ukrainian Social

Democratic Party. The significance of co-operation with the CP(B)U and its help in the party's development were strongly emphasized.[54] A resolutions committee composed of Vasylkiv, Rosdolsky, Koszutska, Próchniak and Volynets probably played a major role in the formulation of positions.[55] The conference elected a central committee composed of: Popel (Lom), Krilyk (Vasylkiv), Vasyl Korbutiak (Vasyl), Rosdolsky (Prokopovych), Prystupa (Polovy), Kazimierz Pyzik (Kasik), Józef Mizes (Józek), Pavlo Ladan (Nedobyty) and Volynets (Etien, Stepan). Alternates were: Panteleimon Kraikivsky (Dresher), Jerzy (Dłuski), Hryhorii Mykhats (Myron), Fedir Bei (Orlovsky), Rozenberg (Lvivsky), Zenon Kuzma (Kuzma)[56] and Serhii Vikul (Serhii).[57] Maksymovych was not elected to the central committee since he was not recognized as a legitimate delegate, but he remained the most influential member of the party. Volynets, recently a member of the USDP, was elected first secretary of the central committee.

Maksymovych summarized the importance of the Fifth Conference:

> Up to the Fifth Conference it may have seemed objectively [sic] as though our party had turned all its attention to the countryside, that such a line flowed from the view that in Western Ukraine the peasantry is the main mover of the revolution and will be the leader in the worker-peasant partnership. I say that objectively such a view could creep into the views of some comrades because they have seen the party's rapid expansion in the countryside without any corresponding lasting expansion among the workers. The conference called attention to this objective *narodnytsvo* [populism], and called for a return from the countryside to the city, from the expansive militance of the peasantry to the factory and to the trade unions.[58]

The decisions on organization accepted by the Fifth Conference caused conflict between the CPWU leadership and its membership in the Boryslav-Drohobych oil fields. Here the party's delegate, Kazimierz Pyzik, reported that the majority of the CWPP delegates missed the proceedings through the machinations of their factional opponents. For the same reason only two former CWPP members had been elected to the central committee. The decision to create a "workers'-peasants' union" as a legal front for the party was interpreted by the Boryslav–Drohobych organization as the conference's attempt to liquidate the Union of the Proletariat of City and Countryside (UPCC), a body led by the CWPP, and composed largely of Poles. The organization was equally offended by the election of Volynets, a member of the party for barely a year, to the position of first secretary.[59] Pyzik's conclusions were confirmed by Hryhorii Mykhats (Myron) who, as a delegate from Boryslav–Drohobych, failed to "make contact" and, like most of the CWPP members, missed the conference; and by Leon Pasternak, the leader of the local organization, its "only intellectual," who was reportedly driven by "disproportionate ambition."[60] The party atmosphere in Boryslav-Drohobych, in the words of Zdziarski, "was buzzing like a beehive." The party organization there passed a resolution calling the conference a usurper and the central committee elected at it illegal. It also demanded the creation of a separate organization in Boryslav and Drohobych subordinate to the CWPP as a truly Bolshevik party, and denounced the CPWU as a nationalist party.[61] Though Pyzik's accusations were far from dispassionate, it is true that after the liquidation of the UPCC, the majority of its members, all from the CWPP, found themselves outside the Ukrainian party.[62]

There were also differences of opinion among Communists in Eastern Galicia on tactics. The workers preferred open struggle, using strikes and demonstrations to provoke direct conflict with factory management. The Vasylkivists, on the other hand, favoured conspiratorial work in the countryside, creating cells distinct from each other and connected only with the party leadership. This tactic went back to the period of the partisan war against the Polish state, but the workers saw it as a sign of "cowardice."

In the summer of 1924 about twenty members of the Boryslav-Drohobych organization attended a conference in the woods outside Truskavets. The CPWU Central Committee sent its secretary, Volynets, while Królikowski represented the Polish party. Królikowski's sharp criticism of the Drohobych group shocked those who had counted on him for support. While Królikowski admitted that many of the organizational moves of the CPWU's Central Committee were inappropriate, he held that the resolutions of the Fifth Conference were correct in principle and should be supported. After a day-long discussion some of the delegates were convinced of the correctness of Królikowski's position, others submitted without being convinced and Pasternak alone resigned his position and left the party.[63]

Królikowski's conduct was typical of the CPP attitude toward the CPWU at that time. In internal party matters the Vasylkivists had complete freedom. Those who were removed from positions were often aided on an individual basis. If the person in question was Ukrainian, he was sent to the USSR for political instruction, if Polish, he was transferred to another area.[64]

On 8–10 June a plenum of the CPWU's Central Committee discussed several problems arising from the Fifth Conference, including the Drohobych affair, and ratified the members of the central committee, except for Kazimierz Pyzik and Roman Rosdolsky.[65] The matter of the UPCC caused a controversy at the plenum. The CPWU wanted to keep it, while the Vasylkivists wanted to create a new organization. Once again Królikowski made an impressive defence of the rights and prerogatives of the Ukrainian Central Committee, but he did not approve its negative attitude toward the UPCC. The plenum affirmed the Fifth Conference's decision that the resolution of the Second CWPP Congress calling for realization of the agrarian reform was not binding on the CPWU since the reform stipulated the colonization of Western Ukraine.[66] The so-called "Berlin Four," that is, the ultra-left opposition in the CWPP, was condemned unanimously.

At the August plenum of the CPWU three persons were added to the central committee: Roman Kuzma (Turiansky), former co-founder of the IRSD who since 1919 had been in Soviet Ukraine, Mykhailo Tesliuk (Ernest), who had come from circles close to the IRSD, and Mirosław Zdziarski, representing the CPP leadership. Tesliuk and Zdziarski joined Volynets in the secretariat.[67]

The decisions of the Fifth Congress of the Comintern (17 June–8 August 1924) shocked the CWPP and had a lasting effect on its membership. In February 1924 the Communist press in Berlin had published a document entitled "On the Crisis in the CWPP and the Most Urgent Problems of the Party," popularly called the "Theses of the Berlin Four."[68] The document's authors were Julian Leński, Henryk Stein-Krajewski [L. Domski], Zofia Unszlicht [Osińska] and Ludwik Prentki [Damowski]. With the exception of Damowski (an ephemeral character in the history of the CWPP), all were well-known members of the former SDKPL who, because they objected to union on an equal basis with the PSP-Left, had not participated in the formation of the CWPP in 1918. Holding important positions in the government and party machines in the Soviet Union, they took no part in the daily life of the Polish party, although as guests at the latter's congresses and conferences they were usually opposed to its positions. Now, in the theses, the four attacked all the CWPP's policies on the agrarian question, on the nationalities question and on a united front with the PSP against the right in Poland. Their criticism openly contradicted the general postulates of the Comintern and could not have been successful had it not been for the vulnerable situation in which the Polish party found itself after its open disagreement with the RCP(B). Aside from the substantial criticism the theses contained practical advice for "a way out of the crisis": remove all former PSP-Left members from the leadership and replace them with former members of the SDKPL.

Despite the unanimous condemnation of the Berlin Four by the central committees of both the CWPP and the CPWU, they and several of their adherents and protectors, former social democrats who did not belong to the CWPP (Unszlicht, for example), were at the congress and participated in the work of the Polish Commission, convened to decide the "Polish affair" in the Comintern and headed by Stalin.

Even before the commission met, the Polish delegation was subjected to pressure from the opposition and even received a visit from Zinoviev. The proceedings themselves were stormy and dramatic, and culminated in a speech by Maria Koszutska.[69] Refuting the accusations of Stalin and the oppositionists, she spoke at length about the problems and deficiencies of the Comintern's work. Again she explained the futility of blaming selected CPG leaders for the November defeat in Germany.[70] What was needed, she declared, was an open assessment of the errors of the entire party and of the Comintern. Only this would ensure the intellectual development of the party and its future success. Self-criticism on the part of the Comintern's leaders would actually strengthen its authority, Koszutska argued. She charged that the cultivation of authority by the Russian comrades had already stifled independent thought in other parties within the Comintern. For example, when Zinoviev appeared before the Polish delegation to attack the "3Ws" (Wera Kostrzewa-Koszutska, Warski and Walecki), members panicked and admitted to errors they had not committed, lost their self-confidence and did not defend the party or their own decisions and resolutions.[71] Koszutska turned to the representative of the Russian party and warned: "Because of your special privileges [the great authority the Russians enjoyed in the Communist movement—J.R.], it is not the people whose bones you can break [Zinoviev's polemical threat against the CWPP-J.R.] who are dangerous in the Comintern but rather those people who have no bones."[72] Koszutska said that if the Comintern's methods continued, they could result in "seasonal leaders and careerists" taking over the party leadership in some countries.[73]

In discussing the accusations against the CWPP the commission upheld only the charges that the united front with the PSP was "opportunist" and, more important, that the CWPP had supported the right wing in the RCP(B) and CPG. In connection with the latter charge, it decided to remove the "3Ws" from the CWPP leadership and to place the oppositionists, Leński and Domski, on its central committee. Domski began at once to play a leading role.[74]

The Fifth Congress of the Comintern and the resulting tactical and political changes had an ambiguous effect on the CPWU. The party was concerned that the leadership of the CWPP had passed to Leński and Domski, who opposed the resolutions of the Second Congress, so advantageous for the CPWU. In an article devoted to the changes, Vasylkiv expressed the fear that "certain elements" in the new leadership had not rid themselves of the SDKPL's contempt for the national and peasant questions and might take an ultra-left and unrealistic position on the united front, insisting on "action entirely from the ranks," i.e., trying to persuade the PSP members to co-operate against the will of their leaders. Vasylkiv also criticized Domski's plans to build the CWPP leadership only from former members of the SDKPL.[75]

But the CPWU made a tremendous gain in the congress resolution on the Ukrainian question which was formulated in exactly the spirit the Vasylkivists had long fought for. The resolution considered it "necessary in Poland, Czechoslovakia and Romania to demand that those Ukrainian lands seized by the imperialists be joined to the Soviet Republic." It pointed out that national autonomy could not be the goal of a Communist party,[76] and approved the resolutions of the Second Congress of the CWPP and Fifth Conference of the CPWU.[77]

The Ukrainian draft resolution called for a "Ukrainian International" composed of representatives of the Communist parties of Soviet Ukraine, Eastern Galicia, the Chełm region, Podlachia and Transcarpathian Rus'. It was rejected by the Nationalities Commission of the Congress because the existence of two leaderships (in Warsaw and Kiev) would have been harmful from the organizational point of view. The commission referred to dangerous tendencies, "particularly strong among the Communists of Eastern Galicia," to undermine the centralized structure of communist parties using arguments about the right of oppressed peoples to self-determination.[78]

The Fourth Plenum of the CPWU Central Committee was held early in November 1924.[79] Representatives of the CWPP leadership in attendance included Stefan Skulski (Stanisław Mertens), to whom Ukrainian party matters had been assigned. The plenum discussed the crisis in the Polish party. The minutes of the plenum show that "one Pole from the CC CPWU," i.e., Zdziarski, defended Warski, Koszutska and Walecki and one Ukrainian abstained from voting on the resolution condemning the "3Ws".[80]

The plenum attacked the "language bill" of the Polish Sejm, which in practice curtailed instruction of Ukrainian and Belorussian children in their mother tongues. But all plans to boycott the schools were dropped. The proposal of the CWPP Central Committee to withhold taxes in the *Kresy* provoked a heated debate. One source states that "the Ukrainians," in defiance of "the Poles," maintained that the call to withhold taxes would lead inevitably to armed conflict with the authorities and, ultimately, to an uprising for which no one was prepared. The Ukrainians pointed out, probably on the basis of their own experience, that the sabotage (insurrectionist) movement would harm the party because it would be inundated by nationalists and thus the distinction between the Communist and nationalist movements would be lost.[81] But the Polish Central Committee pointed to what it saw as the positive insurrectionist practice of the Communist Party of Western Belorussia (CPWB). The Ukrainians, with great reluctance, accepted the resolution that "it is necessary to draw the masses into direct conflict with the authorities...," and "where conditions are favourable (Volhynia), to organize a boycott of taxes and a defence of the masses against its consequences."[82] They refused to go further than this, and resisted Polish pressure to accept a resolution calling for an armed uprising.[83]

The "Polish Affair" again became a major topic at the Sixth Extraordinary Conference (14–17 December 1924).[84] Stepan (Volynets), in his opening address, described the situation in the CWPP and the CPG in accordance with the interpretation of the Comintern and ascribed the errors of the CWPP almost exclusively to the policy of the "3Ws." Zdziarski, however, argued that all Communist parties had erred in united-front tactics, on which the Comintern's guidelines were unclear. Hence the entire party was in error and the Polish leadership more so than others. Without this experience the line of the Fifth Congress could not have been formulated. Zdziarski emphasized, however, that removing "individual opportunists" would not cure the movement. The party was now falling into a "leftist folly," which would be exploited by "non-bolshevik elements" led by Domski.[85] After being roundly attacked, Zdziarski made a second speech in which he stated that he recognized the resolutions of the Fifth Congress, but disagreed with the expulsion of the "3Ws" and certain formulations of the Polish Commission.

Królikowski concurred with Zdziarski that individual persons should not be singled out as being responsible for the errors. Vasylkiv also agreed that "an atmosphere of scapegoating" was unhealthy.[86] Fornal (Aleksander Różański), secretary of the Volhynian district committee (*okruzhnyi komitet*), and Solodky (Nestor Khomyn)[87] supported Zdziarski without reservation. Both had belonged to the CWPP from the period of the factional fights in the CPEG. Others, including former CWPP members (Mojżesz Mandel, Natan Shapiro-Sukhy, Hryhorii Mykhats), accepted the resolutions of the Polish Commission without objection. A delegation was elected to the upcoming Third CPP Congress, consisting of Shapiro, Mandel, Tesliuk, Volynets and Vasylkiv.[88]

The conference resolution is now almost illegible. The few remaining fragments indicate only that there was an attempt to define objectively the reason for the "wave of opportunism" in Germany, Poland and Bulgaria. Only those "who unreservedly supported the Comintern's line" were to remain in the CWPP Central Committee.[89] Ultimately, the resolution adopted by the conference was close to the view of the new CWPP Central Committee.[90] If initially the CPWU was somewhat reluctant to accept the new line of the CWPP on the Polish and international questions, it retained from the first a different view on the Ukrainian question. The new CWPP Central Committee urged insurrection, a tactic similar to that used by the Ukrainians in 1921–3, although now the *Kresy* were to begin what would become a general Polish movement. The CPWU Central

Committee, on the other hand, was inclined to moderation. The party was anxious to emphasize its class basis, thereby breaking with Ukrainian nationalism. The CPWU leadership endeavoured to bring order and stability to the party and, to a greater extent than before, began to emphasize unity with the Polish revolutionary left.[91]

The Third CPP Congress, 14 January–7 February 1925

The final confrontation between the Vasylkivists and adherents of the Polish party came at the Third Congress of the CPP. Stefan Skulski delivered the central committee's report "On the situation in the *Kresy*."[92] He argued against the view held by Vasylkiv and some other members of the CPWU that the insurrectionary movement in Western Belorussia and northern Ukraine (i.e., Volhynia) was not indigenous but engendered from without. On the contrary, he said, the central committee was aware that "it [the partisan movement] is not just partisan border actions," but "a mass armed movement that originated with the Polish occupation of these lands" and which ebbed and flowed and should be channeled into "our" current. The party should be favourably disposed toward an uprising, but not necessarily proclaim one at every opportunity. The motive force of the movement, Skulski added, must be the call for non-payment of taxes, the very slogan to which "the Ukrainian comrades are so vehemently opposed."

Leon Purman, Władysław Stein-Krajewski, Tadeusz Żarski and other CPP leaders spoke in the same spirit. Citing Stalin,[93] they accused the Ukrainians of passivity,[94] and of aiming for "organizational improvement and training cadres" rather than direct revolutionary action.[95] Domski demanded that the call to boycott taxes "be brought to Poland to develop a struggle against the background of [the issues of] ownership of pastures and forests (*serwituty*), agrarian reform, excessive parcellation [of peasant lands] and so forth." And he recommended that the Ukrainians "pile up arms in the factories and take over the railways."[96] CPWU delegates were reminded that without their support the insurrectionist movement in Belorussia would be isolated.

Vasylkiv assured the delegates that there was at present no possibility of an uprising in the *Kresy*. There was indeed a revolutionary partisan movement, but not an insurrectionist one.[97] To use the tax boycott as a general slogan would, in Vasylkiv's opinion, provoke a conflict with the authorities, which would result in an uprising. In many areas, however, the peasants wanted neither the slogan nor the uprising. Such an uprising would be doomed to failure and would destroy the party. In Belorussia, for example, "there is no party ... in the full sense of the word.... It is just now being rebuilt."[98]

Other delegates who did not belong to the new CPP leadership felt that, outside of Western Belorussia, the party would not be in a position to help the peasants against the repression that might follow an attempted uprising.[99] What was needed, then, was to take control of the movement in the *Kresy*, bring it closer to the Polish movement and avoid any premature "spontaneous outbursts."[100] Skrypnyk and Ladan reminded the delegates that what the CPP leaders were proposing had already been undertaken by the Ukrainian party in 1920–2. A repetition was unnecessary since the conditions for an uprising in the whole country were lacking. Although in Belorussia there were "partial outbursts," there was certainly no general uprising.[101] During the discussion the Comintern was asked for advice. Zinoviev declared that the Polish leadership was essentially mistaken in its notion, "let the *Kresy* begin and Warsaw will help. It should be the other way around."[102]

The final resolution adopted at the congress was something of a compromise. It proclaimed the right to self-determination for all nationalities in Poland. At the same time, in accordance with the wishes of the CPWU, the resolution emphasized that "calling for the annexation of Western Belorussia and Western Ukraine to the neighbouring Soviet republics was in the interests of the masses both of these areas and of Poland proper." After pointing out that the polonization policies of successive Polish governments toward the national minorities differed only in method, the resolution went on to note that "resistance against the collection of taxes... has taken on a mass character in Western Belorussia and Volhynia." Although it warned against a premature armed outbreak, the resolution stated that "not only does the party not avoid starting such actions... in the countryside, it energetically initiates and leads them," because only through these actions would the peasants gain experience in the struggle. The anti-taxation action could take various forms: demonstrations, hiding peasant property, boycotting auctions of peasant lands (to pay overdue taxes) and "armed defence against punitive expeditions of the police."[103] The resolution also recommended organizing the rural population into "peasant defence committees."[104] The resolution, then, did not proclaim an immediate uprising, but pointed the way toward it. It defended the partisan movement in Belorussia and Volhynia, probably hoping to preserve it as the "spark to the fires."

How the decision to wage an insurrection was implemented in practice can best be demonstrated from the example of Volhynia. The first Communist organizations were established in Volhynia in the beginning of 1922.[105] Hryhorii (Hryts) Ivanenko came to Volhynia in 1923 and organized them into a single district organization.[106] Like most Volhynians he was a follower of Zatonsky and therefore favoured the CWPP rather than the Vasylkivists. His organizational contacts, however, were more with Kharkiv than with Warsaw, and he was connected with the Foreign Division of the CC CP(B)U, the *Zakordot*.

The activities of the *Zakordot* and the Volhynian Communist organization often overlapped. There was co-operation, but there were also differences of opinion. As mentioned above, the Fifth Conference condemned insurrection, but a resolution alone could not check the activities of the *Zakordot* and its followers. Much depended on the attitude of local leaders. On 16 February 1924 Ivanenko was arrested[107] and the leadership of the Volhynian organization passed to Aleksander Różański, another CWPP member. The latter rebuilt and consolidated the organizations that had been depleted by arrests.[108] In this way, Różański won the trust of the entire Volhynian organization and increased its independence from headquarters in Lviv. The organization had been independent from its inception thanks to contacts with the CWPP and Kharkiv. The insurrectionist spirit continued to flourish in Volhynia, where the events in Belorussia were followed with interest and, still more, the resolutions of the Third CPP Congress found fertile ground.

Różański and his followers established a broad network of military organizations in preparation for an uprising. They were aided by the *Zakordot* and Toma Prystupa, a Communist emissary from Warsaw. The preparations were so intense that party organizations were transformed into military groups. Squadrons of tens (*desiatyny*) and hundreds (*sotni*) were organized and weapons were stockpiled.[109] A military command headed by Viktor Kraits was established. Several thousand persons comprised a network of military organizations throughout Volhynia. The central committee in Lviv was aware of these preparations but was in no position to stop them. Panteleimon Kraikivsky (Dresher) travelled to Volhynia for a meeting with the local leadership,[110] and in 1925 central committee member Tesliuk went there for a conference of the local organization,[111] but their attempts at persuasion did not help. The Volhynians asserted that the insurrectionist movement in Western Belorussia strengthened rather than weakened the party and they accused the central committee in Lviv of opportunism and cowardice. A note written by Zdziarski, after January 1928, showed that although he perceived a large measure of recklessness in Różański's activity, he attributed the latter's differences with the central committee of the CPWU to the Galician Communists' lack of experience in mass work on such a large scale.

Efforts to build a mass insurrectionist organization collapsed in the spring of 1925, with a Polish counteraction. The police (whose agent, Bondarenko, had infiltrated the would-be insurrectionists) arrested around fifteen hundred persons in a quick action. Some of the conspirators, including Różański, managed to flee the country. Nearly all those arrested were beaten, tortured, and sentenced to prison. The largest trial, the so-called "trial of the 151," took place in Volodymyr-Volynskyi from 15 October 1926 to 10 January 1927.[112] Three of the defendants (Nestor Khomyn, Mojżesz Mandel and Viktor Kraits) were sentenced to life imprisonment; four were given fifteen years, thirty-nine were given ten years, eighty-six were sentenced to four to six years and nineteen were set free.[113] Those sentenced to life imprisonment had already sustained serious injuries from the interrogation and were later released to the USSR in an exchange of prisoners. Kraits was also released as part of an exchange just before his death. This tragic end to the "Różański" epic diminished the insurrectionist strategy in the eyes of the party and resolved the differences among the CPWU leadership on this issue. In 1925 the partisan movement in Western Belorussia began to weaken and the local Communist organization proposed an end to armed struggle, in defiance of the partisan leaders. The conflict in 1925 between the Comintern and Domski's group soon overshadowed all other problems.[114]

Disagreements between former CWPP members and Vasylkivists continued in Galicia; in Kolomyia, Przemyśl and Stanyslaviv. In Stanyslaviv the conflict was long-standing and typical of the internal problems faced by the CPWU. There the primarily worker-based organization was headed by a newly-appointed peasant functionary who was controlled by the central committee. This was no isolated instance—the Vasylkivists had few trusted workers in their ranks. The local organizations objected to such appointments, however, and accused the party of subordinating the working class to the peasantry. In the case of the Stanyslaviv organization, members strongly criticized the nomination, asserting that the newcomer was less sophisticated ideologically than the party rank and file. The central committee responded by suspending the entire organization. Like their Drohobych counterparts, the Stanyslaviv Communists applied to the party authorities in Warsaw, demanding disaffiliation from the CPWU and affiliation with the CPP.[115] Only after long negotiation was the conflict settled.

The organization in Kolomyia was disbanded because, against the orders of CPWU leaders, it had co-operated with the PSP in elections to mutual-aid organizations. But the organization in Sambir went unpunished for a similar offence.[116] The removal of former CWPP members from leadership positions on the slightest pretext caused much bitterness and undoubtedly weakened the party. Hryhorii Mykhats (Myron), a former CWPP member, explained this at the Second CPWU Congress: "We must remember," he said, "that all the former CWPP members who are now outside the party once belonged to our labour-union movement ... and their expulsion, sometimes for petty reasons, does great harm to our movement.... In Przemyśl alone there were several examples of scandalous expulsion from the party."[117] According to Mykhats "our comrades [i.e., the CC CPWU] think that if anyone criticizes the organizational structure, then he is dangerous and must be expelled."[118] Zdziarski's speech at the congress was even more pronounced on this question. He cited the suspensions for several months of entire organizations (always local) and gave the pseudonyms of CWPP members who were expelled (Józek, Stefan, Neznaiko), invariably for "discrediting the Central Committee."[119] In their defence the Vasylkivists maintained that the information about the repressions was either exaggerated, or that the persons concerned deserved to be punished for their "divisive activities." (In 1928, when Skrypnyk was defending the pre-1927 policy of the Vasylkivists as correct in principle, he also recalled the expulsion of dissidents.)[120]

At the same time, the Vasylkivists were making a tremendous effort to give the party a greater working-class orientation, which meant that they had to move closer to the Polish working class, where many CWPP members were active. There was further impetus for such a rapprochement in the party's labour-union activities and in the struggle to unite workers of all nationalities in the unions. Evidently their contradictory behaviour resulted from the Vasylkivists' fear of losing control in the party and consequently damaging the West Ukrainian cause in the international Communist movement.

During this period the CPWU carried on a vigorous propaganda and educational campaign to place the Ukrainian question in an internationalist context. The party maintained that only through an all-Polish socialist revolution would it be possible for Western Ukraine to join the Ukrainian Soviet Republic.[121] A maxim of the time was: "the road to Kharkiv goes through Warsaw."

In June 1925 a conflict erupted between the central committee of the CPWU and the ultra-leftist Domski group, which dominated the central committee of the CPP. The dispute arose from a CPP resolution accusing the Communist parties of Germany, France and Bulgaria of opportunism in the united-front tactics. The resolution also led to a new crisis in relations with the Comintern,[122] and came as a surprise to the leaders of the CPWU. The latter lacked information about the international situation, but they did not trust Domski's ideas and did not want a conflict with the Comintern. Vasylkiv, in a letter to Maksymovych of 5 June 1925 about the CPP's criticism of the tactics used by the CPG and FCP, said: "Since the policies of these parties are carried out with the knowledge of the Comintern, the CPP is attacking the Comintern in its resolution. The [proposed] resolution has not yet been adopted. It will first be edited, but when it comes before the council of the Central Committee in June it will certainly be adopted. We do not know about these affairs in enough detail to know what position we ought to take. This matter has surely been discussed ... in the CP(B)U, and you are familiar with such things. Therefore Etien[123] asked me to request that you provide us with exact information on what all this means and what position we should take."[124] Maksymovych answered that the CPP's position was undialectical. The CPP's defiance of the Comintern "throws the party from the rightist frying pan into the leftist fire."[125] Presumably Maksymovych advised the CPWU as to what position it should take.

At the Sixth Plenum of the CPWU Central Committee on 15 June 1925, there was friction between the CPP Central Committee representative, Stefan Skulski, and members of the Ukrainian Central Committee. Skulski proposed the following resolution: "the Plenum of the CPWU Central Committee, after discussing the tactical errors of the CPG, FCP and CP of Bulgaria, is in complete solidarity with the resolution in this matter adopted by the CPP Central Committee in the middle of June of this year."[126] Only Skulski himself voted for the resolution, which read as follows: "The plenum of the CPWU Central Committee, on the basis of the resolution of the CPP Central Committee of June 1925, affirms that within the CPG, FCP and CPB[ulgaria] are certain deviations from the resolutions of the Fifth Congress. The plenum does not agree, however, with the demand for an expanded Comintern Executive since this would be an expression of distrust in the Comintern. At the present moment, with a growing threat of monarchist reaction demanding extraordinary cohesion and manoeuvrability, this is an inappropriate move."[127] This was the first, and a rather moderate and enigmatic, criticism of the international conceptions of the Domski group. This tactic of handling a dispute with a superior authority by accepting general principles and denying specifics was typical of the Vasylkivists. They applied the tactic systematically, and Maksymovych was considered a master at it.

At the Seventh Plenum (6–7 August 1925), when there was no longer any doubt about the Comintern's position (the final condemnation of Domski had taken place on 4 August), the CPWU Central Committee criticized "Domskiism" in the harshest terms.[128] It charged that Skulski had deliberately misinformed previous meetings and plenums. Kuzma-Turiansky (Komar), Maksymovych (Hak) and Vasylkiv saw the actions of the CPP Central Committee as an attempt to create an organized faction within the Comintern.[129] The Vasylkivists also tried to exploit the conflict with the Comintern to gain greater independence from the CPP. They demanded representation on the Comintern Executive Committee and on the Politburo of the CPP Central Committee, claiming a need for reliable information. Skulski, however, would not agree to these demands and proposed instead that Volynets be the representative to the Politburo of the CPP Central Committee.[130] He further suggested that, despite the resolutions of the CPWU to recruit the proletariat into its ranks, its true role was as an agrarian wing of the CPP.[131] This resulted in a heated discussion, in which an angry exchange between Zdziarski and Skulski almost led to the latter's leaving the plenum.

The final resolution differed clearly from the policies of the CPP Central Committee. It expressed the CPWU's own views on the united-front tactic, broke with the "ultra-left tactics of Domski and his comrades," and, in the area of international politics, asserted that the CPG, FCP and CP of Bulgaria had committed no errors, but had followed the correct Comintern line.[132] The resolution also maintained that the CPWU Central Committee should "have its own representative in the Comintern in order to maintain a constant flow of systematic and objective information."[133]

In addition to the conflicts over fundamental questions of current policy, these demands elicited a hostile reaction from the leadership of the Polish party. In August 1925 the outgoing CPP Central Committee passed a pointed resolution stating that "the CPWU's demand for its own representative in the politburo and Comintern is leading the Polish party to consider whether the CPWU should leave the CPP."[134] The CPP maintained that a continuation of the Ukrainian party's policies would lead inevitably to a split, not only in the CPWU but in the entire Polish revolutionary movement. The resolution of the CPP Central Committee "most categorically calls on the CPWU Central Committee to cease its fractious work within the party and asks all comrades in the CPWU to reflect upon the actions of the leaders."[135] The deepening conflict was checked by the Comintern's criticism of the policies of the CPP Central Committee. The Second Congress of the CPWU was devoted to an assessment of the conflict.

Notes

1. *Piatyi vsemirnyi kongress Kommunisticheskogo internatsionala. Stenograficheskii otchet*, part 2 (*Prilozheniia*) (Moscow-Leningrad, 1925), 127.
2. June plenum, CA KC PZPR, 165/1–3, 1: 18.
3. Letter of the ministry of internal affairs on preparations for liquidating the USDP and a circular of the office of the *wojewoda* of Lviv to the *starosty* on the same matter. *Pid praporom Zhovtnia*, 145–9.
4. For details, see chapter four below.
5. O. Vasylkiv, "KPZU i druhyi zizd KPRP," *Nasha pravda*, no. 1 (1923): 5–13.
6. *Ibid.*, 5.

7. *Ibid.*, 7.
8. Information of Ostap Dłusk, CA KC PZRP, 8397, poz. 4, 7.
9. Organizational report (of the CC CPWU) for January-February 1924, AM CA KC PZPR, 1356/7, jednostka archiwalna 15.
10. Vasylkiv, "Na pravylnyi shliakh," *Nasha pravda*, no. 4–8 (1924): 30.
11. Kos, "Proty nastroiv," *Nasha pravda*, no. 1, (1924): 21–5.
12. Bukshovany [O. Ivanovych], "Vid sabotazhu do sotsiialnoi revoliutsii," *Nasha pravda*, no. 2–3 (1924): 60–8.
13. These were officers of the Red Army, Ukrainian Galicians who headed an armed group which in October 1922 crossed into Galicia to initiate a partisan struggle. Petro Sheremeta was killed in a skirmish with the Polish police on 28 October 1922. Stepan Melnychuk was executed by the Polish authorities in Chortkiv on 11 November 1922. *Pid praporom Zhovtnia*, 87–8.
14. P. Kulykovsky, "Revoliutsiia, horozhanska viina i zbroine povstannia (na pidstavi tvoriv Lenina)," *Nasha pravda*, no. 2–3, (1924): 10–24.
15. S. Vikul [I. Pavlyshyn], "Lenin i selianstvo," *ibid.*, 25–53.
16. The "three Ws" were Maria Koszutska (Wera), Henryk Walecki and Adolf Warski. They were the most influential group in the CWPP leadership at that time.
17. P. Ladan [P. Netiaha], "Vid porazhky do orhanizatsiinoi peremohy (v lavakh Komunistychnoi partii Nimechchyny)," *Nasha pravda*, no. 1 (1924): 26–41. Vasylkiv returned to these matters after 1928 in internal discussions and took a similar position. Chapter six below contains more on this subject.
18. *Ibid.*, 33.
19. "Nauka nimetskykh podii," *Nasha pravda* no. 2–3 (1924): 118.
20. Zinoviev in *Pravda*, 7 November 1923, 2.
21. Preobrazhensky in *Pravda*, 28 November 1923, 4.
22. Trotsky, in a series of articles entitled "Novyi kurs," the first of which appeared in *Pravda* on 11 February 1923.
23. *Nowy Przegląd* (organ of the CWPP central committee), 1924–5, reprinted (Warsaw, 1959), 238–50.
24. P.K., "Novyi kurs u vnutrishniomu zhytti RKP," *Nasha pravda*, no. 1 (1924): 42–53.
25. *Ibid.*, 44.
26. *Ibid.*, 50.
27. *Ibid.*
28. *Ibid.*, 51–2. These arguments were put forth in the USSR by N. Kyrylenko who did not belong to the opposition, but called attention to the danger of an overly arbitrary interpretation of the resolution on factionalism. See *Pravda*, no. 284, 5.
29. Vasylkiv, "Natsionalne vyzvolennia a ukrainske dribnomishchanstvo," *Nasha pravda*, no. 1 (1924): 5–11.
30. At this time (1923) the largest Ukrainian party, the Ukrainian National Labour Party, split into several splinter groups including a pro-Soviet one,

and only in 1925 succeeded in achieving formal unity as the Ukrainian National Democratic Union.

31. Vasylkiv, "Natsionalne vyzvolennia," 6.
32. *Ibid.*, 7.
33. "Smert natsionalizmu," *Nova kultura*, no. 2–3 (1923): 1–7.
34. *Postanovy Piatoi Konferentsii Komunistychnoi partii Zakhidnoi Ukrainy* (Lviv, 1924), 3.
35. The minutes of the Fifth Conference are not extant. The information in the text is drawn from materials of the June plenum of the central committee of the CPWU (8–10 June 1924) which contain detailed data on the Fifth Conference. CA KC PZPR, 165/I–3, vol. 2: 3.
36. *Ibid.*
37. *Ibid.*, manuscript of the minutes, 28.
38. *Ibid.*, 3.
39. *Ibid.*
40. *Ibid.*, typescript, 4.
41. *Postanovy*, 12.
42. Królikowski, among others, spoke on this topic at the Second CWPP Congress. See *II Zjazd*, 359.
43. *Postanovy*, 10.
44. *Ibid.*, 13.
45. Information given orally by Rosdolsky on 16 July 1966.
46. *Postanovy*, 9.
47. *Ibid.*, 10.
48. *III Zjazd KPP. Sprawozdanie z obrad* (n.p., [1925]), 46.
49. This is cited in minutes of the Third CPP Congress, AM CA KC PZPR, 158/I–3, page 75.
50. Information given by Trofym Maryshchuk, a conference participant. The general picture of the proceedings is based on information given independently by Maryshchuk and Rosdolsky, which coincides almost completely.
51. Information given by Rosdolsky. It is worth mentioning here that in 1927 Maksymovych, defending Shumsky against accusations of ideological deviation, said that he had helped the CPWU avoid Trotskyist inclinations. (See chapter four.) Skrypnyk, too, at the March plenum in 1928, wishing to emphasize the good influence of the CP(B)U on the fraternal Ukrainian party, said: "Let us remember how influential Trotskyism was in Poland; we succeeded in putting the CPWU on the right road." Skrypnyk in *Dzherela ta prychyny rozlamu v KPZU* (Kharkiv, 1928), 89.
52. Information given by Rosdolsky.
53. *Postanovy*, 5, 16.
54. *Ibid.*, 6.
55. CA KC PZPR, 165/I–3, vol. 2, minutes, 29.
56. Not to be confused with Roman Kuzma (Turiansky).
57. CA KC PZPR, 165/I–3, vol. 2, minutes, 4. In 1911–19 Vikul was a

member of the Ukrainian Social Democratic Workers' Party and supporter of the Central Rada. Later he wrote for the CP(B)U and worked as an editor of *Nasha pravda.*

58. K. Savrych [K. Hak], "Naiblyzhchi zavdannia nashoi partii," *Nasha pravda*, no. 9–12 (1924): 29.
59. At one time Volynets belonged to the right-wing faction of the *drahomanivky* and later was a member of the USDP almost until its liquidation.
60. Mirosław Zdziarski [St. Zawadzki], "Notatki z pracy mej w KPZU," AM CA KC PZPR, 1356/9.
61. *Ibid.*, 76 (internal paging).
62. For the leadership of the UPCC, see *Z istorii revoliutsiinoho rukhu u Lvovi 1917–1939* (Lviv, 1957), 162–3.
63. Pasternak joined the PSP, publishing an appropriate declaration in *Dziennik Ludowy*, no. 150 (1925): 6. Later, however, he emigrated to the Soviet Union.
64. The fate of Tomasz Bando is a case in point. He was active in the UPCC in Stanyslaviv and was expelled from the party for factionalism, but he was afterward transferred to Sosnowiec, where he was active in the CPP.
65. CA KC PZPR, 165/I–3, vol. 1.
66. *Ibid.*, page 4.
67. M.M. Tesliuk, "Na shliakhu bilshovizatsii KPZU (II Zizd KPZU)" in *Na choli vyzvolnoi borotby. Spohady kolyshnikh aktyvnykh diiachiv KPZU* (Kiev, 1965), 61.
68. H. Grudowa, "Sprawa polska na V Kongresie Międzynarodówki Komunistycznej," *Z pola walki*, no. 4 (1962).
69. Maria Koszutska [Wera Kostrzewa], *Pisma i przemówienia*, Vol. II: 1918–1925 (Warsaw, 1961), 285–99.
70. The reference is to an abortive insurrection in late October 1923, resulting in the banning of the CPG on 24 November 1923.
71. Kozutska, *Pisma 1918–1925*, 298.
72. *Ibid.*, 298–9.
73. *Ibid.*, 299.
74. Koszutska and Warski returned to work in the central committee of the CPP after 1925 and together with their followers were expelled in 1929. The more interesting of the two was Koszutska (1876–1939). She was thoughtful and perceptive in her judgments, usually tactful, composed, courageous, politically sophisticated and loyal even in furious factional struggles. These traits together with her personal charm (she was also quite attractive) won the respect and admiration of even her ideological opponents. While in Moscow in 1937 she was arrested and died in prison.
75. O. Vasylkiv, "KPRP na V-mu kongresi Kominternu," *Nasha pravda*, no. 9–12 (1924): 26–7.
76. *Piatyi vsemirnyi kongress*, 127.
77. Skrypnyk wrote the draft for this resolution. See M. Skrypnyk, *Natsionalnyi vopros v programme Kominterna* (Kharkiv, 1929), 59.

78. D. Manuilsky, (Report on the work of the Nationalities Commission), *Fünfter Kongress der Kommunistischen Internationale. Protokoll*, Bd. 11 (Moscow, n.d.), 1004. Abstracting from the obvious political aims of the resolution, there are evident lapses in its argument. The Chełm region and Pidlissia clearly did not constitute a separate country, and did not have the regional peculiarity of Volhynia, which the document does not mention. Manuilsky's report suggests that the Ukrainians readily backed down on their demand, while the American scholar, Roman Solchanyk, shows that a sharp exchange occurred between Manuilsky and Vasylkiv during the discussion on the draft. See R. Solchanyk, "The Communist Party of Western Ukraine, 1919–1938" (Ph.D. thesis: University of Michigan, 1973), 210.
79. A letter has been preserved in which the date of the plenum is given mistakenly as 13 October. According to other sources it was held in November. See "Postanovy IV Plenuma TsK KPZU 9–11 XI 1924," *Nasha pravda*, no. 9–12 (1924), and Plenum of the CC CPWU, CA KC PZPR, 165/I–3 vol. 3, page 1.
80. *Ibid.* Several long excerpts from the Polish draft resolution. See *III Zjazd KPP. Sprawozdania z obrad*, 211.
81. Plenum of the CC CPWU, CA KC PZPR, 165/I–3, vol. 3, page 1.
82. *Ibid.*, 6. Also in *Nasha pravda*, no. 9–12 (1924): 81.
83. *Ibid.*, 2 and "Źdźbło w cudzym oku.Pare słów odpowiedzi tow. Warskiemu," *Nowy Przegląd* 1924–5 (Reprint: Warsaw, 1959), 171.
84. Minutes of the Sixth Extraordinary Conference of the CPWU, AM CA KC PZPR, 1356/3.
85. *Ibid.*, 3.
86. *Ibid.*, 5.
87. *Ibid.*, and Report on the conference proceedings for the CC CPP, AM CA KC PZPR, 933/1 dział 3.
88. Minutes of the Sixth Extraordinary Conference, 22.
89. *Ibid.*, 22. A similar wording was adopted at the Fourth Plenum. See "Postanovy IV Plenumu," 78.
90. Report from the Sixth CPWU Conference, AM CA KC PZPR, 933/1, dział 3.
91. These demands and aims were put very explicitly in the circular. See *Biuleten A[git]propa TsK KPZU* (November-December 1924).
92. On the situation in the *Kresy*, Minutes of the Third CPP Congress, CA KC PZPR, 158/I–3/vol. 3, pages 28–38.
93. Purman [Brunon], *ibid.*, 127.
94. Feliks [Stein-Krajewski], *ibid.*, 60; Oskar (Żarski), 47.
95. Domski, *ibid.*, 130.
96. *Ibid.*, 17 and 19.
97. Vasylkiv, *ibid.*, 115.
98. *Ibid.*, 116.
99. Warski, *ibid.*, 51.
100. Koszutska, *ibid.*, 91.

101. Skrypnyk, *ibid.*, 54; Ladan (Nedobyty), 83.
102. Zinoviev's speech at the Second Congress of the CPWU, CA KC PZPR, 165/I–2, vol. 2, page 17.
103. *Uchwały III Zjazdu KPP* (Warsaw, 1925), 56.
104. *Ibid.*, 58.
105. I. Zabolotny, *Neskorena Volyn. Narys z istorii revoliutsiinoho rukhu na Volyni 1917–1939* (Lviv, 1964), 49.
106. *Ibid.*, 35.
107. Ie. Halushko, "H.V. Ivanenko (Baraba)," *Ukrainskyi istorychnyi zhurnal*, no. 6 (1963): 118–120.
108. Halushko, *Narysy*, 183.
109. Letter to Maksymovych, probably from a Soviet intelligence officer abroad. The letter contains information on the situation in Volhynia from refugees to the Soviet Union. "Uvazhaemyi tov. Maksymovych!" PA IIP TsK KPU, f. 6, op. 6–1, od. zb. 126, page 44.
110. Zdziarski, "Notatki," 11–12.
111. Halushko, *Narysy*, 164.
112. Durach archives, CA KC PZPR, 105/847, page 33 and *Nashe zhyttia*, no. 47 (1926) to no. 4 (1927).
113. *Nashe zhyttia*, no. 4 (1927): 2.
114. Among the peasant masses the insurrectionist mood was slow to die. The secretary of the Kovel local, for example, reports in 1926 that there was a decline of revolutionary feeling among the workers as a result of economic stabilization. The peasants were incomparably more militant, but it was difficult to draw them into the organization because "they do not want to hear . . . that the party sees no possibility of armed insurrection in the near future, within months," and when the necessity of such a tactic was explained to them "they refuse to join the party." See the report of the Kovel local at a party meeting 25 February 1926: *Borotba trudiashchykh Volyni za vyzvolennia z-pid hnitu panskoi Polshchi i vozziednannia z Radianskoiu Ukrainoiu (1921–1939). Zbirnyk dokumentiv i materialiv,* Part 1: 1921–1928 (Lutsk, 1957), 126.
115. Zdziarski, "Notatki," 8–9.
116. Vasylkiv, Speech at Second CPWU Congress, CA KC PZPR, 165/I–2, vol. 3, page 53.
117. Mykhats (Myron), *ibid.*, 165/2, vol. 2, pages 6–7.
118. *Ibid.*, 7.
119. Zdziarski, "Notatki," 78. The first two pseudonyms mentioned by Zdziarski remain obscure. "Neznaiko" was Ivanenko's pseudonym. There is insufficent data on his conflict with the central committee of the CPWU. Ivanenko spent more than two years in prison and after that several months in the Ukrainian Soviet Republic. In December 1928, after the expulsion of the Vasylkivists, he was appointed deputy member of the central committee of the CPWU. In May 1929 he was secretary of the central committee.
120. Skrypnyk, *Dzherela ta prychyny*, 105.

121. K. Savrych-Maksymovych [Hak], "Naiblyzhchi zavdannia nashoi partii," *Nasha pravda*, no. 9–12 (1924): 29–37, P.K., "Revoliutsiia, horozhanska viina i zbroine povstannia," *Nasha pravda*, no. 2–3 and no. 9–12 (1924): 51–66; *Biuleten TsK KPZU*, no. 6 (June 1925).
122. *Materiały egzekutywy Międzynarodówki Komunistycznej w sprawie KP Polski* (Moscow, 1925), 5, or *Z pola walki*, no. 1 (1961): 84, fn. 2. This entire problem was discussed at length at the Fourth CPP Conference.
123. Etien (Volynets) was then the CPWU representative in the CPP.
124. See "Dorohyi Karlo," Vasylkiv's letter of 5 June 1925, PA IIP TsK KPU, f. 6, op. 1, od. zb. 126.
125. *Ibid.*, 42.
126. Sixth Plenum of the CC CPWU, CA KC PZPR, 165/I–3, vol. 5, page 5.
127. *Ibid.*, 5, or a somewhat different version, 10.
128. See Sixth Plenum of the CC CPWU (minutes, manuscript in Ukrainian), CA KC PZPR, 165/I–3 vol. 6.
129. *Ibid.*, 18–19.
130. *Ibid.*, 14–15.
131. *Ibid.*, 10.
132. *Ibid.*, 57–9.
133. *Ibid.*, 60.
134. See Zdziarski's speech, Minutes of the Second CPWU Congress, CA KC PZPR, 165/I–2, vol. 2, page 71, and Cichowski's (second speech), 28.
135. Quoted by Skrypnyk in *ibid.*, 165/I–2, vol. 2, page 92.

Chapter Three

The Second Congress of the CPWU and the Fourth Conference of the CPP, October–November 1925

Second Congress of the CPWU

The CPWU had been functioning for several years, yet had never held its own congress. Although what is called the Second Congress was, in fact, the first congress of the party, it was officially known as the second, the St. George Conference in 1921 being considered the first. An important reason for calling the congress was the crisis in the CPP and the resulting weakening of that party both internally and externally (within the Comintern). Former CWPP members within the CPWU were disoriented, and it was an opportune moment for the Vasylkivists to reduce CWPP influence and strengthen their own position both in the party and in the Comintern.

Justifying the congress, Vasylkiv wrote to Maksymovych: "Now as never before we are strong both in the centre and in the outlying regions. We have at our disposal both good organizers and people of intelligence.... At this moment conferences are being held, the inevitable result of which will be the election of an overwhelming majority of our delegates, i.e., twenty-five delegates, more or less, with a deciding vote and maybe five or six factionalists [CWPP members] but they won't have either the courage not to vote with us or the strength to form a faction."[1]

The same reasons that drove the leaders of the CPWU to push for a quick convening of the congress caused members aligned with the CPP to try to avoid a congress altogether. The CPP representative in the

Comintern, Wacław Bogucki, tried to veto the congress, claiming that it had been convoked without consultation with the Polish party leadership. However, owing to the objections Mykhailo Tesliuk of the CPWU Central Committee lodged with the Comintern's executive committee, Bogucki's veto was overruled.[2]

Following the disputes with the Polish party, Comintern leaders seemed to show more interest in the CPWU as a relatively independent, influential and loyal internal division of the CPP. With this in mind, the CPWU decided to give its congress a high profile.

The proceedings took place in a Moscow suburb on 11–28 October 1925. At the congress the CPP Central Committee was represented by Kazimierz Cichowski, Edward Próchniak, Wacław Bogucki and Aleksander Danieluk (Stefański).[3] The Comintern was represented by Grigorii Zinoviev and Vincas Mickevičius-Kapsukas, director of the Polish-Baltic *Landessekretariat*.[4] Oleksander Shumsky, Mykola Skrypnyk, and later Volodymyr Zatonsky represented the CP(B)U Central Committee. Many guests from the West European parties also attended. Thirty-three voting delegates (not counting those with advisory votes) represented 3,243 party members, about 1,500 of whom were in prison.[5] Of the thirty-three delegates, nineteen represented the peasantry, eight the working class and five the intelligentsia and middle class.[6] Their actual social positions were somewhat different—fifteen intellectuals, ten peasants (living and farming in the countryside) and eight workers. The CPWU activists were very young, with only four delegates over thirty-five years of age. By nationality there were twenty-nine Ukrainians, three Poles (of whom one was the CPP delegate Zdziarski and one was from Western Belorussia) and one Jew.[7] The party affiliations of the delegates before joining the Communist party were varied: eleven came from the USDP, one from the Ukrainian section of the Social Democratic Party of America, one from Poale Zion, one from the PSP-left and four from International Revolutionary Social Democracy. The remaining delegates had no previous party affiliation.[8] Thus a plurality of the delegates were former Ukrainian social democrats in Eastern Galicia.

The congress took place just after the "ultra-left deviation" in the CPP was liquidated and passions were still hot. The CPWU emerged from that crisis relatively unscathed. It had resisted the "leftist" drive of Domski and his supporters from the beginning and was the first to oppose it openly. The CPWU leaders were proud of this and wanted to use it to further their political aims. The performance of the main CPP Central Committee speaker, Kazimierz Cichowski, afforded them an opportunity to do so. Cichowski broke with Domski on fundamental questions but tried, in regard to the CPWU, to salvage something of the former CPP policy. He asserted that the CPWU demand to have its own representatives in the

Comintern's central committee and in the Politburo of the central committee of the CPP was contrary to the organizational principles of the Communist party and motivated by factionalism.[9] Cichowski stated that, unlike the CPWB, the CPWU was permeated by organizational separatism which was evident even in relations among comrades.[10] Cichowski's opponents simply identified him with Domski or ascribed to him a covert sympathy with Domski's views.

The Comintern executive's chairman, Zinoviev, criticized the CPWU's position on the national question, but supported the party in its conflict with the CWPP. He told the delegates: "You are an important component part of the party and so you must take care to see that the comrades [from the CC CPP] work in co-operation and solidarity with the RCP(B) and the Comintern, that they do not think themselves too wise, that they do not try lurching first in one direction and then in another.... We must create a central committee for the [Polish] party that is willing to learn from the Comintern."[11] Zinoviev agreed that the CPWU should have its own representative in the Politburo of the CPP Central Committee and also in the executive committee of the Comintern (as a part of the Polish representation).[12] As for Domski, Zinoviev said that the executive of the Third International would "agree to Domski's candidacy for the party leader only in the event of his unanimous election to the Central Committee at the [Third] Congress."[13]

Zinoviev's speech intensified the criticism leveled at the CPP by most of the delegates. In a caustic and emotional speech Vasylkiv addressed the CPP: "I ask, when did you ever contribute anything positive to our work, or ever give us an answer to a single question? No, you contribute nothing positive, and it even offends you to see a CPWU slowly and gropingly grow. We did not get leadership from you; we were pushed around and ordered about for petty reasons."[14]

Zdziarski's speech introduced new points of dispute. On the question of the conflict with the Polish Central Committee (Domski), he fully supported the CPWU's distrust of the CPP Central Committee. But he attacked the CPWU leaders' persecution of former CWPP members.[15] After Zdziarski's speech, which was interrupted several times, the Vasylkivists rose one by one to defend their leaders in the strongest terms. They either denied the alleged discrimination against CWPP members or attributed it to the latter's own factional activity. Korbutiak was particularly bitter and suggested that the CPP and its followers had done only harm in Western Ukraine. Among the guests, Skrypnyk was conspicuous for his thoroughgoing attack on the CPP, in which he listed its "sins" (right-wing deviation, defence of Trotsky, ultra-left-wing deviation) and referred to its activity as permanent blundering. The CPWU, according to Skrypnyk, had taken a correct pro-Comintern position on all matters.[16]

Vincas Mickevičius-Kapsukas and Oleksander Shumsky disputed Skrypnyk's views. Mickevičius-Kapsukas maintained that Skrypnyk had painted a picture of an ideal party that had never existed in the Comintern. He recalled that the CPWU's first resolution on the question of the united-front tactic in the West, though more moderate than that of the CPP, was no less erroneous. At the meetings of the CC CPP, the CPWU representative, Stepan Volynets, had often taken an incorrect position. As for the internal situation of the party, Mickevičius-Kapsukas pointed out that Korbutiak's negative evaluation of the CPP revealed the party's unhealthy tendencies toward "separatism and federalism."[17]

Shumsky took a similar approach. He noted that despite an illustrious past, the CPP had its weaknesses. Thus the Polish party was now being "beaten," but there should be limits to this punishment. Had such a treatment been applied to the CPWU during its Fifth Conference the entire organization "would have gone to pieces," Shumsky said. He also pointed out that some of the old Ukrainian factions, constantly referred to themselves as "we" and to the Poles as "they." This was particularly evident in the speeches at the congress. Such tendencies, said Shumsky, had to be overcome.[18]

More complicated was the dispute over the main strategic formula: whether or not to abandon the demand for annexation of Western Ukraine to the Ukrainian Soviet Republic. This problem had a long history in the CPWU. Negotiations were taking place for a diplomatic rapprochement between the USSR and Poland, a fact the delegates were well aware of.[19]

A dispute had already erupted before the congress at a meeting of an ideological commission considering proposed congress resolutions. Present at the meeting were Stanisław Budzyński and Mickevičius-Kapsukas, who noted that the proposed resolutions said much about joining Western Ukraine to Soviet Ukraine but completely ignored the slogan calling for a "government of workers and peasants." During the ensuing discussion Vasylkiv explained to Mickevičius-Kapsukas that the demand for the creation of a workers' and peasants' government in Poland was not relevant for Western Ukraine, since the latter was to be annexed to the Ukrainian Soviet Republic.[20] This assesrtion was not disputed by the other members of the CPWU Central Committee, and Mickevičius-Kapsukas concluded that Vasylkiv had voiced the opinion of the entire central committee.[21]

On 13 October 1925 the Politburo of the RCP(B) Central Committee decided that the slogan calling for annexation of Western Ukraine to Soviet Ukraine was an error.[22] Returning to this question at the Second Congress of the CPWU, Zinoviev said that national problems were gaining importance and that mainly in connection with them "the PSP has won away from us [*otvoevala*] the working masses."[23] Now, then, was the time to deal with these problems. In regard to Western Ukraine it was necessary to find the source of the demands for secession, which in Zinoviev's opinion lay outside the party. It was well known, he said, that a fairly numerous Ukrainian petty-bourgeois intelligentsia favoured joining the Soviet Union, mainly because in Soviet Ukraine there was a great demand for professionals in the labour market. But in calling for annexation the intelligentsia certainly did not have revolution in mind.[24] The Ukrainian peasants, Zinoviev said, had similar tendencies. They had no idea when the Polish revolution might come, but annexation to Soviet Ukraine "could happen as a result of the Red Army's intervention or a new war.... The peasant masses are peasant masses because they expect their salvation from others... but should we leave them those illusions?"[25] Turning to the congress delegates, he explained, "One shouldn't imagine that tomorrow there will be war or that tomorrow we will fight Poland. Neither will happen tomorrow, and, if it depends on us, we will do everything to avoid starting a war."[26]

Zinoviev noted the delegates' concern over the rapprochement between Poland and the Soviet Union. They were unpleasantly surprised by Chicherin's refusal to receive a delegation of the national minorities during his visit to Warsaw. The delegates had perceived everything in terms of the annexation of the *Kresy*, to the point that they counted on an armed conflict between Poland and the USSR.[27] This was also the source of the party's erroneous position on the main slogan. Zinoviev felt that the slogans should link the revolutionary energy of the West Ukrainian masses with the Polish proletariat and orient both toward an internal revolution; for example, slogans calling for "a Soviet Poland," "a Poland of workers and peasants" and "a government of workers and peasants." But a demand for secession from Poland was not a unifying slogan; on the contrary, it expressed separatist sentiments. Zinoviev recommended a demand for self-determination for Western Ukraine without specifying the form it would take, although union with the Ukrainian Soviet Republic was most likely.[28] "We have the feeling," Zinoviev declared, "that you forget that, besides black Warsaw, there is also red Warsaw"; and that the latter, at the right moment, "will say the decisive word with the help of Lviv and other centres." Zinoviev therefore demanded "not a formal change" but a much deeper "correction of the error."[29]

The representatives of the CPP supported him, especially on withdrawing the demand for secession. Stefański argued that this demand had been correct during the Second Congress of the CWPP, but had now lost its relevance and was harmful.[30] Mickevičius-Kapsukas also defended Zinoviev with great conviction and polemized with his opponents. If the opponents were right in thinking that without the secessionist slogan the party would "perish," then the slogan was not secondary, but primary, and the centre of the movement and political orientation of the CPWU would move from Warsaw to Western Ukraine.[31] Moreover, he pointed out, the masses could not always be counted on to support this slogan. In the Vilnius region they had no desire to join the Soviet Union, and in Estonia the slogan, together with the uprising in Tallin, led to a dramatic decline in the party's influence and increased animosity toward the USSR.[32] Mickevičius-Kapsukas justified further the Comintern's position on this question. Noting that the CPWU was a peasant party both in its membership and in its ideology, he challenged it to move closer to the proletariat of Lviv and other centres dominated by the PSP. The slogan calling for re-Ukrainianization would not win many workers. Instead, it was necessary to come to terms with the CPP, and the secessionist slogan was a hindrance.[33]

In Shumsky's view, the slogan calling for annexation to Soviet Ukraine went back to Zatonsky in 1920 (i.e., when the Red Army occupied Ternopil) and had never lost its relevance for the masses. One member of the CPWU had asked Shumsky, "Why do we need a government of workers and peasants? We already have such a government, we only need to move its borders somewhat to the west." Thanks to that slogan, Shumsky said, "the masses stand with their backs to Warsaw, waiting and keeping a lookout for the Red Army."[34] He also considered it the basis of the party's espousal of sabotage. All the guests who took part in the discussion, except Skrypnyk, supported Zinoviev's position. Skrypnyk was in favour of retaining the slogan[35] as were all the Vasylkivists. Several CPWU members who favoured the position of the CWPP did not speak out.

The Vasylkivists had several arguments in defence of their position. Since the Fifth Conference the secessionist slogan had not been the main slogan for mobilizing the masses. Repeatedly, the party had instructed that union with the USSR could only result from a victorious Polish revolution. But this slogan was essential to help the Polish worker rid himself of the vestiges of "PSP nationalism." The Vasylkivists maintained that one could not overcome nationalism by indulging it and that the CPP should use the slogan to re-educate the Polish proletariat.[36] Moreover, programmes and slogans were not advanced on the whim of the party leadership. The secessionist slogan was put forth by the masses; it embodied their desires and could not be replaced simply by a vague call for self-determination that they did not understand. In the minds of the masses the matter was already settled.[37] The strategic aim was the all-Polish revolution, but the slogan that would mobilize the masses' support for the party was secession. Without it the party would lose its influence; the masses would rally behind non-Communist groups who would espouse secession. "We will be but a handful without the masses."[38] The Vasylkivists also pointed out that anti-Polish feeling was very strong among the masses; they distrusted Poland or could not force the normalization of relations. Too much hatred had accumulated.[39] The CPWB delegate, Salomon Miller, shared these views.[40] Finally the question was referred to a special commission which, however, did not reach an agreement.

The CPWU delegates defended union with the USSR. It was proposed that the Politburo of the RCP(B) Central Committee be approached a second time. This time the bureau complied with the request of the congress delegates.[41] The final text of its resolution stated that national liberation and the realization of self-determination were possible only as a result of an all-Polish revolution, but that in the present historical circumstances of Western Ukraine, self-determination would mean union of the region with Soviet Ukraine.[42]

Two additional problems discussed at the congress are worthy of mention: the future of the right-wing Ukrainian parties and the organizational form of a future legal political front to be created by the CPWU. The first was discussed in connection with the changing situation in Western Ukraine. We have already mentioned the crisis in the bourgeois camp caused by the decision of the Council of Ambassadors of the Entente in March 1923 that recognized Polish domination of Eastern Galicia, and by the split in the Ukrainian National Labour Party.[43] In July 1925 the UNLP reunited and again became the most powerful Ukrainian party in Eastern Galicia. Before the split the UNLP had been cautiously but clearly sympathetic toward Soviet Ukraine perhaps because it had no chance of rapprochement with the Polish government. Once the party had restored unity, the pro-Soviet faction was in a minority.[44] Most party members preferred to work out a modus vivendi with the authorities in Warsaw.

Naturally, Ukrainian Communists could not remain indifferent to the renewed consolidation of the bourgeois camp and the reconstruction of its largest party. The CPWU had discussed this problem in previous plenums and returned to it again at the congress. A large number of CPWU members were inclined to belittle the UNLP, feeling that a conciliatory policy had no chance of winning broad support among Ukrainians. "There is no need to discuss at length whether conciliation has a base.... No petty-bourgeois party currently has a base in the countryside,"[45] Kraikivsky, who was elected to the central committee at the congress, assured the delegates. Vasylkiv was somewhat more cautious. He perceived that some consolidation was taking place among Ukrainian nationalists, "which was not the case in previous years."[46] But he added that unlike the extreme right-wing Polish nationalists, the *Endecja*, which, in Congress Poland, had support among the large landowners, clerks and artisans, the petty-bourgeois Ukrainian parties were based on the intelligentsia, part of the peasantry and even a section of Ukrainian workers. The Ukrainian Communists could take that base away from them, but only by using authentic arguments instead of insults.[47]

Vasylkiv, however, did not appreciate the degree of differentiation in his own society and the economic basis for co-operation between the Ukrainian right and the Polish government. Later at the congress he declared unexpectedly that "in the future both the radicals and the *Selsoiuz* will co-operate with the Polish authorities."[48] But the delegates felt that this was blurted out accidentally, since it did not fit the general train of his thought.

Próchniak took an opposing view, noting that "Vasylkiv does not appreciate the danger of conciliatory tendencies." He agreed, however, that the Galician countryside was poor and that 80 per cent of the farms had no more than two hectares of land. "But there are still 20 per cent of the farms that are not dwarf-holdings... there are large groups of the intelligentsia and priests who have influence on the peasant masses. There still remain therefore social groups... for whom conciliation is a matter of life and death and who have considerable economic importance and influence on the masses."[49] Próchniak ventured that the pro-government conciliatory movement would get stronger, since the authorities had an interest in its existence and could do much for it both economically and politically, in the latter case by offering, for example, Ukrainian autonomy.

Mickevičius-Kapsukas supported Próchniak. He thought that the CPWU's position was misguided, that it overlooked "the partial stabilization of capitalism" in Poland. "From the opening of the congress to the end," he said, "we have heard from many of the most outstanding Ukrainian comrades that there is absolutely no chance of a serious reconciliation in Western Ukraine. The same thing was said in the first draft of the congress resolutions."[50] Mickevičius-Kapsukas felt that such views could weaken the party's influence and draw opposing classes into co-operation with the Communist party. These arguments did not convince the CPWU. It recognized that despite the partial economic stabilization in Poland since 1923,[51] which fostered conciliation, the Polish government could not compete with the Soviet government in solving the Ukrainian question.[52] Therefore conciliation would not acquire a mass base.

Concerning the creation of a legal front party, the delegates recognized the need to channel the pro-Soviet mood of the Ukrainian peasantry, but differed on the form such an organization should take. Vasylkiv proposed the creation of rural committees that would defend the interests of the peasants.[53] Others spoke of a Union of Poor Peasants. Shumsky proposed Committees of the Rural Poor.[54] Próchniak argued for the creation of a legal party that would defend all the peasants. Such an organization would not be confined to sporadic action—such as insurrection—which Próchniak felt was implied in the speeches of several delegates.[55] Mickevičius-Kapsukas also agreed that a legal party was needed. Although its supporters would not be 100 per cent communist, Communists would have the dominant influence in such a party. He considered Shumsky's proposal useless because "at present, intensifying the class struggle in the countryside is not in our interest." Thus Mickevičius-Kapsukas was for drawing the entire countryside into conflict with the regime. He urged a greater tolerance for those elements that were vacillating, criticized the negative attitude of the CPWU toward the Volhynian *Selsoiuz* and stressed the necessity of penetrating such parties and capturing them from within.[56] Finally the delegates agreed that the best form of organization would be one "that operated legally and embraced the wide strata of the peasantry; one that, under the influence of the Communist Party, paralysed the influence of other organizations following the petty-bourgeois parties."[57]

Generally the congress' resolutions criticized Domski's "ultra-leftist" policies in the CPP Central Committee, thus echoing other documents from the period, including the resolution of the CPP's Fourth Conference. The congress resolution accented the CPWU's positive role in that conflict.[58] It also reproached the leadership of the CPP with "persisting in the insurrectionist line, even though the central committee was corrected on the question of insurrection in the *Kresy* by the Comintern at the Third Congress of the CPP, and calling for a tax boycott as the central slogan for the CPWU and the CPWB, which would inevitably press these parties into an armed uprising regardless of the state of the class struggle in Poland."[59]

With regard to the CPWU the resolution stated:

> The party remains peasant in character.... In spite of the special emphasis placed by the Fifth Congress on making the party proletarian we have not so far succeeded in acquiring sufficient strength among the workers.... Undoubtedly there is no need to fear a large percentage of peasants in the party or their continued influx as long as there is both a strong proletarian core and base within the party. But if we don't acquire this core and the party takes on a primarily peasant character, then the dangers that will threaten it are all too obvious: the ideology and practice of sabotage, which has still not been completely eradicated.[60]

The resolution repeatedly emphasized the need to fight the terrorist deviation. Also condemned were the "views on liberation of Western Ukraine by the Red Army," which persisted in the party.[61]

The congress obliged party members "to wage an intense struggle against certain comrades who try... to sow distrust in the CPWU toward the CPP and within the CPWU toward the leadership."[62] It also recognized that since the resolution of the Fifth Conference on the question of labour unions had been implemented only in its propaganda aspect (convincing party members)[63] and since the majority of the Ukrainian proletariat remained "outside any sort of class organization,"[64] it was necessary to unite all national unions in one class organization.

The political struggle with the PSP in Western Ukraine acquired new aspects in the resolution. The goal was no longer merely to break its influence over the Polish proletariat and its monopoly in the labour unions.[65] The resolution stated that the PSP in Western Ukraine was significantly more anti-Ukrainian than it was elsewhere,[66] that it was more closely connected with the police, that it was responsible for the polonization within the labour unions which frightened away the Ukrainian worker[67] and that it made the organization of the Farmers' Union in Ukrainian regions impossible.[68] The congress saw the united-front tactic as a method of "snatching [the working class] away from reformist and opportunist influences."[69] It defined "Fornalism" (Fornal was Różański's pseudonym) as a manifestation of the mistaken view that the revolution could be accomplished without the working class.[70] The ultra-leftist group in the Union of Communist Youth of Western Ukraine, which defended Domski at its conference, had deviated because of its non-worker membership.[71]

The comprehensive resolution on the national question was edited in such a manner as to preclude charges of separatism. The resolution defined the question thus: social and national liberation could be achieved only through a victorious all-Polish revolution. Liberation could not come from outside and spreading such illusions was extremely harmful. The border question would be solved easily on "the day after the revolution." The revolution would be victorious only as a result of co-operation between workers and peasants of all nationalities in Poland.[72]

Despite occasional acute differences and the congress' rejection of certain demands of the Comintern and the central committee of the CPP, the latter bodies viewed the congress positively. Even later, in the period of the split, when the party's past was examined critically, the resolutions of the Second Congress provided no basis for condemnation.

According to police sources, a temporary intensification of factional divisions took place during elections to the CPWU's central committee. The election commission, headed by Shumsky, was handed two lists of candidates, one put forth by the Vasylkivists, the other presented by Adolf Ursaki on behalf of members aligned with the CWPP. The latter list bore the names of Hryhorii Mykhats, Leon Przeorski, secretary of the *okruzhnyi komitet* in Przemyśl, Zdziarski and two more persons with the pseudonyms Czop and Hawman.

Mickevičius-Kapsukas demanded that more workers be included among the candidates, and he added the names of Shapiro, Prystupa and several others.[73] Despite the objections of Vasylkiv and Turiansky, all nominations were accepted. Elected by secret ballot to the central committee were: Fedir Bei, Osyp Krilyk (Vasylkiv), Roman Kuzma (Turiansky), Panteleimon Kraikivsky, Vasyl Korbutiak, Petro Lyshega, Stepan Volynets, Mykhailo Tesliuk, Illia Kaliatynsky, Natan Shapiro (Sukhy), Bartolomii Kopach (Kovalsky), Mirosław Zdziarski, Karlo Savrych (Maksymovych) and Toma Prystupa. Ivan Khlon and Zenon Kuzma were elected as alternates. Of these only Zdziarski, Shapiro and Prystupa did not belong to the inner circle of Vasylkivists.

The Position of the CPWU at the Fourth Conference of the CPP, December 1925

The themes of the CPP's Fourth Conference overlapped on many questions with those of the CPWU's Second Congress: the "Domski affair," the international situation, the problem of secession for the *Kresy*. What was new, however, was the discussion of a proposed resolution defending Poland's independence. Nikolai Bukharin opened the discussion in the name of the Comintern and not only proposed new slogans and demands but explained the guiding motives of the Comintern.[74]

He noted first the growth of England's influence at the expense of France. British imperialism, by nature more reactionary and aggressive, was winning out over its French rival in Europe. This was clearly felt in Poland, where indebtedness to England was increasing and there were plans to sell the nation's resources.[75] Bukharin recognized the Piłsudskiites as advocates of a pro-English orientation, and he considered them "half fascist." This new orientation in foreign policy was threatening to transform "independent Poland into a vassal half-dependent on English capital";[76] increased exploitation of the working class and its possible economic ruin would follow. Thus the situation was most favourable for a defence of Poland's independence, which would attract the support of a majority of the Polish proletariat. It was good, Bukharin emphasized, that the CPP had a strong influence among the national minorities, but the chief aim, the revolution, was unattainable without a majority of the Polish proletariat on the side of the party.[77]

Bukharin's speech contained several interesting formulations. He declared that, "as during the First International, independent Poland is again becoming an important factor in the development of the international revolution." But he compared Anglophile Polish economic circles to "new *targowiczanie*[78] trying to save themselves in a way that will mean not only the end of Poland's independence, but the beginning of slavery for its toiling masses."[79]

A group of party leaders, among them Adolf Warski, Maria Koszutska, Mirosław Zdziarski, Wacław Bogucki and Mickevičius-Kapsukas, firmly supported Bukharin's position, and ultimately he received the support of the majority of the Polish delegates. But on the question of Poland's threatened economic position and independence, the speakers debated what attitude the party should take toward the present borders and whether earlier resolutions of the CPWU and the CPWB calling for annexation of the *Kresy* to the Soviet republics were correct. Stanisław Budzyński, for example, thought that the CPP should demand autonomy for the *Kresy* in its resolutions but not question in principle the Ukrainian and Belorussian parties' resolutions.[80] Koszutska stated that, after the failure of the revolution in Germany and the general retreat from revolution, the slogans calling for secession of the Ukrainian and Belorussian territories had lost their meaning. She declared that secession of the *Kresy* would not advance the revolution, but, on the contrary, could be accomplished only through the revolution.[81] The Ukrainian delegation, however, wanted to retain the demand for secession in its programme and insisted on its inclusion in the resolutions of the CPP.

Vasylkiv's views on the defence of Poland's independence were quite original. He approved discussion of the "Polish question" and thought that it should have been put on the agenda earlier. But in laying out the problem, the party had drawn closer to the nationalism of the Polish petty bourgeoisie. This had proved unsuccessful because the masses did not believe that the Communists wanted to defend the independence of bourgeois Poland or her boundaries. It was possible to deceive individual persons, but not entire classes. Vasylkiv felt that any thesis on the defence of Poland's independence and her national existence must clearly show revolution to be the only defence possible. Vasylkiv bitterly criticized Budzyński's proposal, calling it opportunist.[82] Other CPWU delegates, Volynets and Korbutiak, and the CPWB Central Committee representative, Mikalai Arekhva, defended Vasylkiv's arguments in all their ramifications.[83]

On the question of secession of the *Kresy*, Domski also supported Vasylkiv. In his opinion the CPP resolution should reflect the clear and universal desire of the Ukrainian and Belorussian people to join the Soviet republic. Domski advocated the concentration of all energies on the defence of the western borders, which would probably become an object of political barter in spite of the feelings of their residents.[84] Zdziarski firmly demanded the inclusion of independence and patriotic demands in the CPP programme, but proposed that the secessionist slogan for the *Kresy* be included only in a CPP resolution, with the CPWU and CPWB confining themselves to "self-determination" formulas.[85] Later, however, he amended his speech in the minutes, so that his position on the Eastern *Kresy* corresponded with that of the other CPWU delegates.[86]

The Fourth Conference did not accept the position of the CPWU delegates, though in many points the latter's views influenced the final form of the resolutions. According to Leński, who gave the report on the question, the majority of the delegates understood the defence of independence as a struggle against the politics of Locarno and the threat of war. The resolution also called for defence of the existing borders, but only, as Leński noted, the western borders.[87] The resolution, however, was less clear on the question of defending the independence of bourgeois Poland than Leński and others implied. It declared independence possible either through revolution and the establishment of a worker-peasant government, or through fundamental reforms that would bring the country closer to the Soviet Union economically.[88] Although the thesis had been moderated for the benefit of the Vasylkivists, they still did not approve it and it became a source of new conflict between the CPP and the CPWU. Another factor in inter-party differences was the conference's desire for economic rapprochement between Poland and the Soviet Union. Ukrainian Communists had already reacted nervously to the signs of such a rapprochement at their Third Congress. Though the CPWU's concern was never stated explicitly, this fear must have increased its opposition.

The Fourth Conference took a less rigid and perhaps more fruitful stand on the conciliatory parties, particularly the peasant ones, than the Ukrainian congress. The Polish Communists followed events closely, perceived emerging differences within the parties, and outlined means of exerting influence over these parties. The Ukrainian delegates raised no objection, and probably approved these aspects of Polish Communist activity. They were also satisfied by the retention of the thesis on the right of the Eastern *Kresy* to "self-determination, including secession, as a result of a revolution in Poland, which will mean their annexation to their paternal Soviet republics."[89]

The Comintern leadership attached great importance to this demand. They returned to it in their own discussions, and a year later adopted the following resolution: "Comrades are advised not to play down the slogan of 'a nation's right to self-determination, including secession,' and should not put forth the slogan calling for annexation of Western Ukraine and Western Belorussia to Soviet Ukraine and to Soviet Belorussia."[90] This resolution was not reflected in this period either in the practical activity or in the ideology of the CPWU and was implemented only later after a change in the party leadership.

Notes

1. Vasylkiv's letter to Maksymovych dated 16 May 1925. PA IIP TsK KPU, f. 6, op. 6, od. zd. 126, page 35.
2. Tesliuk (Ernest), "Na shliakhu," 65.
3. Stefański's speech has not been preserved in the minutes, but many delegates made reference to the points he made.
4. *Landessekretariat* (German): organizational unit in the Comintern, responsible for one or several countries. The Polish-Baltic *Landessekretariat* included Poland, Lithuania, Latvia and Estonia.
5. Tesliuk, "Na shliakhu," 6.
6. Zawadzki, Report of the mandate commission, Minutes of the Second CPWU Congress, CA KC PZPR, 165/I–2 vol. 4, page 102.
7. *Ibid.*, 103. It is clear from the questionnaires that the local Polish proletariat was not represented at the congress. This was pointed out to the Ukrainians at the Fourth CPP Conference. See Żarski's report in *IV Konferencja Komunistycznej Partii Polski (24 XI–23 XII 1925). Protokoły obrad i uchwały*, part 1 (Warsaw, 1972), 75.
8. Minutes of the Second CPWU Congress, 165/I–2, vol. 4, page 104.
9. *Ibid.*, 165/I–2, vol. 2, page 30.
10. There were many charges along this line. The Ukrainians were accused of keeping to themselves during the breaks at Polish plenums and councils. See Vasylkiv's speech, *ibid.*, 165/I–2, 2: 61. A typical incident also took place at the Second Congress itself. During a break in the proceedings Zdziarski entered a room where Skrypnyk and Vasylkiv were sitting with a group of Ukrainian activists evidently holding their own meeting. Zdziarski, who was a member of the central committee of the Ukrainian party, but from the CPP, was asked to leave. Offended, Zdziarski did so, but asked for an explanation during the congress proceedings. (Related by Mykhailo Korolko, a conference participant. This incident is indirectly referred to in the minutes, during speeches by Skrypnyk and others.) Skrypnyk had to explain himself several times. He recalled, however, that the CPP activists had at one time not allowed a member of the CPWU to attend their plenum; CPP delegates replied that the person in question had not been a full member.

    In his memoirs on his work in the CPWU (1928), Zdziarski wrote that the Vasylkivists always came to central committee meetings with established positions and a draft resolution and always voted together. The other members were impressed at first, seeing in this an example of Bolshevik unity. (Zdziarski, "Notatki," 94.) Also, unlike the Belorussians, the CPWU maintained its own, separate guest houses in Gdańsk, with the result that it had fewer contacts with comrades from the CPP or CPWB (information given by Maria Pieczyńska, 1965).
11. Minutes of the Second CPWU Congress, 2: 35.
12. *Ibid.*, 40.
13. *Ibid.*, 1.
14. *Ibid.*, 63.

15. For details on the speeches of Zdziarski and Mykhats, see the preceding chapter.
16. Minutes of the Second CPWU Congress, 95.
17. *Ibid.*, 121, 129–30.
18. *Ibid.*, 136–8.
19. Negotiations began in the latter half of 1924 and an agreement was reached on border disputes on 3 August 1925. In September, Chicherin paid a diplomatic visit to Warsaw. See *Dokumenty i materiały do historii stosunków polsko-radzieckich* (Warsaw, 1965), 4: 442–8.
20. Bogucki, Minutes of the Second CPWU Congress, 2: 96; Mickevičius-Kapsukas, 122.
21. *Ibid.* Somewhat later (see *IV Konferencja KPP*, part 2 [1965]) Vasylkiv objected to the idea that he had denied the need for a slogan calling for a government of workers and peasants. He recalled that he himself had put this slogan forth at the Fifth Conference, and claimed that the Comintern delegate had misunderstood him. Mickevičius-Kapsukas, for his part, rejected this explanation. Turiansky, Vasylkiv's closest co-worker, said that the lack of objections from other members of the central committee did not necessarily mean solidarity with Vasylkiv. Turiansky declared that "Vasylkiv's view is his personal view which I have discussed before the Commission and the Congress." Minutes of the Second CPWU Congress, CA KC PZPR, 165/I–2, vol. 13, page 1. Turiansky repeated this declaration a few years later.
22. See Zinoviev's speech at the Second CPWU Congress, CA KC PZPR, 165/I–2, vol. 2, 18, and Mickevičius-Kapsukas in *IV Konferencja KPP*, part 1, 586.
23. Zinoviev, Minutes of the Second CPWU Congress, vol. 2, 15.
24. *Ibid.*, 31.
25. *Ibid.*, 29.
26. *Ibid.*, 38.
27. *Ibid.*, 37–8.
28. *Ibid.*, 32.
29. *Ibid.*, 53.
30. *Ibid.*, 165/I–2, 3: 27. Turiansky quoted Stefański.
31. Mickevičius-Kapsukas, 165/I–2, 2: 123.
32. *Ibid.*, 126.
33. *Ibid.*, 128.
34. *Ibid.*, 143.
35. Not long after his speech Skrypnyk was recalled from Moscow where the congress was being held and Zatonsky replaced him. Zatonsky was more favourably disposed toward the arguments of the Comintern and the CPP. (See his speech, *ibid.*, 165/I–2, 3: 83.) This was interpreted to mean only one thing in the lobbies of the congress. The CPWU delegates made up the following song about Skrypnyk's replacement by Zatonsky:

Vradovalys kapepivtsi
Tai na tuiu zminu,
Shcho poikhav Diadia Skrypnyk
Ta na Ukrainu.

"Nie będzie już stary skakać
I zębami zgrzytać,
A towarzysz Zatoński,
Pójdzie razem z nami."

(The partisans of the CPP were gladdened
Over the change,
When Uncle Skrypnyk left
For Ukraine.

"The old man won't be jumping around now
And gnashing his teeth,
And Comrade Zatonsky
Will go along with us.")

Skrypnyk returned for the end of the congress.

36. Turiansky, *ibid.*, 165/I–2, 3: 1–2.
37. Vasylkiv, *ibid.*, 65.
38. *Ibid.*, 66.
39. Borysov (Bardaś?), delegate from Volhynia, *ibid.*, 116.
40. Miller [Szłomka], *ibid.*, 48.
41. M. Tesliuk, "Na shliakhu," 71.
42. *Postanovy II zizdu Komunistychnoi partii Zakhidnoi Ukrainy* (Lviv, 1925), 25.
43. *Ibid.*, 51.
44. The question of relations with the Ukrainian Soviet Republic led to a split in the Ukrainian National Democratic Union in 1927. The pro-Soviet faction led by Ievhen Petrushevych, former leader of the Western Ukrainian People's Republic, created a separate Ukrainian Labour Party. The ULP considered the existence of a Ukrainian national state (the Ukrainian SSR) to be of utmost importance for the entire Ukrainian movement. The question of its socio-political system was secondary. The system doubtless had its positive aspects, since it gave priority to the masses who were Ukrainian. Monthly report of the Ministry of Internal Affairs on national minorities, April-May 1927, AAN, 961, 38–9.
45. P. Kraikivsky (Dresher), Minutes of the Second CPWU Congress, CA KC PZPR, 165/I–2, 4: 1–2.
46. Vasylkiv, *ibid.*, 59.
47. *Ibid.*, 60–1.
48. *Ibid.*, 49.
49. Próchniak, *ibid.*, 165/I–2, 3: 96.

50. *Ibid.*, 104.
51. *Postanovy II Zizdu*, 14–15.
52. *Ibid.*, 24.
53. Vasylkiv, Minutes of the Second CPWU Congress, CA KC PZPR, 165/I–2, 3: 56.
54. Shumsky, *ibid.*, 80.
55. Próchniak, *ibid.*, 80.
56. Mickevičius-Kapsukas, *ibid.*, 107–8.
57. *Postanovy II Zizdu*, 31.
58. *Ibid.*, 8.
59. *Ibid.*, 3–4. Implied here is criticism of Różański's activities in Volhynia.
60. *Ibid.*, 45.
61. *Ibid.*, 35.
62. *Ibid.*, 10.
63. *Ibid.*, 9.
64. *Ibid.*, 27.
65. *Ibid.*, 18.
66. *Ibid.*
67. *Ibid.*, 28.
68. *Ibid.*, 18. It should be remembered that the national autonomy for Western Ukraine proposed by the PSP was firmly opposed by the Eastern Galician organization of the party. See A. Tymieniecka, *Polityka Polskiej Partii Socjalistycznej w latach 1924–1928* (Warsaw, 1969), 54.
69. *Postanovy II Zizdu*, 28.
70. *Ibid.*, 46.
71. *Ibid.*, 95–8. In the discussion there were those who pointed out that the UCY WU had a majority of Jewish youth and for that reason the entrance of young Jews into the organization should be restricted. Korbutiak [Vasyl] criticized this view. Minutes of the Second CPWU Congress, 165/I–2, 4: 21–3.
72. *Ibid.*, 95–8.
73. Polish police report on the proceedings of the Second CPWU Congress, CA KC PZPR, 256/III–47, 24.
74. *IV Konferencja KPP*, part 1, 18–25.
75. It should be remembered that this took place at the time of the Locarno Agreements which were considered by all Polish parties to be harmful to the cause of independence.
76. *IV Konferencja KPP*, part 1, 21.
77. *Ibid.*, 380–2.
78. The reference is to a confederation of conservative Polish magnates who allied themselves with Russia in order to oppose reforms within Poland.
79. Quoted from an article by the secretary of the CPWU Central Committee, Leon Kotowicz-Klonowicz. The article was cited during a heated discussion. The authenticity of the quotes was not questioned. L. Kotowicz-Klonowicz

[K. Viniarsky], "Z pryvodu pevnoi pomylkovoi kontseptsii," *Nasha pravda*, no. 1–3 (1930): 58.

80. Budzyński's statement on autonomy of the Eastern *Kresy* is not preserved in the minutes, but is known from evidence given by several delegates: Bogucki, *IV Konferencja KPP*, part 1, 566; Koszutska, 596; Vasylkiv, 606.
81. *Ibid.*, 596.
82. Vasylkiv, *ibid.*, 516–17, 606.
83. Arekhva, *ibid.*, 527; Korbutiak, 535; Volynets, 557–8.
84. *Ibid.*, 476–8.
85. *Ibid.*, 553–4.
86. In a typescript of the minutes, Zdziarski, to the words "not putting forth the secessionist slogan," added "as a militant slogan." CA KC PZPR, 158/I–4, 3: 102.
87. Leński's summation, *IV Konferencja KPP*, part 1, 614–19.
88. *Uchwaly IV Konferencji KPP* (Warsaw, 1926), 354–5, 360, 364–6. The final text of the resolution on the national question was edited by Warski. See Kotowicz-Klonowicz, "Z pryvodu," 61.
89. *IV Konferencja KPP*, part 1, 365.
90. Minutes of the meeting of the secretariat of the executive committee of the Comintern, 5 October 1926. Arkhiv Instituta marksizma-leninizma pri TsK KPSS (Moscow), f. 495, op. 61, e. kh. 4.

Chapter Four

Ideological Discussions (1926-7) and the Emergence of Selrob

Disputes over the Autonomy of the Eastern Kresy

The domininant political mood at the Fourth CPP Conference did not suit the leaders of the CPWU. The next sign of discord came from Oleksander Shumsky, a CP(B)U leader ideologically close to the Vasylkivists, who used the Fourteenth Congress of the RCP(B) as a forum to criticize the new political direction outlined by the Fourth CPP Conference. He charged that the CPP's "new line of struggle for an 'independent Poland' [Shumsky's quotations marks] . . . of a powerful Poland, having [within her borders] up to 50 per cent [*sic*!] of its population of other nationalities" would mean a drifting of the Polish party to a PSP position.[1] Though Shumsky's interpretation was bitterly opposed by Manuilsky,[2] the matter was still not settled. What worried Vasylkiv and his comrades most was the possibility that the CPP would propose autonomy for the Eastern *Kresy*.

The PSP had discussed various proposals of autonomy for Ukrainians and Belorussians since 1921.[3] But the Communists showed no interest in the proposals until the end of 1925. In January 1926, during the Third Conference of the CPWB, the Comintern delegate Góralski stated: "We consider the call for autonomy a necessary revolutionary slogan,"[4] because "Poland cannot grant autonomy."[5] He was supported by Piotr (Mikalai Arekhva), a member of the CC CPWB.[6] The conference resolution declared that "At the present time the CPWB supports all partial demands of oppressed peoples' toiling masses, including the demand for a local Diet and autonomy."[7]

On 3 February 1926 the central committee of the CPWU held a special plenary session to discuss the results of the Fourth Conference of the CPP and Third Conference of the CPWB (in the minutes the Ukrainians referred to the Third Conference as the First Congress of the CPWB). The plenum asserted that an atmosphere existed in the CPP which fostered rightist deviations on the national question. This atmosphere was evident at the Fourth Conference of the CPP in "statements which treated the slogan of Poland's independence not as something to be realized exclusively by the socialist revolution and [the establishment] of a worker-peasant government in Poland, but as . . . a concession to the nationalist ideology of the petty-bourgeois masses."[8]

The Ukrainian plenum also felt that although the resolution of the CPWB's Third Conference to introduce autonomy "might yield certain positive results, it does not justify attempts to drop the slogan of union with the Belorussian and Ukrainian Soviet Republics via revolution. Besides, the slogan is essential for educating the Polish masses in the spirit of internationalism."[9] The Belorussian Communists, on the other hand, did not make "attempts to drop the slogan of union." They demanded self-determination for the Belorussians which "in the concrete situation of Western Belorussia will mean being joined to the Belorussian SSR."[10] At the close of the plenum the CPWU referred the matter to the Comintern, and sent a letter explaining that the Ukrainian masses did not at the present time demand autonomy. Among the political parties, the CPWU stated, only the group in UNDU that put out the journal *Polityka* was making such a demand.[11] About a month later the Comintern was also told that Warski's first speech in the Sejm, in which he spoke of the need to defend the country's independence, while passing over the national question in the *Kresy*, was received with hostility in progressive Ukrainian circles.[12]

A plenum of the CPP Central Committee, also held in February 1926, replied that "the resolution of the IV Conference contained no tendencies that to any degree were a concession to petty-bourgeois ideology" and no revisions of "our" present position "on self-determination including secession by replacing it with the opportunist slogan of autonomy."[13] According to the plenum, the Fourth Conference placed the national question in Poland in the context of the revolutionary struggle of the proletariat and peasantry and linked the defence of Poland's independence with the struggle for a socialist revolution and the self-determination of nations, including secession. The plenum's resolution stated that "the Third Conference of the CPWB fights for the demands put forward by the masses, that is for a national school system, for equal rights in the administration and the courts, for the election of self-governing bodies, for a local Diet and for autonomy. These are partial demands which do not at all negate demands for self-determination including secession or the struggle for the dictatorship of the proletariat."[14] An executive commission of the Comintern discussed this matter, probably late in February. Present at the meeting were Georgi Dimitrov, Bohumir Šmeral, Dmytro Manuilsky, Oleksander Shumsky, Mykola Skrypnyk, Roman Turiansky, Pavlo Ladan and Julian Leński. The latter delivered the report defending the CPP position,[15] and stated that autonomy would constitute an attack on the existing regime and would weaken the position of the landed gentry in the area.[16] Turiansky, Shumsky and Skrypnyk, however, thought that the CPP was trying to revise the resolutions of the Fifth Conference on the Ukrainian question. Manuilsky, in turn, saw no danger to the adopted resolutions and considered it a matter of approach. He proposed a resolution which was rejected.[17] Ultimately no resolution was adopted and the commission referred the whole matter to the presidium of the executive committee of the Comintern.[18] At the ECCI's Sixth Extraordinary Plenum, Skrypnyk and Leński introduced the problem, but did not reach a solution.[19]

New arguments were put forth at the March Plenum of the CPWU's central committee. The plenum addressed a letter to the Comintern leaders assuring them that any change on the question of autonomy would alienate the masses. The party was already having difficulties in its discussions with Selsoiuz, and barely managed to dissuade the union from adopting a resolution hostile to the Communist party. The party was also under attack from UNDU and others.[20]

The May issue of the party's central organ carried a lengthy article by Turiansky on the question of autonomy, submitted on 10 April.[21] Turiansky admitted that autonomy would weaken the *szlachta* in the *Kresy*, but thought that it would strengthen the existing regime by easing the internal situation and protecting Poland's integrity. It was for this reason that the PSP and the Polish Peasant Party (PPP) ("Liberation") supported autonomy. Communists should not demand autonomy, because the revolution was approaching and it was not time to fight for reforms.[22] If national autonomy were achieved in the *Kresy* the party would not oppose it, but it could not be a goal of the Communist programme.[23]

After the May revolution, when "right-wing opportunism" seemed particularly threatening, these matters came up repeatedly. At a conference in June 1926 Vasylkiv said: "We must review certain resolutions of the Fourth Conference, since they were formulated in specific political circumstances. The slogan calling for an independent Poland was based on the erroneous premise of 'opposition to the bourgeois drive to sell Poland out.' This was a manoeuvre to win over the patriotically-inclined worker and peasant. Another [correct] method would be to demonstrate to that worker that there is no independence now and that it is attainable only after the socialist revolution."[24]

The conflict was settled by the Comintern. The Comintern's executive committee stated that Communist parties should not call for national territorial autonomy if this was the goal of the upper classes of the national intelligentsia rather than the masses.[25] Thus the CPWU's position was vindicated. On the other hand the Comintern accepted the resolutions of the Fourth Conference on the Polish question as a partial programme. According to the Comintern this did not contradict the notion that the Polish problem would be solved only after the socialist revolution.[26] Subsequently, the problem of autonomy was confined to internal discussions and was pushed into the background for several years by other matters on the Communist agenda.

The CPWU and the "Majority and Minority" within the CPP.

In May 1926, Piłsudski overthrew the centre-right government in a coup d'état. The coup was not a complete surprise. Preparations for it were known not only among the parliamentary left, but also within the CPP. The Piłsudskiists were not the only ones threatening a coup d'état: their right-wing *Endecja* opponents were more openly pro-fascist and called for a "strong arm" government as the only way out of the country's political and economic impasse.[27] Just before the coup the Piłsudskiists had extended their flirtation with the left to the CPP. In several confidential talks with the Communists they suggested that they were moving toward leftist radicalism and indicated that they might carry out a democratic revolution.[28] The PSP was given the same impression concerning the planned coup. The workers still considered Piłsudksi a democrat, whereas the right's epithet for him was "red radical."

The CPP leadership began a lively discussion of the situation and of the course it ought to take. Several leading figures of the CPWU, including Turiansky, also took part in this discussion. Turiansky wrote that the CPP'S use of the terms "right and left fascism" was unproductive and could induce the Communists to take a neutral position in the coming conflict much as the Bulgarian party had done during the struggle between the Bulgarian fascists and Stambolists.[29] Instead the CPP should consider the threat of "black reaction" and draw the masses from the Piłsuskiist camp into struggle against it. Turiansky did not doubt that elements of "black reaction" were present in the Piłsudski camp, and that Piłsudski was capable of acting like Tsankov in Bulgaria. Still, he said, "our task ought to be to disarm the reaction within Piłsudski's camp and break . . . its influence over the masses."[30] He held that no agreement could be reached with the Piłsudskiists, but that Communists should follow the example of the Bolsheviks in Ukraine during the uprising against the hetman: "They supported the Petliurites in their struggle against the hetmanate."[31]

These views were fairly typical of the Communists who universally feared a coup d'état by the *Endecja*. Their practical effect was the so-called "May error." At the beginning of the coup, the CPWU acted in accord with the CPP Central Committee. The CPWU declaration about the Piłsudski coup began with the words: "The joint effort of the army and the working class has overthrown the Chjeno-Piast government." It termed the coup a partial victory and called for the continuation of the revolutionary struggle.[32] Somewhat later the party's Politburo supported Piłsudski for president.[33] Individual CPWU members actively participated in the coup. The secretary of the Communist faction in the Sejm, Fedir Bei (formerly a member of the CC of the CPEG and follower of Vasylkiv), for example, took part in the fighting in Warsaw on the side of the rebels.[34]

By the beginning of June, the CPP leadership realized that it had gone too far in its support of the coup, referring to "Piłsudski's revolutionary forces" and calling for the "next stage" of the revolution, thereby suggesting that the coup was the democratic "first stage." The Comintern wanted only to push Piłsudski to the left by ceasing serious criticism temporarily.[35] When the anti-democratic nature of the coup became apparent, the CPP began to discuss seriously the source of its errors, and a new factional struggle began which had serious implications for the CPWU. On 17–19 June the CPWU held its first meeting devoted to the events of May.[36] Much of the middle-level membership attended this meeting. The leaders advanced the thesis that the "error" committed in May was not a chance occurrence, but the result of the erroneous perspective of the CPP Central Committee. Examples given were the autonomy proposal and the position taken on the Polish question by the CPP's Fourth Conference.[37] Many of those attending the meeting were field workers who agreed that errors were committed, but considered them unavoidable.[38] Three delegates—Aleksander (P. Minc), "Zaleski" and "Antonovych"[39]—even proposed a separate resolution stating that the party's policy of 13–15 May 1926 was correct, but had failed because the party lacked influence among the masses. The resolution was defeated by 15 votes to 3 and Vasylkiv's resolution was accepted (12 votes for, 3 against, 3 abstentions).[40] The resolutions were not published and the entire matter re-emerged at the CC plenum of 1–3 July.[41]

The plenum participants maintained the position taken at the June meeting. Only Aleksander remained in opposition ("Zaleski" and "Antonovych" were probably not present at the plenum). He claimed that it had been necessary to support Piłsudski, but not to restrict the party's activities to go beyond this. He disagreed with Vasylkiv's view that at the moment of the coup the CPWU should have called for a worker-peasant government, since the masses would never have supported such a slogan.[42]

The dispute, however, did not get heated, especially since the participants did not want further changes in the CPP leadership. The plenum specifically discussed the situation in the Ukrainian camp and heard the Comintern's decision on autonomy.[43]

The adopted resolution reiterated that the May error was a logical result of the erroneous views of the Polish party leadership. One such misconception was that Poland was on the eve of a bourgeois democratic revolution led by the petty bourgeoisie,[44] and that to come to terms with the latter, the Polish party had advanced a partial demand for autonomy. No connection was ever made between Poland's independence and the self-determination of the Ukrainian and Belorussian peoples.[45] This slogan was blurred by talk of "national freedom" and "national equal rights."[46] The document warned against another leadership crisis, which would be extremely harmful,[47] and called for the error to be corrected "without organizational shocks" that "in the present moment would strengthen only the ultra-leftist tendencies." This last fear became more serious for the CPWU as the factional struggle within the CPP grew more bitter.[48] At this time the Communist movement in Poland split into two factions:

1. the majority, supported by the CC CPWU and led by Koszutska, Warski, Danieluk, Królikowski and Próchniak;
2. the minority, led by Leński, Henrykowski, Skulski, Korczak and a large part of the CC CPWB.

There were bitter disputes over a broad range of issues that arose from the discussion of the "May error"; we will limit our analysis to the position taken by the CPWU.

On 18–23 October 1926 the CPWU Central Committee held another plenum,[49] at which Adolf Warski spoke on behalf of the majority and Julian Leński represented the minority. A fierce argument broke out between Leński and Vasylkiv, the latter accusing the minority leader of demagoguery, political vagueness and hair-splitting.[50] Vasylkiv was supported by Bukshovany, Stepan Volynets, Illia Kaliatynsky, Bartolomii Kopach, Karlo Maksymovych, Stepan Rudyk, Petro Lyshega and, among the guests, Królikowski. Less committed, but also on the side of the majority were Aleksander (P. Minc), Natan Shapiro-Sukhy and Zakhar (Adriian Hoshovsky). The only CPWB representative, Iosif Lahinovich (Korchyk), defended the minority position and tried unsuccessfully to introduce his own draft resolution.

The plenum supported the CPP Central Committee's position on the May error and the present tasks of the party, and stated that "the so-called minority of the CPP Central Committee does not have a political line of its own, but its activity is based on various secondary 'considerations' and 'declarations' composed, as in the case of the September resolution of the CC, six weeks after the plenum."[51] Later, the CPWU occasionally supported the majority in its press,[52] but feared that factionalism might spread into its own ranks.

Later the Sixth Plenum of the CPWU Central Committee (25–28 January 1927) accused the minority of:

1. sabotaging the resolutions of the CC CPP,
2. tendentiously and falsely representing the resolutions of the CC CPP and the CC CPWU,
3. applying "unheard of methods" of factional fighting and attempting to infiltrate certain organizations in order to oppose its leadership; for this reason the plenum passed a resolution warning against "divisive activities" of the opposition.[53]

The Seventh Conference of the CPWU (5–7 April 1927) appealed to the party masses to support the majority of the Central Committee of the CPP.[54]

The Formation of Selrob

In the Polish question the CPWU took a position similar to that of the extreme elements in the CPP. In relation to the PSP it accepted the tactical instructions of the leadership,[55] but in relation to Ukrainian parties, the CPWU developed a more flexible policy than the one outlined in the party's resolutions.

The CPWU carefully observed all the internal dynamics, differences and centripetal tendencies in UNDU and the radicals (from 1926 on—the USRP). A pro-Soviet faction had emerged in UNDU (the faction was called Rada; in 1927 it became an independent party, the ULP). The CPWU hoped that it would join the Communist movement. Because a potentially friendly leftist current had emerged within the USRP, the CPWU leadership took a more positive attitude toward that party.[56] There were also plans to create a mass, legal, pro-Soviet organization as a counterweight to the Ukrainian right.[57] The problem of non-Ukrainian minorities inhabiting Western Ukraine, however, was not taken up systematically and in fact was often ignored altogether. The CPWU did not publish a Polish-language periodical,[58] nor did it discuss the Polish question in Western Ukraine. Aleksander [Pinkus Minc],[59] who had been sent to the Ukrainian party in 1926 to head its Jewish Section, raised these problems at the June meeting. He emphasized the need for work among the Polish proletariat and to oppose the anti-Semitic campaign conducted by UNDU (the Ukrainian public was then focusing attention on the trial of Schwartzbart, Petliura's assassin, in Paris). At first the majority of those who attended the June meeting were not inclined to accept Aleksander's arguments, feeling that the UNDU campaign was purely conjunctural and tactical.[60] But eventually Turiansky supported him[61] and the July plenum passed a resolution, which expressed the need for "a struggle against the anti-Semitic drive unleashed as a provocation by UNDU, which sees in anti-Semitism its last hope of maintaining a vestige of its influence among the peasant masses."[62] But the Jewish question had always received more consideration in the work and even in the writings of the CPWU[63] than had the Polish question, probably because the party's central committee had long had a Jewish Section, but no Polish Section had ever existed. To the question of work among the Poles raised by Aleksander, Vasylkiv answered "We will not win the Polish worker quickly, but we must not strive to win him at the expense of gains made in the national or *organizational* question"[64] [emphasis added—J. R.]. At the conference the CPWU membership was informed of the emergence of the PSP-Left in Ukrainian areas in a manner that suggested the Ukrainian party had been unaware of and had had nothing to do with the creation of this organization in Eastern Galicia.[65]

The economic crisis and unemployment, which disrupted the masses in this period, also caused a decline in party discipline.[66] Several members of the central committee, including Vasylkiv, called for a purge.[67] A temporary loss of contact with sympathizers, exacerbated by repression, resulted in very subdued May Day celebrations in 1926. Spurred on by these events, the CPWU leadership made energetic efforts to rally progressive Ukrainian groups around the party and to find new organizational forms. It attempted to unite the People's Will and Selsoiuz into a single Communist-directed organization. The CPWU had approved this measure in an earlier resolution, but had begun its implementation only in 1926. Both the People's Will and Selsoiuz played an important role in the difficult years 1927–8 and it is relevant to examine their political formation.

Besides "normal" nationalism, the Ukrainians of Eastern Galicia reacted to national oppression with another, more peculiar form of protest. From the second half of the nineteenth century, Russophilism began to spread among Galician Ukrainians.[68] The basic ideas of the movement were the denial of Ukrainian national distinctiveness[69] and the view that the Ukrainian language is a Russian dialect or a variant of vernacular Russian. In 1874 the Russophiles organized the Kachkovsky Society which became the centre of their political life. They published widely and had representatives in the Galician Diet.[70] As a whole, Russophilism was reactionary in its views (defence of the tsar and a "one and indivisible" Russia, anti-Ukrainian nationalism). The tsarist administration sometimes openly supported the movement, and used it to sabotage the Ukrainian independence movement and foster aggression. In spite of this, the movement had considerable influence, especially among the peasant masses of Transcarpathia and the Lviv and Ternopil regions, who reacted to national oppression and humiliation by identifying with a related and powerful people.

Russophilism had gained a firm and lasting tradition among the peasants. It was rooted in the faith that the Russian tsar was concerned with the fate of the peasants and that if he took power in Galicia he would dispossess the Polish landowner in favour of the peasantry.[71] The masses added to Russophilism the doggedness characteristic of a populist movement. Russophile peasants were often ready to suffer for their views. This was evident in the persecutions of the 1880s and especially during the First World War when the Austrian authorities carried out numerous executions and imprisoned thousands of people for pro-Russian sympathies and collaboration with the Russian army.[72]

Before the First World War, certain currents close to the progressive movement in Russia began to take form among the Russophile intelligentsia and sought links with the peasantry. In 1908 a group formed around and named after the Lviv newspaper *Volia naroda* expressed views that were, according to its leader Kyrylo Valnytsky, similar to both Marxism and SR ideology.[73] According to Soviet historians, by 1913 this group bore the name "Galician-Russian Socialists."[74] In addition to Valnytsky, its leaders were Mykhailo Zaiats and Kuzma Pelekhaty. Austrian repression during the First World War greatly weakened Russophilism, and the October Revolution and the establishment of the Ukrainian Socialist Republic split the movement.

In the first postwar years the Russophiles slowly rebuilt their organizations. In September 1920, Valnytsky's group resumed publication of *Volia naroda*[75] in Ukrainian and Russian, and joined the Russian executive committee,[76] forming its leftist faction. The left Russophiles, unlike the right, were not implacably hostile toward Ukrainians. They supported the Ukrainian boycott of the 1922 elections to the Sejm and collaborated with the illegal Ukrainian university by establishing a chair of Russian culture and language.[77]

There is little information available on the internal ideological evolution of Valnytsky's group. According to a resolution of the CPEG in 1923 condemning the group, it had sided with Denikin and Wrangel in 1920–1,[78] but this accusation is not supported by other sources. During this period, however, the group maintained contact with Kerensky and other SRs,[79] and Valnytsky travelled to Uzhhorod to meet with the SR Vladimir Zenzinov.[80] These contacts were later broken.[81] According to police information a conflict broke out in 1923 between the People's Will and other left Russophiles over the former's "bolshevism."

Early in the 1920s the People's Will produced a programme entitled "The Provisional Statute of the Galician-Russian Socialists" (*Vremennyi regulamin Galitsko-Russkikh Sotsialistov*). This document stirred the revolutionary camp and provoked the reaction of the CPEG outlined in the resolution mentioned above.[82] The programme reflected the group's significant move toward the left and formulated the following theses:

> the aim of the Galician-Russian Socialists is the union of the landless and small-holding peasantry with the working class and the working intelligentsia of "Galician Rus' " into one common socialist organization;
>
> the complete liberation of the "Galician-Russian" people is closely connected with the economic liberation of the toiling masses and peasants in other countries;
>
> the source of exploitation is the capitalist system based on the private ownership of the means of production;
>
> the Organization of Galician-Russian Socialists will strive to introduce the socialist system based on the social ownership of the means of production;
>
> this aim is attainable through the class struggle in solidarity with the working classes of other nations.

On the national question the People's Will held that a "narrow nationalism" weakened class consciousness and contaminated the masses with bourgeois ideas, which split them into hostile national groups. The document went on to state that the Russian socialists in Eastern Galicia considered local demands for the creation "of independent nations out of the Russian tribes a contradiction of natural development and an expression of backwardness." The document further stated that "Russian culture and the Russian literary language were the common creation of all Russian tribes" and thus "there is no need to give up this culture and language." In the bylaws the document states that "any Russian born in Eastern Galicia, having a socialist world view" and not belonging to a "non-socialist party," could be a member.[83]

Thus in its social programme Valnytsky's group was formally radical socialist, while its views on the national question expressed the Russophile denial of the Ukrainian people's existence. The latter contained elements of tolerance toward Ukrainians that were completely alien to classical Russophilism, but stressed the national, Russian character of the organization.

The CPEG Central Committee reacted angrily to these views, and in a resolution accused this "handful of intellectuals" of sympathizing with Denikin and Wrangel in 1920–1, of not yet having broken completely with reactionary Russophilism, and therefore of being a continuation of the Russian Black Hundreds.[84] Earlier the group had defended a "one and indivisible" Russia and now, like the *smenovekhovtsy*,[85] it defended Soviet Russia. Finally the CPEG Central Committee felt obliged to oppose the Galician-Russian Socialists and strongly protested the "support of this group behind the back of the CPEG by certain Russian figures."[86] At the Second CWPP Congress, Jerzy Czeszejko-Sochacki called the People's Will "*smenovekhovtsy*" in a positive sense. He considered it a manifestation of a pro-Soviet trend in Western Ukraine similar to that in Western Belorussia.[87]

In 1924 the People's Will produced a new draft programme which its First Congress adopted basically unchanged in 1926.[88] After 1924 the official name of the organization was the People's Will Party (PWP) and it moved closer to the Ukrainian movement, declaring its readiness to join the latter's liberation struggle. It ceased publication of the Russian language edition of *Volia naroda* and published the paper only in Ukrainian. The loss of subscriptions from Russophile readers hurt it financially for a time. Many readers who were faithful to Russian culture were prepared to pursue a Communist course with them, but not a Ukrainian one.[89] According to Polish security forces, "the greater part of [*Volia naroda*'s] subscriptions in Ruthenian villages, especially in Lemkivshchyna, have been cancelled; but at the same time the paper has gained new potential."[90]

The rejection of Russophilism by the People's Will in 1924 was not, however, whole-hearted. At that time Valnytsky introduced his "two in one" theory of the Ukrainian-Russophile movement. In 1928 (after he had already abandoned the concept) he explained that the movement had manifested itself in two mutually hostile currents, which nevertheless remained elements of the Ukrainian national movement.[91] The police files contain Valnytsky's accurate, if laconic description: "The Russophile movement is the second phase of the same movement as the Ukrainian movement."[92]

In 1925 and early 1926, *Volia naroda* held a discussion on the Ukrainian question with *Kultura*, the unofficial organ of the CPWU. *Kultura* made *Volia naroda* explain its position, which gradually moved closer to that of *Kultura*.[93] In a report written in 1925, the CPWU Central Committee wrote that "the People's Will has evolved considerably from the left wing of the Bobrinsky party,[94] where it once stood. Once in contact with the peasantry, the group abandoned its 'black-hundreds' view on the national question. There is a CPWU representative on the editorial board of *Volia naroda*."[95] There is some doubt about this latter statement. CPWU documents and the party's later development do not indicate that the party had inside information on the People's Will (as it did on the Selsoiuz, over which it had considerable influence).

The first People's Will Party (PWP) Congress was held in Lviv on 25 April 1926. Fifty-two persons took part, including forty-eight delegates from twenty-three districts of Eastern Galicia. Despite a strong effort, the group did not extend its influence beyond Eastern Galicia. The congress elected a fifteen-member central committee and a presidium which included Kyrylo Valnytsky as chairman, Hryhorii Dmukhar as deputy chairman and Nestor Pryslopsky as treasurer. The chief secretariat consisted of Maksym Biliansky, Meliton Holinaty, Mykhailo Zaiats, Kuzma Pelekhaty and Nestor Pryslopsky.[96]

The dearth of biographical data on the PWP leadership does not permit a complete characterization. It is certain that Valnytsky was the unquestioned leader of the party, and he was probably of peasant origin. The Russophile attacks on him suggest that he came from the impoverished Polish nobility. He received an education in law, but his personality was formed under the influence of classical Russian literature to which he always remained attached.[97] He was very knowledgeable about the agrarian problems in Eastern Galicia.[98] Another outstanding member of the group, Kuzma Pelekhaty, took part in the Drohobych uprising (April 1919), led by the Communists.[99]

The First Congress adopted the programme drafted in 1924.[100] Apart from disputes over the national question, the programme did not provoke any dissension at the congress. In general it was Communist in spirit and contained the following points:

1. The People's Will is a union of small-holding and landless peasants, workers and working intelligentsia.
2. The ideology of the party is based on "scientific socialism."
3. The aim of the party is social and political liberation. Any freedom that impedes liberation of workers from the oppression of capital is a fraud. The means of achieving this aim is the class struggle in union with the toiling masses of the entire world.
4. The PWP struggles for the destruction of the colonial system, the replacement of the regular army by a people's militia, freedom of speech, press, conscience and civil rights regardless of race, religion, nationality or sex.

Among its immediate demands the PWP called for compulsory, free, secular elementary education in the native language, separation of church and state, agrarian reform in favour of small-holding and landless peasants, free medical aid and the eight-hour working day in the towns. On the national question the PWP called for complete equality among peoples, and considered the federated union of all peoples to be in the interests of socialism. But in the current situation an application of the "principle of self-determination" was necessary to solve the national problem in Western Ukraine.[101] The programme did not mention that the PWP was a Ukrainian party, nor did it cite the 1923 by-law prohibiting membership for all but Galician Russians. Anyone accepting the party's programme could become a member, thus the PWP emphasized the internationalism of the party.

The first issue of the PWP organ to appear after the congress dealt with the national question somewhat differently.[102] It informed readers that at the congress almost all had erred in attempting to solve this controversial problem. War and revolution, the paper said, had tested many assumptions, including those about nationalities. The Ukrainian movement had passed that test and achieved its own national state (the Ukrainian SSR). Russophilism, on the other hand, was an outdated and defeated concept.

> We know very well that many people joined the Russian movement at a cost of great sacrifices and it will be difficult for them to break with their views.... Whoever individually, personally wishes to remain a Russian will do so, that is his right and we have no intention of fighting him; but whoever wants to take an active part in political life must reconcile himself to the fact that practical activity and the cultural and social reality of our people is going the way of the Ukrainian movement.... Members of a socialist party must see things as they really are. We are free of prejudices and antiquated ideas and have no need to renounce or avoid calling ourselves Ukrainian. We do not want the Ukrainian national movement to become a monopoly of the priests and nationalists; it is the dominant progressive forces, which we as a socialist party are obliged to support.[103]

Finally the paper noted that the People's Will had long followed this line, which had been confirmed at the party congress.

A month later the paper returned once again to the national question, outlining the party's official position. It condemned the party's own Russophile past, noting that many outstanding Ukrainian activists like Ivan Franko and Mykhailo Pavlyk had been part of that movement in their youth. Next it gave a Leninist interpretation of the national question. As "internationalists (not social-patriots)" the PWP opposed all national oppression. Not every national movement, however, was to be supported; only those that were objectively progressive. A progressive national movement was an ally of the socialist movement. The Ukrainian movement had been shown by revolution and war to be such a movement. "As members of this people we should be the first to remember this."[104]

This PWP position basically satisfied the CPWU. The PWP made preparations to join with the Selsoiuz active in Volhynia. Later, during the split in the party, when the Vasylkivists accused the PWP of joining the Ukrainian movement to compete with it, the above-cited position was seen to contain remnants of Russian nationalism concealed within national nihilism and a refusal to admit to a Ukrainian identity. In terms of the Communist theory of that time the PWP position was essentially correct. However, the emphasis on the secondary nature of the national question as a means of attaining purely social aims at just the time that the PWP joined the national movement could not help but awaken suspicion and distrust among Ukrainians.

Selsoiuz, the precursor of Selrob, originated in different social classes and developed differently. Its creators were a group of leftist Ukrainian deputies elected to the Sejm in 1922. The Galician Ukrainians had, of course, boycotted these elections,[105] but things were different in Volhynia, Chełm and Polissia. From the "Bloc of National Minorities" created there the Ukrainians elected twenty deputies and six senators who organized the Ukrainian Parliamentary Representation, often simply called the Ukrainian Club. On 23 May 1923 nine members of the Ukrainian Club formed the independent Socialist Faction.[106] The Galician USDP, which unofficially represented the CPWU-Vasylkivists, immediately established contact with the Faction. Ukrainian socialists from Eastern Galicia were eager to extend their influence to the other areas inhabited by Ukrainians. Consequently, a council held at Lutsk on 17 November 1923 created the local USDP council, a new party organization for Volhynia, Chełm and Polissia. The council included members of the Ukrainian Club's Socialist Faction in the Sejm.

At the suggestion of the USDP that the Socialist Faction represent that party in the Sejm, the Faction broke away from the Ukrainian club and formed its own club. The members of the Socialist Faction were thus forced to define their political stance in conferences from December 1923 to February 1924.[107] At the conference held on 16–17 December 1923 the Faction members together with USDP deputies unequivocally supported the Communist programme and the demands adopted by the USDP.

The leader of the Faction, Pavlo Vasylchuk, firmly opposed an alliance with the Communists. He thought that Communism disregarded the needs of small peoples. "We cannot be Communists if for no other reason than because we are Ukrainians." He considered the Communist slogan calling for joining Western Ukraine to the USSR erroneous and a hindrance to political activity. Instead he proposed the resolution: "We will create a socialist party organizationally independent of the Communists. We will be guided by the principle of loyal co-operation with them." The resolution was defeated.[108]

In subsequent conferences several other Socialist Faction members sided with Vasylchuk. Maksym Chuchmai and Andrii Bratun spoke of the need for "an evolutionary way and not dictatorship."[109] Stepan Makivka was opposed to joining the pro-Communist USDP, because he considered it inappropriate "to be led by a party which does not know our needs." He also mentioned the advantages of legal activity and immunity enjoyed by deputies to the Sejm.[110] Ultimately, a split occurred within the Socialist Faction at a meeting on 6 February 1924. The formal reason for the split was the dissension of the four above-mentioned deputies on the question of creating a separate USDP club.[111] But the decisive factor was the government's repression of the USDP at the end of 1923 and the beginning of 1924, which effectively destroyed the party's hopes of functioning as a legal organization.

On 22 February 1924 the deputies Vasyl Mokhniuk, Andrii Pashchuk, Osyp Skrypa, Toma Prystupa and Iakiv Voitiuk announced to the Marshal of the Sejm their intention to leave the Ukrainian Club and form the USDP Club.[112] Several months later (7 November 1924) all except Mokhniuk joined the Communist Faction.[113] In March 1924 other members of the Ukrainian Club's Socialist Faction—Bratun, Chuchmai, Makivka and Vasylchuk—had created the Ukrainian Socialist Peasants Union, known as Selsoiuz.

Pavlo Vasylchuk was an outstanding organizer of Selsoiuz. Originally from Chełm, he had studied commerce in Kiev. He was a high official in Petliura's government during the civil war in Ukraine and later represented that government in Kovel. After Volhynia was taken by the Polish forces he was arrested many times, once in Chełm in 1920 for publishing the paper *Nashe zhyttia* together with his brother. He was one of the chief organizers of the Bloc of National Minorities in the 1922 elections to the Sejm.[114] In this same year he collaborated with Makivka in publishing the original organ of the Ukrainian Deputies' Club, which later became the main organ of Selsoiuz.

The other organizers of Selsoiuz were peasants by origin and teachers by profession. Makivka came from the Chełm region, Chuchmai and Bratun from Volhynia; all were active in the Ukrainian SR movement in Eastern Ukraine. Bratun served in Petliura's army and was later chairman of Prosvita in his native province. Chuchmai filled the same post in Dubno.[115] Makivka wrote short essays on peasant life for *Nashe zhyttia* and became the paper's editor in 1924.

The first regional Congress of Selsoiuz was held in Chełm on 17 August 1924.[116] This was in effect the founding congress that adopted the party programme and outlined its policies. Vasylchuk opened the congress, while Makivka, H. Novosad, V. Hul, P. Prokopiuk, Bratun and others participated in its activities. The party programme stated that Selsoiuz "is a class party of Ukrainian peasants," which seeks to abolish "the exploitation of poor Ukrainian peasants." Its ultimate aim was the overthrow of the capitalist system and the establishment of socialism. That aim was to be attained "by methods of struggle appropriate to the political situation." In the fight for self-determination for all peoples, the party would represent the Ukrainian people. The programme also contained general democratic demands including the struggle against clericalism and for national, secular elementary education.[117] The congress considered the main problem of the party to be land redistribution and agrarian reform. Redistribution without compensation would be carried out by local peasant committees. Since such demands could be realized only by a government "composed of peasants together with workers,"[118] Selsoiuz proclaimed a struggle for such a government.

The party extended its activity to Polissia and Volhynia in October and December 1924, organized local Selsoiuz congresses in Brest[119] and Volodymyr,[120] and created local organizations. The membership of the new party grew rapidly. Serhii Kozytsky and Serhii Nazaruk moved over from the Ukrainian Club to the Selsoiuz faction in the Sejm.[121] Soon Selsoiuz became the most popular Ukrainian party in Volhynia and Polissia.[122] The party had no competition from large legal Ukrainian parties here as it did in Eastern Galicia, and was able to overcome pro-government right-wing organizations of the Petliurite type.

The programme adopted at the congress, however, did not really reflect the ideological make up of Selsoiuz, which was much more moderate, less class-oriented and more nationalist than the programme might suggest. The ideology of the party was best expressed in its organ *Nashe zhyttia*. In February 1924, for example, the paper published an article by Makivka which called for a "united front of all Ukrainians."[123] Up to 1926 *Nashe zhyttia* did not attack the Ukrainian right and even allowed its representatives to use the newspaper for their attacks on the left.[124] Despite the demands of the party's programme, the paper did not fight Ukrainian clericalism. Defending Orthodoxy against the government, the paper emphasized ties with Orthodox tradition (holy days, for example) over ties with the socialist tradition of the workers movement. The fact that members of the Ukrainian club crossed over to the Communist faction was seen as evidence that extreme centralization of the Communist movement would result in neglect of the Ukrainian cause.[125]

The paper did not normally attack either Ukrainian or Polish Communists openly, but it devoted a great deal of space to criticism of the PSP, which was considered a false friend of the Ukrainian cause[126] for supporting the Polish element in the *Kresy* by organizing Polish libraries, courses and theatres there.[127] *Nashe zhyttia* also criticized the PSP for its inconsistent and conciliatory stance toward the Polish right, though Selsoiuz was itself well disposed toward the Ukrainian right. The paper took a great interest in the life of the peasants and their problems, defending them in matters both large and small. It criticized the proposed agrarian reforms, condemned colonization and propagated the development of co-operatives in the countryside.

Nashe zhyttia emphasized the national cause, and sometimes showed a nationalist antipathy for the *moskali*, as the Russians were pejoratively called. "Aside from indulgence and sentimental muttering [and] . . . hatred in the past and present, we haven't seen or heard much from our brother *moskal*."[128] Such statements were rare, however. Selsoiuz, initially took a wait-and-see attitude toward the Soviet Union and Soviet Ukraine. But it moved quickly toward a positive relationship with Soviet Ukraine and even took a lively interest in the cultural life of that country.

Selsoiuz held a conference in Warsaw on 13–14 March 1926. The conference resolution declared that by their daily struggle and work the Ukrainian masses were making Soviet Ukraine into a true state of the Ukrainian toiling masses.[129] The conference condemned both the Polish reaction and the Polish democratic camp (Liberation, PSP, the Labour Club, the Peasant Party) for fostering the polonization of Ukrainians. It felt that the "Polish revolutionary camp is not currently playing the decisive role in political life." The conference announced that Selsoiuz would struggle against "all Polish parties active in Ukrainian territories regardless of their political or social colouring" because "even those acting under radical and socialist slogans are trying to draw the non-conscious elements of our people into their ranks."

Regarding the political groups of other national minorities in Poland, the conference stated that the rightists collaborate with the Polish bourgeoisie, while the leftists strive for a united front "against the Polish chauvinist camp." Thus Selsoiuz considered co-operation with the toiling masses of other nationalities to be possible in principle, "if these masses recognize the national and social demands of the Ukrainian people completely and without reservation."[130] The conference advanced the slogan of a "national front of the Ukrainian toiling masses against the front of the Ukrainian bourgeoisie and clergy." Despite this the party found it necessary for the defence of national demands to remain with the right in a coalition of the Ukrainian Parliamentary Representation as long as it defended the Ukrainian peasantry.[131]

The first serious conflict between Selsoiuz and UNDU[132] began in 1926 and was followed by sharper attacks on the Ukrainian right.[133] At this time Selsoiuz clearly if inconsistently moved toward the revolutionary left. Its inconsistencies were due to its vacillation in seeking allies and internal contradictions.

Almost from the beginning of its existence Selsoiuz negotiated with the Radicals,[134] a peasant party having much in common with them, but further to the right and anti-Soviet. On the other hand, contacts with the CPWU inclined Selsoiuz toward the left. Within the CPWU, Selsoiuz was seen as pro-Soviet, but vacillating, unsure and tainted with nationalism.

Initially, the CPP looked more favourably on Selsoiuz and induced its Ukrainian comrades to adopt a more tolerant attitude toward the party.[135] The Comintern representative also thought that the CPWU took too rigid a position on this group.[136] Nevertheless, the Second Congress of the Ukrainian party rebuked Selsoiuz for allegedly trading on national interests, but at the same time promised the creation of a legal left Ukrainian peasant organization.[137] In connection with the latter, the communists became more tolerant toward the vacillations of Selsoiuz in 1926.

The 1925–6 report of the CPWU Central Committee describes a joint URP-Selsoiuz meeting that took place in Lviv.

> No agreement was reached because the Radicals opposed a pro-Soviet orientation and Selsoiuz could not agree to this opposition. The CPWU is anxious to prevent the consolidation of the petty bourgeoisie and has taken steps in this direction. The CP has contacts with Pavlo Vasylchuk through Voitiuk (a Communist). By skilful manoeuvring and with some material aid, we can draw Selsoiuz into struggle against the rest of the national camp. The CPWU is striving to prevent a rapprochement between Selsoiuz and the Radicals and is providing some financial aid to the Selsoiuz organ *Nashe zhyttia* toward that end. This policy convinced Selsoiuz to reject the Radicals' position on the Soviet Union.[138]

Somewhat later the Communists maintained their contact with Selsoiuz through Makivka who represented a leftist tendency and, together with Chuchmai, was gradually moving into a leadership position. The right wing was represented primarily by Vasylchuk, whose position, activity and influence declined visibly in this period. In early 1926 a new leadership, the Presidium of the Central Committee, was constituted. The Presidium consisted of Chuchmai as chairman, Makivka as vice-chairman and Bratun as secretary.[139] Vasylchuk was left out. From March to October 1926 Selsoiuz became further radicalized. Ultimately, it took a position in defence of Soviet Ukraine and polemized bitterly with the UNDU press. The leaders, however, did not accuse UNDU of nationalism. The use of this term in a pejorative sense was generally avoided and Selsoiuz never referred to itself as an internationalist party.

The posture of the People's Will was quite different on the eve of its union with Selsoiuz. It was avowedly Marxist, publishing Marx in popular editions[140] and reporting on the Polish and foreign workers' movements in its press. There was much in its press not only about Soviet Ukraine but also about Soviet Russia, including the problems of the Soviet Union as a whole, which were presented clearly with a peasant and worker emphasis. The People's Will propaganda, more than that of other Communist parties, stressed the secondary nature of the national question and the bourgeois origins of national movements.[141] The People's Will was condescending toward its Selsoiuz allies, chiding them, at times publicly, for nationalist errors and later for opportunism.[142]

The CPWU was the mediator in the union of the two parties. Adriian Hoshovsky (editor of *Profesiini visti*)[143] and occasionally Stepan Rudyk (editor of *Kultura*) spoke for the CPWU in negotiations. Selsoiuz was usually represented by Chuchmai, Makivka and P. Shcherbak, while Valnytsky, Holinaty and Zaiats spoke for the People's Will.[144] The first (unsuccessful) meetings were held in Gdańsk in the beginning of 1926. Valnytsky accused Selsoiuz of nationalism and was himself accused of nihilism on the Ukrainian question.[145] This exchange was sparked by Selsoiuz's proposal to use the term "Ukrainian" in the name of the united party.[146]

Prior to the unifying congress the central organs of both parties popularized the idea of the union. *Nashe zhyttia* explained the need for the party to go beyond the "Sokal cordon," that is to extend its influence to Eastern Galicia for the struggle with UNDU. Of the People's Will it wrote: "No one can doubt that it is a socialist party"; and of its Russophilism: "This original sin of the parents ... will surely disappear from the party in time."[147]

On 10 October 1926 a joint congress of the two parties, held in Lviv, accepted the motion to merge. On the same day a congress of the new party convened, but proceedings were curtailed when the police broke up the meeting. The parties did manage to elect a joint central committee on the basis of parity. The central committee consisted of Chuchmai, Makivka, Kozytsky, Valnytsky, Zaiats and Pelekhaty. The new party, at the suggestion of the CPWU, was called Ukrainske seliansko-robitnyche obiednannia or Selrob.[148]

In March 1926 the party published a brief programme.[149] In the introductory chapter the social demands of the People's Will and national demands of Selsoiuz were repeated in a few sentences. The programme considered the Ukrainian question in Poland an important issue and stated that the party, "recognizing the right of all peoples to self-determination, will fight to make this right effective for the Ukrainian people."[150] The rest of the programme concerned partial demands. There were no nationality restrictions for membership in the party.

A small splinter group of former Selsoiuz members led by Vasylchuk and Nazaruk soon formed. In December 1926, Vasylchuk, who had abstained from the vote on uniting,[151] left Selrob together with members of the Chełm and Volodymyr organizations, and reorganized Selsoiuz and its organ *Selianskyi shliakh*. Both during and after the split the reborn right-wing Selsoiuz bitterly attacked Selrob, but was unable to stem the latter's growing influence.

The newly-formed Selrob began its development in difficult circumstances. The membership was aware of differences on the national question among Ukrainian Communists, which greatly hampered the consolidation of Selrob's disparate elements. The two groups retained their factional distinctiveness and reacted to current political events according to their own traditions. Selrob was also severely strained by the government's policies toward the Slavic minorities after the May coup. These policies were on the one hand repressive (liquidation of the Hramada in Western Belorussia in January 1927) and on the other conciliatory (with an attempt to woo the minorities). We will devote some space to the minority policy since it later became a major and lasting preoccupation of party ideologues.

The Government's Policy and the Communists' Attitude toward the Ukrainian Minority after the May Coup

All national minorities in Poland had high expectations after the May coup. The "Belvedere camp," leftist parties in the parliament that had supported Piłsudski in his struggle for power, was known for its opposition to the nationalities policy of the Polish right. The Piłsudskiists made no secret of their alliances with Petliura and had first sought a means of meeting Ukrainian demands through their representative Hołówko in 1921.[152] Later, on the eve of the coup, Hołówko published an article severely critical of the national oppression in Volhynia.[153] The Piłsudskiists had many direct links with Ukrainian leaders through Leon Wasilewski and through right-wing members of the former USDP. This was not demagoguery. On taking power the Sanacja considered a more tolerant policy toward the minorities. In August 1926 this matter was discussed at a meeting of the Council of Ministers.[154] The council set up a Commission of Experts, which included such well-informed persons as Wasilewski and Hołówko. Probably at the end of 1926 the commission drew up the "Guidelines of the Polish internal nationalities policy,"[155] which was sent to the *wojewody*.[156] The chief aim of the approach was "state assimilation of the national minorities (forming a citizen who possesses his rights and knows his obligations) and an abandonment of national assimilation, especially linguistic assimilation."[157] Regarding Belorussians and, especially, Ukrainians the document recommended several conciliatory steps. Except for the districts that were, for various reasons, to be polonized (these districts constituted a bridge between Lviv and ethnically Polish areas), Ukrainian territories were to receive "complete equal rights, de jure and de facto, for Ukrainians in the areas of self government, the economy, language and culture."[158] Even in the regions to be polonized (the Chełm region, for example), the polonization was not to take the form of a struggle against the local language, but was to support simply the "cultural, educational and economic-civilizing effort of the Polish state or society."[159] The document recommended widening the network of Ukrainian schools as well as the establishment of Ukrainian humanities sections at Lviv University and Ukrainian gymnasia in Volhynia.

These efforts to improve relations with Ukrainians were not disinterested. They assumed the emergence of a pro-Polish Ukrainian movement and "the awakening of a Ukrainian national movement in Soviet Ukraine in the spirit of Western European culture and civilization."[160] They also tried to foster Hutsul and Volhynian regionalism.[161] These half measures did, in fact, have some influence on certain sections of Ukrainian society and diverted them from what the Sanacja called "an idle negation of the Polish reality."

The following changes were effected: Ukrainians began to be accepted for graduate study at Lviv University;[162] Ukrainian economic institutions received credits and subsidies;[163] there were many Ukrainians among the settlers in Volhynia;[164] the more hated officials in the *Kresy* were dismissed and a number of Ukrainian officials were employed in the administration.[165] CPP sources noted these measures, but usually point out that they were an attempt to "buy off" the Ukrainian bourgeoisie, wealthy peasantry and upper middle class,[166] and sometimes even the "upper strata of the middle peasantry."[167]

Soviet Ukrainians took a pessimistic view of these events and their influence on West Ukrainian society. Skrypnyk stated that "with Piłsudski's accession to power the blind, mindless policy of the large bourgeoisie has changed. In place of antagonism toward the bourgeoisie of the national minorities it is pursuing a far-sighted, truly class-based, fascist policy... Piłsudski will succeed in rallying all the forces of bourgeois Poland under his leadership and prepare them for an attack on the Soviet Union."[168] The Kharkiv publicist and member of the party's central committee, Andrii Khvylia wrote: "The political factor that clearly formed the [new] orientation of Ukrainian bourgeois circles was the fundamental change Piłsudski made in Ukrainian national policy,... now even the Polish schools in Western Ukraine teach the Ukrainian language. This undoubtedly has a great psychological significance."[169] This exaggerated assessment of Sanacja influence resulted largely because the analysis ignored the influence of the changes taking place in Soviet Ukraine on the mood of Western Ukraine. Later events prove that this was by far the most important factor (the 1930s saw a decline in pro-Soviet organizations in Western Ukraine and even in pro-Soviet tendencies in Ukrainian art).

In the purely political realm the Polish authorities succeeded in taming UNDU, which lost its influence among the masses. In turn, the significance of OUN and UMO increased, especially after the pacification of 1930. These organizations opposed the Communists as much as Poland. The CPP called attention to the increasing influence of UMO at its Fifth Congress in 1930. Jerzy Sochacki, in the opening speech at the congress, said: "The second plenum of the CPWU's Central Committee (January 1929) pointed out the increasing role of UMO... the particular danger of UMO lies in the fact that it has access to areas which neither UCO [Ukrainian Christian Organization], nor UNDU, nor individual detachments of social fascism can penetrate... it is our serious opponent in the struggle for the Ukrainian masses. The influence of UMO has undoubtedly increased recently not only among bourgeois youth, over which it has almost complete control, but even among the peasants and proletariat, especially the youth." By the end of 1929 "UMO was the actual organizer of a broad anti-Soviet campaign of public meetings."[170] There were many such statements aimed more at Eastern Galicia than at Volhynia but even in the latter area a similar process was gaining strength. Among the Communists the Vasylkivists were the least inclined, both before and after May 1926, to fear the attraction of the government's national minorities policy.

Clearly Sanacja influence was greater on the central parties than on the left. Nevertheless, its influence extended even to the Selrob leadership, which saw the possible benefits of operating legally, such as parliamentary immunity and guarding the elementary rights of the Ukrainian people.

The Municipal Elections in Western Ukraine

The first real test for Selrob came with the municipal elections in the summer of 1927. A pre-election meeting was held among the Workers' Left (the CPWU's legal front), the PSP-Left (represented by Władysław Gomułka), Poale-Zion-Left and Selrob. The latter's representative, Zaiats, refused to sign the official declaration of the formation of a bloc among the participating parties. Such a move, he though, would result in the delegalization of Selrob and, moreover, would contradict his central committee's instructions. Despite the urging of Kraikivsky (a member of the CPWU Central Committee and the Selrob leadership), Zaiats insisted that co-operation among the parties should be clandestine. As it transpired, this was not the opinion of the entire central committee of Selrob, but only of former PWP members. The planned bloc was dropped and Selrob campaigned in the elections separately. The Workers' Left fielded candidates in the towns and in some areas of the countryside.

It is difficult to establish the precise results of the elections in the Eastern *Kresy* because of the contradictory information from the revolutionary and government presses, as well as from internal police documents. According to official data, in the Volhynian countryside where the former Selsoiuz was active, the Ukrainians won 71 per cent of the seats. Of this number, Selrob candidates made up the largest minority among the political parties (24.5 per cent), with the remaining seats going to independents and other parties.[171] Internal police documents state that, of the total Ukrainian seats (71 per cent), independents won 66.4 per cent, Selrob—18.2 per cent, the CPWU—1.8 per cent, UNDU—6.6 per cent, the USRP—4.9 per cent and others—2.1 per cent. In the Volhynian towns the Ukrainians won fifty seats (14.6 per cent), of which sixteen were won by Selrob (32 per cent).[172] The initial calculations of Selrob, based on incomplete data, revealed that Selrob took 516 of the 694 seats won by Ukrainians or 74.3 per cent. Of that 516, 370 seats were won by party members and 146 by sympathizers.[173]

The differences in the results derived from the way independents and sympathizers were counted. Police documents certainly made no distinction between them, counting sympathizers as independents; in this way Selrob received only 54.7 per cent of the seats. Also the police did not include invalidated mandates, whereas the party did. Regardless of these differences, it is certain that Selrob was the strongest party in the Volhynian countryside.

In the Chełm region, Selrob and the CPWU together took 69 of the 120 rural Ukrainian seats, or 57.5 per cent.[174] For Eastern Galicia official results were as follows: UNDU—about 50 per cent, independents—approximately 16 per cent, USRP—about 13 per cent, the Ukrainian National Union[175]—about 8 per cent, Selrob—about 3 per cent, with no data on the CPWU.[176] The 3 per cent for the Selrob does not give an accurate picture of its influence, since Selrob won seats in the third and fourth curias, which represented the vast majority of the voters, but did not win any in the first and second curias, where the same number of seats represented a much smaller number of voters (sometimes as few as twenty).[177] It is a fact, though, that neither Selrob nor the CPWU had much success in Eastern Galicia.

The central organ of the CPWU carried an article which conceded "that the majority of workers did not vote." Analysing the reasons for this, the article's author rather unconvincingly denied the role of the PSP, which had called for a boycott of the elections in Eastern Galicia.[178] But he ascribed the failure of the Workers' Left in the oil basin to, among other things, "the years of disruptive work by the PSP" and its "poisonous influence," and to the difficulties the CPWU had experienced in reaching the urban workers who "were mainly of Polish nationality."[179] The article noted the success of the party in obtaining 11,338 votes in the nine largest towns of Eastern Galicia. If one adds to this number the several thousand disqualified votes, the CPWU received about 30–50 per cent of the total.[180]

In Eastern Galicia a sizable majority, 70–80 per cent of eligible voters, did not participate in the election. Despite its optimistic prognoses, the above article concluded that "as the elections in Eastern Galicia have shown, the workers' camp has clearly yet to attain its goal of winning over the peasant masses,"[181] and that only the first steps had been taken in winning over the working class. The refusal of Selrob to form a bloc with the left and the fact that UNDU did form such a block with Polish and Jewish parties were perceived correctly as a negative influence on the election results.

The party journalists did not discuss dissension within Selrob or the reasons for the waning influence of the Ukrainian revolutionary camp in Eastern Galicia, though they were well known. The debate over the national question, which had erupted in Soviet Ukraine in 1926, had a greater impact on Eastern Galicia than it did on Volhynia. Within a few months this debate would throw Selrob and the entire Ukrainian Communist movement into a long and difficult crisis.

Notes

1. *XIV Sezd Vsesoiuznoi Kommunisticheskoi partii (bolshevikov). 18–31 XII 1925. Stenograficheskii otchet* (Moscow, 1926), 684.
2. *Ibid.*, 697–8.
3. *Robotnik*, no. 295 (1921), no. 24 (1922). For the later period, see A. Tymieniecka, *Polityka*, 51–4.
4. Minutes of the Third CPWB Conference. Góralski's [pseudonym] speech, AM CA KC PZPR, 1425/9, 762.
5. *Ibid.*
6. *Ibid.*, 789.
7. *Postanovleniia III Konferentsii Kommunisticheskoi partii Zapadnoi Belorussii*, (1926), 31.
8. Resolution of the CC CPWU plenum, 3 February 1926, CA KC KPZR, 165/I–3, 7: 1, and *Nasha pravda*, no. 1–4 (1926): 94–9.
9. Resolution of the plenum, 1.
10. *Postanovleniia III Konferentsii KPZB*, iv, 11.
11. Resolution of the plenum, 2.
12. *Ibid.* This undated document is among the material of the February plenum but it was written in March of the same year (it mentions Warski's speech in the Sejm on 3 March 1926 during the debate on ratification of treaties with France and Germany). See A. Warski, *Wybór pism i przemówień* (Warsaw, 1958), 2: 297–308.
13. CC CPP plenum, CA KC PZPR, 158/III, 4: 27.
14. *Ibid.*, 28.

15. Report of Komar (Turiansky) at the CC CPWU plenum, 27–9 March 1926 on the discussion in the ECCI, CA KC PZPR, 165/I–3, 8: 2.
16. Turiansky [Komar], "Do dyskusii z pryvodu pytannia avtonomii," *Nasha pravda*, no. 5 (1926): 40.
17. Information given by Ladan at the CC CPWU plenum, 27–9 March 1926.
18. *Ibid.*, 3.
19. *Shestoi rasshirennyi plenum Ispolkoma Kominterna. Stenograficheskii otchet* (Moscow, 1927), 239–43.
20. CC CPWU plenum, 27–9 March 1926, 24–5.
21. Turiansky, "Do dyskusii."
22. *Ibid.*, 40–1. Probably Turiansky considered the period before the May coup to be revolutionary. Hence the editors' notes on when the article was received, since the issue appeared after May.
23. *Ibid.*, 43.
24. Expanded meeting of the CPWU, CA KC PZPR, 165/I–3, 9: 13.
25. "Pro natsionalno-terytoriialnu avtonomiiu (Postanova poshyrenoho plenuma Vyk KKI)," *Nasha pravda*, no. 6–7 (1926): 96–7. Reprinted in *Pid praporom Zhovtnia*, 208–9. The information that this is the resolution of the sixth expanded plenum of the executive committee of the Comintern held in March is probably mistaken. The resolution of that plenum does not contain the resolutions cited in the Ukrainian sources. See *Shestoi rasshirennyi plenum*. Internal documents of the CPWU indicated that the decisions cited came later. The party's representative in the Comintern informed the central committee of the latter's decision at the July plenum (1–3 July). He stated that at the meeting of the Comintern executive, a commission on the national question was established at Stalin's suggestion. This commission, headed by Manuilsky, consisted of representatives of the Communist parties of Poland, Ukraine, Romania and Bulgaria. It concluded that, in the debate on autonomy, the CPWU line "corresponds to the Comintern line," and that the resolutions of the CPWB and CPP were wrong (CA KC PZPR, 165/I–3, 10: 5). But this same commission examined questions stemming from Piłsudski's coup so that the meeting could not have taken place earlier than the latter half of May 1926.
26. "Pro natsionalno-terytoriialnu avtonomiiu," 97. *Pid praporom Zhovtnia*, 207–8.
27. For more on this see J. Kowalski, "Rozwój sytuacji wewnętrznej w KPP po przewrocie majowym 1926 (o sporze między 'większością a mniejszością')," *Z pola walki*, no. 4 (1963): 123–55.
28. The impending conflict between the Piłsudskiists and the Polish right was sometimes described in Communist circles as a conflict between left- and right-wing fascism. See H. Walecki, *W sprawie prawego i lewego faszyzmu. Wybór pism* (Warsaw 1967), 2: 289–91.
29. On 9 June 1923 a coup d'état took place in Bulgaria. The Stamboliski government, which had carried out agrarian and other democratic reforms, was overthrown. Tsankov established a military dictatorship. In the course of

the coup the central committee of the Bulgarian Communist Party declared the party neutral in the struggle between the "urban and rural bourgeoisie."

30. Turiansky's letter of 25 April 1926, PA IIP TsK KPU, f.6, op. 2, od. zb. 46, 4.
31. *Ibid.* The letter refers to the following events: the Ukrainian Central Rada was losing its war with the Soviets and turned to Germany for military aid. The Germans invaded Ukraine and engineered a coup that put Hetman Pavlo Skoropadsky in power. Skoropadsky, protected by the occupation forces and tied to reactionary tsarist officers, revoked all the democratic reforms introduced by his predecessor in Kiev. In November 1918, when the Germans began to leave Ukraine, a group of former Central Rada supporters headed by Petliura and Vynnychenko (the so-called Directorate) led a revolt against Skoropadsky's government. The Bolsheviks and Borotbists supported the revolt.
32. *Z istorii revoliutsiinoho rukhu u Lvovi*, 263. See also the document in the resolutions of the plenum of the central committee of the CPWU (1–3 July), "Majowe wystąpienie Piłsudskiego i taktyka naszej partii," *Nowy Przegląd*, (1926) (reprinted: Warsaw, 1961), 514. The full resolution: "Maiskyi vystup Pilsudskoho i taktyka nashoi partii," *Nasha pravda*, no. 8 (1926): 89–97.
33. Mykola Popov [Lovytsky], Report to the Third CPWU Congress, CA KC PZPR, 165/I–3, 1: 10.
34. Information given verbally by A. Hoshovsky.
35. Kowalski, *Zarys historii*, 137.
36. Expanded meeting of the CPWU, CA KC PZPR, 165/I–3, vol. 9.
37. *Ibid.*, 13. Vasylkiv's speech.
38. *Ibid.*, 17, 23, 25, as well as Vasylkiv's information on the conference at the plenum of 1–3 July.
39. Unidentified pseudonyms.
40. Expanded meeting, 65 and 73.
41. Plenum of the CC CPWU, 1–3 July 1926, CA KC PZPR, 165/I–3, vol. 10.
42. *Ibid.*, 15.
43. Iarema's statement (Volynets or Turiansky), 14.
44. Resolution of the plenum of the CC CPWU in *Nowy Przegląd* (1926 reprinted: Warsaw, 1961), 512. Note that the date of the plenum given in the text is wrong. The errata states June 1926, which is also wrong. The correct dates are given in CA KC PZPR, 165/I–3, 10: 10.
45. *Ibid.*
46. *Ibid.*
47. *Ibid.*
48. An example of the kind of factional dispute that arose in the CPP concerns the nature of Piłsudski's regime. Both factions considered the regime fascist, because of its links with the "petty bourgeoisie"; "its" parties, Liberation and especially the PSP. The minority, citing Lenin's thesis on the dependence of the petty bourgeoisie, said that these parties were not only incapable of effecting their own social programmes, but had no intention of doing so.

Thus, it considered the growing opposition of these parties to the Piłsudski regime a mere pretence. Neither in Poland nor in Italy would the social democratic opposition parties be represented by the dictatorship. The majority, on the other hand, held that the fact that "up to now Piłsudski's fascism has not persecuted the PSP does not mean that it will not in the future. Though it has subordinated itself to fascism a hundred times, it nevertheless cannot go all the way with it. Whoever imagines that the Second International can go all the way with fascism, renounce its democratic programme and relinquish its petty-bourgeois content is fooling himself and others." A. Warski, *Wybór pism i przemówień* (Warsaw, 1958), 2: 403. The minority's views, incidentally, were close to the Comintern's "social fascism" concept.

49. CA KC PZPR, 165/I–3, 11: 1.
50. *Ibid.*, 10 and 16.
51. *Ibid.*, 89. For an abbreviated version see *Nowy Przegląd* (1926), 470.
52. See, for example, Kuzma [T-i], "Na manivtsiakh ultralivoho oportunizmu," *Nasha pravda*, no. 11–12 (1926): 51–70.
53. "VI plenum TsK KPZU. Orhanizatsiina rezoliutsiia," *Nasha pravda*, no. 1–3 (1927): 127, 129–30.
54. *VII Konferentsiia KPZU. Rezoliutsii* (Lviv, 1927).
55. In June the Lviv organization of the CPWU was sharply criticized for deciding on common action with the socialists after the PSP had accepted its conditions for co-operation (joint struggle for the unity of trade unions; for reacceptance into the Central Commission of Trade Unions of the Central Organization of Chemists, which had earlier been expelled; for the release of political prisoners). See Expanded meeting, 100.
56. *Ibid.*, 28, and materials of the July plenum (1–3 July 1926), 13.
57. Expanded meeting, 28.
58. The Vasylkivists published only two issues of *Komunistyczny Sztandar* in Polish. The first issue appeared on 1 October 1926 (see J. Daszkiewicz, "Polska nielegalna prasa KPZU," *Z pola walki*, no. 4 (1960): 40). One should note that the CPWU conference in Stryi passed a resolution calling for the publication of pamphlets in Polish as well as Ukrainian. See the police report for the fourth quarter of 1926, in *Pid praporom Zhovtnia*, 278. Of course, publications of the CPP were easily accessible to Poles in Western Ukraine.
59. Pinkus Minc (1895–1966?) was a member of the Kombund in 1921–3. Together with this organization he entered the CPP. In 1927–8 he was a member of the CPWU Central Committee, and during the thirties was active in a Trotskyist organization in Warsaw. He died in Brazil where his memoirs were published in Yiddish.
60. Expanded meeting, Kraikivsky, 34; Adriian Hoshovsky (Lemko), 18.
61. *Ibid.*, 28.
62. "Rezoliutsiia plenumu TsK KPZU." "Maiskyi vystup Pilsudskoho," 45.
63. See, for example, P. Minc [A], "Zhydivske seredovyshche i zavdannia

KPZU," *Nasha pravda*, no. 8 (1926): 58–62.

64. Proceedings of the plenum of 1–3 July 1926, CA KC PZPR, 36.
65. Vasylkiv's report explained the matter as follows: "Recently the PSP-Left was formed. We will have to pay close attention to this [new] process in order to guide the left in winning over the Polish worker." Expanded meeting, 13.
66. "Rezoliutsiia plenumu TsK KPZU," 155.
67. Plenum of 1–3 July 1926, 36.
68. The situation was similar in Transcarpathian Ukraine.
69. Initially there were two currents in this movement: Russophiles proper and those who did not completely identify with the Russians, but claimed a certain distinctiveness within "the one Russian people"; the latter were called Old Ruthenians or simply Ruthenians.
70. See M. Andrusiak, *Narysy z istorii moskvofilstva* (Lviv, 1935), 78.
71. M. Pavlyk, *Moskvofilstvo ta ukrainofilstvo sered avstro-ruskoho narodu* (Lviv, 1906), 10–16.
72. M. Baczyński, *Kwestia mniejszościowa* (Lviv, 1935), 8. On the basis of Daszyński's interpellation in the Viennese Parliament, Baćzyński concludes that around 30,000 persons were hanged and another 80,000 imprisoned. According to other sources the numbers were larger. See *Voennye prestupleniia gabsburgskoi monarkhii 1914–1917 gg. Galitskaia golgofa*, Book I (Trumbull, Conn., 1964).
73. K. Valnytsky, *Do istorii pravo- i livo-selrobivskykh ukhyliv*, (Lviv, 1928), 8.
74. M. Humaniuk, "Nash Kuzma," in *Za voliu narodnu* (Lviv, 1956), 277.
75. See the commemorative article, "Radisna pakhota," *Volia naroda*, no. 300 (1926): 1.
76. "Selrob-Jedność" (police report), 14 November 1930, CA MSW, 227, t. 36b, 46.
77. *Ibid.*, 47.
78. AM CA KC PZPR, 1477, 4.
79. K. Valnytsky, *Do istorii*, 12.
80. Related by Hoshovsky. CA KC PZPR, record of memoirs about the CPWU, 7 May 1962, 20. At one time Hoshovsky was on friendly terms with Valnytsky.
81. K. Valnytsky, *Do istorii*, 12.
82. AM CA KC PZPR, 1477. The microfilm contains a CPWU resolution related to the *regulamin* of the Valnytsky group and a copy of that document in the original Russian. Both documents are undated but were produced before 9 September 1923.
83. *Ibid.*, 1.
84. *Ibid.*
85. This term comes from the name of the journal, *Smena vekh* (Change of Signposts) published by a Russian emigre group that defended Soviet Russia after the introduction of NEP. For Communists the term often had pejorative

connotations and referred to a vacillating, insincere ally, a false Communist and often a hidden Russian nationalist.

86. *Ibid.*, 3. In the typescript of the CPEG Central Committee's resolution, the word "Russian" has been inserted over an erased word. Probably the authors of the resolution were thinking of contacts between People's Will members and Soviet diplomatic representatives. At the CPWU's Third Congress in 1928 the party leaders defended the unpopular decision of the central committee to accept Valnytsky into the party and emphasized that "he was always close to the party and carried out its directives." Minutes of the proceedings of the Third CPWU Conference, CA KC PZPR, 165/I–3, 1: 26.
87. *II Zjazd KPRP*, 334.
88. The text is reprinted in M. Feliński, "Ukraińskie Selańsko-Robitnycze Socjalistyczne Objednanie (Selrob)," *Sprawy Narodowościowe*, no. 5–6 (1927): 496. The original could not be located.
89. Memoir on the CPWU recorded 30 November 1962, related by J. Zawadzki, CA KC PZPR, R. 123, 32.
90. "Selrob-Jedność," 227, t. 366, 49.
91. K. Valnytsky, *Do istorii*, 13.
92. "Selrob-Jedność," 45.
93. R. Kuzma [N. Lazarkevych], "Vid obiednannia do uhody," *Kultura*, no. 6–7 (1925): 85–7; R. Kuzma [Turiansky], "Apolohiia i apolohety moskvofilstva," *Kultura*, no. 8–9 (1925): 45–53; R. Kuzma [Turiansky], "U vidpovid 'Voli naroda'," *Kultura*, no. 10–11 (1925): 108–10. K. Valnytsky, "U vidpovid 'Kulturi'," *Volia naroda*, no. 250 (1924): 3–4 and no. 254 (1925): 2–3; Valnytsky, "Po dyskusii," *Volia naroda*, no. 255 (1925): 3.
94. The Counts Bobrinsky were an aristocratic family whose members were known for their chauvinistic and russifying activities. Vladimir was a leader of the Russian nationalists in the Third Duma. Georgii was governor in Eastern Galicia after it was occupied by tsarist forces in 1914. He carried out a policy of forced russification and destroyed the existing Galician autonomy which had guaranteed minimum national rights.
95. Monthly report of the CC CPWU from 1925), AM CA KC PZPR, 1356/7, no date.
96. "Pershyi Kraievyi Zizd Partii Narodnoi Voli," *Volia naroda*, no. 286 (1926): 3–4.
97. Information given orally by T. Maryshchuk and J. Zawadzki.
98. Related by A. Hoshovsky. CA KC PZPR, R. 123, 20.
99. Ie. Halushko, *Narysy*, 18.
100. *Volia naroda*, no. 286 (1926): 3–4.
101. *Ibid.*
102. "V natsionalnii spravi," *Volia naroda*, no. 287 (1926): 3.
103. *Ibid.*
104. "Nashe stanovyshche v natsionalnim pytanni," *Volia naroda*, no. 295 (1926): 2.
105. Father Mykola Ilkiv's group of five broke with the boycott and were elected

to the Sejm with the support of the government and PPP-Piast. The group called itself Khliboroby (farmers), but the Ukrainians called it "Khiliboidy" (bread eaters). The Poles were also antagonistic toward this group. See W. Witos, *Moje wspomienia* (Paris, 1965), 3: 26; A. Chernetsky, *Spomyny*, 54; "Khruniada," *Nashe zhyttia*, no. 10 (1926).

106. *Parlament Rzeczypospolitej Polskiej 1919–1927* (Warsaw, 1928), 326.
107. See the minutes of the meeting of the Socialist Faction of the Ukrainian Deputies' Club, AM CA KC PZPR, 1366/7.
108. *Ibid.*
109. Minutes of the Socialist Faction meeting, 20 December 1923, *ibid.*
110. Minutes of the Local Council of the USDP of Volhynia, Chełm and Polissia held in Lutsk, 26 January 1924, *ibid.*
111. Minutes of the Socialist faction meeting, 6 February 1924, *ibid.*
112. *Parlament Rzeczypospolitej*, 327.
113. In May 1925 Mokhniuk returned to the Ukrainian Club.
114. *Parlament Rzeczypospolitej*, 334. In this and many other publications Vasylchuk's name is misspelled "Vasynchuk."
115. *Ibid.*, 331–3.
116. "Kholmskyi povitovyi Zizd Selianskoho soiuzu," *Nashe zhyttia*, no. 35 (1924): 2.
117. *Ibid.*
118. *Ibid.*
119. "Zizd Selianskoho soiuzu v Bresti," *Nashe zhyttia*, no. 41 (1924): 1.
120. "Zizd Selianskoho soiuzu v Bresti," *Nashe zhyttia*, no. 50 (1924): 3.
121. *Parlament Rzeczypospolitej*, 327.
122. *Ibid.*, 328.
123. Untitled article, *Nashe zhyttia*, no. 7 (1924): 1.
124. I. Khrutsky, "Posly USDP v roli prorokiv," *Nashe zhyttia*, no. 29 (1924): 2.
125. "Dva kroky," *Nashe zhyttia*, no. 47 (1924): 1.
126. S. Makivka, "Zemelna reforma," *Nashe zhyttia*, no. 3 (1926): 1.
127. "Krasnoie znamia v Lunyntsi," *Nashe zhyttia*, no. 5 (1926): 2.
128. S. Liubotets, "Shevchenko—patron natsionalnykh i sotsiialnykh zmahan ukrainskoho narodu," *Nashe zhyttia*, no. 11 (1926): 13.
129. "Ukhvaly konferentsii," *Nashe zhyttia*, no. 14–15 (1926): 3.
130. *Ibid.*, 5.
131. *Ibid.*
132. S. Makivka, "Iednaimosia, ale iak?" *Nashe zhyttia*, no. 5 (1926): 2.
133. A. Bratun, "Natsionalyi front," *Nashe zhyttia*, no. 10 (1962): 1. The article condemns the idea of a united front with the Ukrainian right.
134. S. Makivka, "Krainia pora," *Nashe zhyttia*, no. 36 (1926): 1–2.
135. *IV Konferencja (KPP)*, part 1, 74–5. (Żarski's report.)
136. Mickevičius-Kapsukas at the Second Congress of the CPWU. See ch. 2.
137. *Postanovy II Zizdu KPZU*, 88.
138. CPWU report on the situation in Western Ukraine, no date, AM CA KC PZPR, 1356/7.

139. "Prezydiia Tsentralnoho komitetu," *Nashe zhyttia*, no. 6 (1926): 2.
140. "Z temriavy narodnykh relihiinykh viruvan," *Volia naroda*, no. 286 (1926): 2; "Iak povstav kapitalizm," *Volia naroda*, no. 289 (1926): 2; "Chy ie potribni rizni politychni partii," *Volia naroda*, no. 294 (1926): 1.
141. See, for instance, "Iak povstaly natsionalni rukhy," *Volia naroda*, no. 286 (1926): 7.
142. *Volia naroda* reacted sharply to the derisive way in which *Nashe zhyttia* reported a beating received by deputies of the Independent Peasant Party (IPP) in Chełm. "If *Nashe zhyttia* considers that IPP deputies as Poles should not appear in Chełm because they might encounter the distrust of the Ukrainian peasant, it should say so clearly without being sarcastic about the beating of two representatives of a movement motivated by ideals." "Nefortunna zamitka," *Volia naroda*, no. 287 (1926): 3.
143. The unofficial trade union organ of the CPWU.
144. "Selrob-Jedność," 50.
145. Memoirs of A. Hoshovsky, recorded 30 November 1962, CA KC PZPR, R 123, 3.
146. "Rozbyvachi seliansko-robitnychoi iednosty," *Nashe zhyttia*, no. 38 (1927): 1.
147. S. Makivka, "Krainia pora."
148. "V dobryi chas," *Nashe zhyttia*, no. 42 (1926): 1.
149. *Prohrama i orhanizatsiinyi statut Ukrainskoho seliansko-robitnychoho sotsiialistychnoho Obiednannia. "Sel-Rob"* (Lviv, 1927), 24.
150. *Ibid.*, 3.
151. "Komunikat," *Nashe zhyttia*, no. 12 (1927): 2.
152. See for example T. Hołówko, "Mniejszości narodowe," *Trybuna*, no. 43, 48 and 49 (1921).
153. T. Hołówko, "Stosunki administracyjne na Wołyniu," *Robotnik*, no. 65 (1926): 1.
154. "Dokumenty w sprawie polityki narodowościowej władz polskich po przewrocie majowym," *Dzieje Najnowsze*, no. 3 (1972): 138–60.
155. AAN, sygn. 995, manuscript without date. The same document is found in typescript in the Lviv archives and appears in Ukrainian translation in the collection of documents *Pid praporom Zhovtnia*, 226–35. There are some differences among these versions.
156. The typescript kept by the Lviv *województwo* administration gives evidence of this.
157. In the Lviv typescript the corresponding sentence ends with the words "by way of force."
158. *Pid praporom Zhovtnia*, 232.
159. *Ibid.*
160. *Ibid.*, 231.
161. *Ibid.*, 232.

162. For the announcement that Ukrainians would be received into institutions of higher learning, see T. Hołówko, "Metody i drogi sanacji stosunków we Wschodniej Galicji," *Droga*, no. 7–8 (1926). In the years 1928–9 Greek Catholic (and hence Ukrainian) students made up 4.6 per cent of the students in institutions of higher learning, while Orthodox (either Ukrainian or Belorussian) made up 1.9 per cent. *Mały Rocznik Statystyczny 1939*, 334, Table 40.
163. Maksymovych at the Fourth CPP Congress, CA KC PZPR, 158/III, 22: 52.
164. *Ibid.*, 53.
165. Skrypnyk's report, 7 June 1927, 41.
166. J. Czeszejko-Sochachi, *Na drogach nacjonalizmu, oportunizmu i zdrady* (Lviv, 1928), 6. One should remember that this was a period of good grain prices and growing prosperity for the peasants. The number of estates parcelled also grew as did the number of peasants buying land. Z. Landau and J. Tomaszewski, *Zarys historii gospodarczej Polski*, 135–40.
167. The Comintern perceived the problem in this way. This is discussed further below.
168. M. Skrypnyk, "Dopovid na plenumi TsK i TsKK KPbU, 13 III 1928," in *Budivnytstvo Radianskoi Ukrainy. Zbirnyk*, Vyp: I; *Za leninsku natsionalnu polityku* (Kharkiv, n.d.), 243.
169. A. Khvylia "Zradnyky," *Bilshovyk Ukrainy*, no. 7 (1928), cited in *Nasha pravda*, no. 3–8 (1928): 104.
170. J. Sochacki's report to the Fifth CPP Congress, CA KC PZPR, 158/I-5, 5: 49.
171. "Wybory komunalne w województwie wołyńskim w roku 1927," *Supplement to Dziennik Urzędowy Województwa Wołyńskiego*, no. 2 (1928): 8.
172. Report of the Ministry of Internal Affairs on national minorities in the latter half of 1927, AAN, sygn. 961, 105.
173. "Shche na vyborchomu fronti," *Nashe zhyttia*, no. 32 (1927): 2.
174. Report of the Ministry of Internal Affairs on national minorities in the latter half of 1927, page 106.
175. Ukrainskyi narodnyi soiuz—a pro-government Ukrainian organization.
176. See "Wybory samorządowe," *Sprawy Narodowościowe*, no. 4 (1927): 399. Police material on each of the three *województwa* in general corroborate the figures cited.
177. In contrast to Volhynia and the former Congress Poland, where the number of seats was proportionate to the number of votes, in Eastern Galicia the old Austrian curial system was still in effect. In this system all voters were divided into four curias according to wealth and membership in the "estate" of landowners, merchants, civil servants, etc. Each curia elected a quarter of the seats, though in the third and fourth curias (lowest) the number of voters was sometimes more than ten times greater than that of the first and second curias. This electoral system must have particularly distorted the picture of political influence in the towns, where "estate" differentiation was greater.
178. S.Vikul [I. Pavlyshyn], "Pidsumky vyborchoi borotby," *Nasha pravda*,

no. 6–7 (1927): 37–47. The boycott of the elections was a protest against the reactionary curial system. Vikul mistakenly says that the PSP did not propagate its decision to boycott the elections. The fact that some members of its local organization in the Lviv *województwo* took part in the elections is not of relevance here.

179. *Ibid.*, 39, 40.

180. *Ibid.*, 37. The estimates cited above are unlikely since the Ukrainian parties together with the CPWU got only 24–9 per cent of the seats. The strongest party, UNDU, acquired 50–70 per cent of the seats, but only 12–17 per cent of the total vote by all nationalities.

181. *Ibid.*, 43.

Roman Rosdolsky, 1920s

Roman Kuzma (Turiansky), 1925

Osyp Krilyk (Vasylkiv), 1925

Mykhailo Tesliuk, 1925

Hryhorii Mykhats

Vasyl Sirko, 1927

Mirosław Zdziarski (Zawadzki), 1925

Panteleimon Kraikivsky, 1926

Mykola Skrypnyk, 1931

Maksymilian Horwitz (Henryk Walecki)

Adolf Warszawski (Warski)

Chapter Five

The National Question in Soviet Ukraine

The ethnic structure of Dnieper Ukraine was similar to that of Eastern Galicia except that here the Russians, rather than the Poles were the dominant minority group. Ukrainians constituted about 75 per cent of the population. In 1920, 84 per cent of the population were peasants and of these, 85 per cent were Ukrainians. Ukrainians made up only 32 per cent of the urban population, behind the Russians (33 per cent) and ahead of the Jews (29 per cent). Poles were a mere 2.4 per cent.[1] Linguistically Russian was predominant since a large number of urban Ukrainians spoke Russian as their mother tongue[2] and other nationalities used it either as their first or second language. This was the inevitable consequence of living in a Russian cultural milieu. In general the larger the town, the greater the dominance of Russian culture.

The proletariat in Ukraine consisted partly of native Russians who had settled in the South West during the period of capitalist industrialization in the 1870s and partly of russified Ukrainians. Volodymyr Zatonsky explained this feature: "In Ukraine capitalism did not develop gradually on a native basis as happened in other countries, even in Russia. Here the capital was foreign and brought with it foreign master craftsmen and skilled workers from more developed Russia. Industry drew Ukrainian peasants into the towns where, in a Russian environment, they quickly became russified. For these reasons . . . the proletariat in Ukraine for the most part felt itself Russian and was not interested in the national question."[3] These facts explain the position of the working class on the national question. Zatonsky explained that there was no analogy between the position of the English working class, who benefited from the colonial policy of the English bourgeoisie and were hence loyal to it, and that of the Russian workers. The proletariat in Ukraine took an implacable class position. "But the fact remains that the russified workers adopted not only the Russian language but also, to a certain extent, a contemptuous attitude toward all things Ukrainian."[4] "Being either of Russian descent or Russian by culture, the majority of the proletariat before the revolution, at least before 1917, took little interest in Ukraine or the Ukrainian question."[5]

Working-class Russophilism had an important influence on the Bolshevik position. From the first, the Ukrainian movement won mass support only in the countryside. During the revolution of 1905 national slogans played a minimal role in the struggle of the peasant masses. The February Revolution in Russia, however, was reflected in a strong national liberation movement in Ukraine. In March 1917 the Ukrainian Central Rada was created by Ukrainian SRs and SDs. The Rada proclaimed a broad national autonomy within the framework of the Russian state and a social programme close to that of the Provisional Government in Petrograd.[6] In the elections to the all-Russian Constituent Assembly in October 1917, the two Ukrainian parties mentioned above received more than 50 per cent of the votes in Ukraine.[7]

Before the October Revolution, the Bolsheviks treated the Ukrainian movement as an ally. In the dispute over autonomy between the Central Rada and the Provisional Government the Bolsheviks firmly supported the Ukrainians.[8] After the October Revolution, the Communists in Kiev recognized the authority of the Central Rada for a time and even sent to it their representative, Zatonsky.[9] The Rada, in turn, attempted to attain Soviet recognition, even calling the Soviet government by telephone.[10] Despite these efforts, however, a conflict quickly grew. The Central Rada's decision to break ties with Soviet Russia was unpopular in Ukraine, where the majority of the urban population were more opposed to the Kiev government than the Bolshevik leaders.[11]

The national question played an enormous role in the civil war, but the Communists did not fully appreciate it at first. They fought against the Central Rada, that is, against the Ukrainian national liberation movement, without proposing any separate national state for Ukraine. Later, they created the Ukrainian Soviet Government, and still later, after the German invasion, the CP(B)U. The latter move was motivated by the separation of Ukraine from the Soviet state by the Brest treaty. Both creations were motivated by tactical considerations, although both had been discussed previously among Communists in Ukraine, and two currents had emerged within the party.

The so-called "Kievans," Georgii Piatakov, Zatonsky and Andrei Bubnov, wanted to establish an all-Ukrainian Bolshevik organization with a degree of autonomy (they disagreed over how much). Opposed to this idea were the "Katerynoslavians," Emmanuil Kviring, Vasilii Averin and others,[12] who ignored Lenin's frequent defence of the "national" course in

Ukraine.[13] Zatonsky maintained that "undeniably the proletariat and its party in Ukraine have committed an error, historically unavoidable, but an error nevertheless.... Absorbed in this great struggle, the Ukrainian workers did not perceive the importance of the national question in Ukraine.... Thus the peasant masses were left almost entirely under the influence of the Ukrainian nationalists."[14] With the help of their Borotbist allies, the Bolsheviks managed to break this influence.

The Borotbists had a considerable influence among the Ukrainian peasants.[15] They opposed the Central Rada, took up arms against Skoropadsky's regime and, as allies of the Bolsheviks, against the directorate, and ultimately made an outstanding contribution to the victory of Soviet power. Bolshevik influence, on the other hand, was mainly confined to the poorer, less educated peasant classes who had little sense of national distinctiveness. Zatonsky relates stories about peasants and sometimes leaders of partisan units who, in letters written in Ukrainian, brand Ukrainian itself a "counter-revolutionary language."[16] This demonstration of anti-Petliurism revealed the low cultural level of the pro-Bolshevik peasants.

After the civil war the Ukrainian question remained crucial.[17] The prerevolutionary discrimination had ended, but the party still had no positive programme of its own. There were two conflicting currents within the party: one demanded Ukrainianization of the towns with the direct assistance of party and state. This group consisted largely of Ukrainian activists who had come to the Communist party from other leftist political parties and organizations.[18] Most important were the former Borotbists. Among the Bolshevik leadership Skrypnyk subscribed to this view. Zatonsky also supported it, but he was more sensitive to the dangers of Ukrainian nationalism.[19] The other current, initially the larger, opposed Ukrainianization and felt that the party should take a neutral position on cultural developments.

These differences of opinion quickly assumed the nature of an ideological struggle. The premier of Ukraine at that time, Khristian Rakovsky,[20] reported that "Ukrainian Mensheviks and SRs are adding to the demands of the Russian Mensheviks and SRs a national one: the dominance of the Ukrainian language in state institutions. They support this rather than the slogan of equal rights for Ukrainian and Russian which is the programme of the government. But the dominance of Ukrainian would mean the dominance of the Ukrainian petty-bourgeois intelligentsia and Ukrainian kulaks."[21] At the Fifth CP(B)U Conference in Kharkiv (17–22 November 1920), Zinoviev, representing the Politburo of the CC RCP(B), advised: "Act in such a way that no one will ever suspect us of wanting to forbid the Ukrainian peasant to speak Ukrainian ... we think that the [Ukrainian] language should develop freely. After many years the language will triumph that is more deeply rooted, culturally stronger and more firmly a part of life."[22]

The Borotbists objected to such a statement. At the same conference, Oleksander Shumsky and Vasyl Blakytny charged that their party (the CP[B]U) was being inundated with a petty-bourgeois element from Russia which was alien to Ukraine and did not understand it.[23] In spite of the bitter debate at the conference, the final solution—a few sentences—was enigmatic: "The national question in Ukraine is a most important and tumescent problem. Without a proper solution to this problem the victory of the proletarian revolution in Ukraine would be impossible."[24] The resolution recommended a struggle "against both Ukrainian chauvinism and Russian nationalism."[25]

The Tenth Congress of the RCP(B) (March 1921) focused on the national question. It affirmed the necessity of a state and party apparatus in non-Russian areas that would operate in the native language of the inhabitants.[26] This was a new step toward breaking with the assimilationist views that formerly ran deep within the Bolshevik party.[27] But the congress' resolution on the Ukrainian question failed to resolve the ideological debate. The question was complicated by Soviet fear and party prejudice toward a national movement that had so recently been anti-Soviet. It was further exacerbated by a large Russian minority which considered itself the bearer of a more revolutionary, proletarian and sometimes a more advanced and richer culture.[28] Among the Communists this view was clearly and frequently expressed by Dmitrii Lebed,[29] secretary of the CP(B)U. He was especially vocal on the eve of the Twelfth Congress of the RCP(B) (April 1923). "We know theoretically," he said, "that the struggle of the two cultures is inevitable. In our Ukraine it is a result of historical conditions that the culture of the towns is Russian while that of the countryside is Ukrainian."[30] Therefore,"a vigorous Ukrainianization of the party and working class would mean descending to the lower culture of the countryside from the higher culture of the town."[31] Thus, Lebed concluded, "no marxist, no economist can say 'I am for the victory of Ukrainian culture' since that culture would hamper our progress... for Communist internationalists the national question as a fundamental problem does not exist."[32] Lebed also feared that national slogans would strengthen the enemies of Soviet power (the kulaks and petty-bourgeois intelligentsia) and repel the workers, who, as experience had shown, reacted positively only to class slogans.[33]

Among the Bolsheviks, strongest opposition to such views came from the popular and influential Mykola Skrypnyk, a member of the CP(B)U Politburo. He condemned Lebed's Russian nationalism, propagating Lenin's views on the revolutionary significance of national liberation movements and castigating attempts to limit the autonomous rights of the

Ukrainian Soviet Republic.[34] In 1923 Skrypnyk opposed the creation of a monolithic Soviet state with a single foreign policy.[35] Following the resolutions of the Twelfth RCP(B) Congress he suggested nationalizing the Red Army in the individual republics[36] (draftees would serve in their own republic, with commands in the language of the republic). At a party forum he demanded the annexation of the Kursk, Voronezh and Kuban regions to Ukraine.[37] At times his comrades, even while supporting Ukrainianization, felt compelled to dissociate themselves from his views.[38]

The Twelfth RCP(B) Congress decided in favour of the national orientation.[39] The congress supported the development of national cultures and the creation of native leadership in the republics and rejected assimilationist attitudes toward either majority or minority peoples. It condemned the notion of the superiority of Russian culture as a covert attempt by the Russian members to maintain a privileged position. The congress considered Russian nationalism the greatest national threat to the development of socialism in the USSR.[40] The congress' views were not unanimous, however, and discussion continued.

The Eighth Conference of the CP(B)U (4–10 April 1923) met under the influence of Lenin's "Testament" and prepared a draft resolution for the Twelfth all-Union Party Congress. The conference was pro-Ukrainianization in tone and rejected Lebed's position, but there were no definite achievements in practical policy. Moreover, Zatonsky reported that the rebuilding of Ukrainian schools would be delayed because they were far behind Russian schools in revolutionary, progressive culture.[41]

A turning point came in April 1925, when the central committee of the CP(B)U for the first time passed a clearly stated resolution calling for Ukrainianization.[42] In May 1925 Lazar Kaganovich became first secretary of the party, replacing Emmanuil Kviring who had once been an active Luxemburgist on the national question. The new party secretary energetically began Ukrainianization.[43] Unlike his predecessors (Piatakov, Viacheslav Molotov, Stanislav Kosior, Feliks Kon, Dmytro Manuilsky and Kviring), Kaganovich (a Jew) spoke Ukrainian fairly well and used it publicly. It was striking that a movement with such outstanding representatives as Skrypnyk, Zatonsky, Shumsky and Vlas Chubar had to take its leaders from without, especially after the decision to make a radical change in the national policy. Toward the end of 1925 and the beginning of 1926, the CP(B)U passed a series of long-range resolutions. Opponents of the new policy (Kviring, Lebed and others) were removed from leadership positions in the CP(B)U. The Ukrainian party now declared openly that the greatest harm to the building of a Ukrainian socialist culture came from Russian nationalism, and the party's central press organs like *Komunist* and trade union papers that were previously published in Russian began to appear in Ukrainian.[44] Intellectual workers were given a time limit for switching to Ukrainian. In 1927 the number of Ukrainian periodicals increased six times over the number published in 1924. The number of local party secretaries of Ukrainian nationality grew from 30 to 56 per cent[45] over the same period, and the percentage of Ukrainians in the CP(B)U rose from 33 per cent in 1924 to 38 per cent in 1925 and to 49 per cent in 1926.[46] Many Ukrainian activists previously connected with the Central Rada or the Directorate returned at this time and many intellectuals from Eastern Galicia emigrated to the Ukrainian Soviet Republic.[47]

However, although Ukrainianization had made progress and was beginning to take on the characteristics of a national renaissance, its development was not smooth. On the contrary, it proceeded in an atmosphere of covert opposition in the party ranks and sometimes open struggle. Thus the advocates of Ukrainianization, despite their achievements, were still uncertain of victory. Their greatest worry was the negative attitude prevalent among the urban population, the majority of whom were culturally Russian and had many ties with the party leadership. There were instances of entire delegations at congresses or conferences (from the Donets basin and even Kiev) declaring that they represented Russia and not Ukraine.[48] There were mass cancellations in working-class environments of subscriptions to newspapers that began to appear in Ukrainian.[49] Protests against alleged and actual Ukrainianization began to appear in the Russian press.[50] Well known Soviet journalists, artists and writers came to the defence of "Russian culture."[51] Larin, a well known activist in Moscow, synthesized these views in an article published in the central theoretical organ of the Russian party during the dispute with Shumsky.[52] On the basis of letters from Russians in Ukraine, Larin stated that "there is growing dissatisfaction [among Russians] not because they have to learn Ukrainian, but because at the same time Russian is being eliminated even where it is the language of everyday practical business."[53]

The protests culminated, as often happens, in discussions about literature. A debate began around attempts to define specifics of the newly forming Ukrainian literature, but quickly took on political aspects. Mykola Khvyliovy, the most outstanding Communist Ukrainian literary critic of the time,[54] formulated the demands of Ukrainian literature in an article published in 1926.[55] He also demanded the rapid Ukrainianization of the working class, without which Ukrainian culture, deprived of a social base, would be unable to develop as a Communist culture.

A question much discussed at that time was which of the great world literatures should the young Ukrainian literature look toward. Khvyliovy wrote: "In any case not to Russian literature—definitely not. Political alliances should not be confused with literature. Ukrainian poetry should flee from Russian literature and its style as quickly as possible. The Poles would never have produced Mickiewicz had they not moved away from Muscovite art. The fact is that Russian literature has weighed on us for centuries, forcing us psychologically into a position of slave-like imitation. To raise our youth on this would be to stop its development. Proletarian ideals are known to us without Moscow's art, and, moreover, as a young people we will quickly give these ideals artistic expression."[56] Hence Khvyliovy introduced slogans such as "away from Moscow" ("het vid Moskvy") and "welcome Europe" ("daiesh Ievropu"). He noted also that:

> If Ukrainian Soviet culture becomes dominant in Ukraine that does not mean that it cannot be a Communist culture, but if no understanding is reached in its struggle with the competing Russian culture then it will pass into the petty-bourgeois camp.... Blurring the idea of independence with an empty pseudo-marxism conceals the fact that until Ukraine goes through the natural development through which Western Europe passed when its national states were formed, it will remain a bridgehead of counter-revolution.... To put it bluntly, but clearly: the struggle for the literary market, for hegemony on the cultural front in Ukraine of two fraternal cultures—Russian and Ukrainian—is a fact of life, a prose far from sentiment and romanticism and which is becoming daily clearer.... Moscow is today the centre of the all-Soviet philistinism, with proletarian oases, the RCP(B) and the Comintern.[57]

Condemnation of Khvyliovy's views, which were the subject of bitter political debate within the party leadership, was almost universal. Shumsky, a former Borotbist and now commissar of education in Ukraine and a member of the central committee's organizational bureau, did not concur with the condemnation of the literary critic. Although he disagreed with many of Khvyliovy's conclusions, including the slogan "away from Moscow" and condemned the latter's exaggerated polemics, Shumsky felt that the critic had been affected by the many negative phenomena in the political and social life of the country. At a meeting of the Politburo devoted to literature, Shumsky defended Khvyliovy: "It is in the interest of Soviet Russian culture to co-operate with Ukrainian culture on an equal basis.... But co-operation cannot be achieved with a haughty, contemptuous and ironical attitude toward Ukrainian culture or by needling. You won't get co-operation with a whip. Of course, this will not be a smooth process. There are many reasons for this.... But it is essential that rivalry should not turn into a struggle of the two cultures. Russian culture [must be] tolerant toward Ukrainian culture and respect its civil rights. Otherwise a struggle for these rights and the sort of extremism that now and then breaks out in Khvyliovy's speeches are unavoidable." In the heat of the debate Shumsky also made some negative remarks about the situation in the party which he would later have to smooth over.[58] He reportedly stated, for example, that "the dominant Communist in the party is a Russian, suspicious and distrustful of Ukrainians, who has the support of the abject and selfish type of "Little Russian" (nurtured under tsarist oppression) who was always hypocritical, devoid of principles, boasting of his indifference to everything Ukrainian and ready to spit on it if it would serve him and gain him a warm place."[59]

The debate became so important in the the party that a special commission on the national question was set up, consisting of Zatonsky, Chubar, Hryhorii Petrovsky, Kaganovich, Shumsky, Mykola Popov, Skrypnyk and Mykola Demchenko. The commission adopted unanimously several theses at a special plenum of the central committee called to discuss the matter.

The plenum was held in June 1926. Zatonsky's opening speech presented the national question in Ukraine in historical perspective. He justified Ukrainianization as a means of maintaining ties between the proletariat and the peasantry. At the same time, he said that it was essential to take a different approach toward the working class.[60] Ukrainianization of the working class must not mean its derussification (renunciation of Russian culture). According to Zatonsky the Ukrainianization of the proletariat would proceed at a pace and in a manner similar to the reassimilation of the germanized proletariat of Czechoslovakia, Hungary and Latvia into their respective national cultures. Zatonsky perceived an increase in both Ukrainian and Russian nationalism as a result of the NEP. He saw Khvyliovy as a reflection of Ukrainian nationalist tendencies, which were connected unconsciously with the bourgeois path of development. Expounding the view of a struggle between Russian and Ukrainian culture inflamed nationalism on both sides and was therefore to be avoided. After Zatonsky's speech the discussion became bitter, particularly after a stenographic report of the Politburo's 12 May meeting, citing the Shumsky controversy, was circulated.

Shumsky took the floor many times at the plenum. First he argued against characterizing Khvyliovy as a nationalist. The situation in Ukraine was especially complicated because of the national problem. "The youth are racking their brains trying to understand a turbulent process of development while the party, culturally Russian, using Russian in its internal life, stands on the sidelines and takes no creative part in this process.... A tiny number of Ukrainian Communists ride the surface of the turbulent Ukrainian rebirth."[61] They were in no position to lead or even influence it, hence the vacillation of the Ukrainian membership. Shumsky was "of the profound conviction" that Khvyliovy was a true Communist, but one without a clear perspective of the development of Ukrainian culture or literature. From the party perspective, he was unable to take a broad view of the Ukrainian enlightenment,[62] tried to guide it and made mistakes.[63]

The CPWU representative, Karol Maksymovych,[64] cautiously defended Shumsky as did the local activist, Solodub. But all other speakers, especially central committee members, disagreed with Shumsky. Skrypnyk spoke against him, as did, even more strongly, Chubar, Andrii Radchenko and Petrovsky.[65] The latter considered Shumsky's reference to the type of "Little Russian" a reference to all Ukrainians on the central committee and thus to himself. He accused Shumsky of playing up to nationalist circles and intrigue and pointed out that many native Russians (Popov, for example) had contributed more to Ukrainianization than had the commissar of education.

In his summation, Kaganovich tried to moderate the tone of the debate. He declared that Ukrainianization would remain the party's most important task. But although "we have made certain achievements in the area of Ukrainianization, ... clearly the present cultural development of the country is proceeding more widely and faster than the party can keep up with."[66] He conceded that many of Shumsky's comments were correct.[67] The party had lagged behind the turbulent development of Ukrainian culture, but would make greater efforts toward Ukrainianization. He recalled, however, that even before the debate among the party literati, the party was aware of its defects. The first secretary objected to demands for a broader discussion with Shumsky since it was not right "to persecute this or that comrade" because he had said something in good faith that was not in the party's interest. Moreover, "business and serious political discussion has been replaced here [at the plenum] by vitriolic polemics ... [into which] has been injected a personal element. The Politburo does not want such polemics and prefers to avoid them."[68] Kaganovich also objected to the division of party members into former Bolsheviks and non-Bolsheviks (Borotbists) in the debate.[69] He cited Khvylia, a former Borotbist who opposed Shumsky's views, as an example to emulate.[70] Kaganovich recognized Russian chauvinism as the main danger in Ukraine but also considered Ukrainian nationalism, represented in the party by Khvyliovy, to be extremely dangerous.[71] Referring to Shumsky's "errors," Kaganovich neither accused him of nationalism directly, nor charged him with responsibility for Khvyliovy's nationalism (as Petrovsky had suggested), but instead struck a conciliatory note by saying that, since the resolution had been passed unanimously, "there are neither victors nor vanquished."[72]

The plenum resolution stated that "the utmost effort and will of the party must go into further Ukrainianization"[73] since "the main difficulties have yet to be overcome."[74] It recommended great caution in Ukrainianizing the working class, the majority of whom "use the Russian language."[75] The document also declared the party in favour of the independent development of Ukrainian culture, which might avail itself of world achievements, and thus for "a decisive break with the traditions of provincial narrowness and slave-like imitation."[76]

Agreement, however, was short-lived. Shumsky was asked to write an article for the party press to dissociate himself from Khvyliovy's errors and to calm passions inflamed by the debate. Shumsky suggested rather that he confine himself to a report of the speech he had already made on this subject, but Kaganovich demanded the authorized article. Shumsky's speech, Kaganovich pointed out, had many flaws: he had avoided controversial issues and concentrated on literary phenomena without mentioning their political roots. Moreover he had mistakenly stated that the fight against Russian chauvinism was begun after the defeat of Ukrainian nationalism and that the civil war in Ukraine was also a national war. Kaganovich also suggested that he use the article to publicly agree with Stalin's criticism.[77] In fact, the article met only part of the leadership's demands.[78] Thus in a critique written immediately after its publication,[79] Skrypnyk wrote that Shumsky attributed Khvyliovy's deviation not to Ukrainian social processes but to Ukrainian reaction to "the intolerant posture of Russian culture." The party could not agree with this statement. Shumsky furthermore had said nothing of the special role of the proletariat and party in Ukrainianization, implying that he did not recognize it.

The debate was back to square one and Skrypnyk began to take an ever more active part in it. Earlier he had attacked Khvyliovy, but evidently he had said little at the June plenum (1926) when Shumsky was criticized. His restraint was probably due to his disagreement with Zatonsky. Only after the elimination from the draft resolution of those sections about which he had reservations did he become more active.[80] A year later Skrypnyk maintained that he had been the first to realize Shumsky's errors and oppose him.[81] Indeed later he became the most active opponent of Shumsky in the press, at plenums and in the Comintern and CPWU, at times he formulated the most drastic organizational sanctions against Shumsky and his followers in the CPWU.

The debate involved not only theoretical but also practical problems. An emigre Ukrainian historian who was at one time close to former Borotbist circles writes: "Kaganovich was sent from Moscow and assigned as secretary of the CP(b)U in May 1925 for the purpose of strengthening a policy of Ukrainianization. With respect to the question of Ukrainianization it would seem that there could be no real differences between Kaganovich and Shums'kyi; however, for reasons unknown to the author, Shums'kyi opposed Kaganovich's appointment. It was rumored that Shums'kyi, heading a 'conspiracy' against Kaganovich, had proposed that Chubar be appointed party secretary, and that the former Borot'bist Hryn'ko replace Chubar as Chairman of the Ukrainian Council of People's Commissars.... Andriy Khvylya...informed against Shums'kyi, [and] Kaganovich learned of the 'conspiracy'.... "[82]

Other sources generally confirm this account. After the Second CPWU Congress (October 1925) a group of activists from that party together with Shumsky had a meeting with Stalin. During the conversation Shumsky asked Stalin why the Ukrainian party in Kharkiv was not led by a Ukrainian (since May 1925 Kaganovich had held the position of first secretary). There was certainly no lack of highly trained Bolshevik Ukrainians, like Chubar or Skrypnyk. Stalin responded that it was still too early for such a step.[83] Several months later Shumsky and Stalin had another conversation on the same subject, which resulted in a letter from Stalin to Ukrainian party members.[84] The letter reveals that Shumsky had criticized Kaganovich's methods and insisted that he be replaced by Chubar. For premier he had suggested Hrynko. Otherwise Shumsky saw no possibility of his working in Ukraine.[85] He had thus given an ultimatum. Stalin rejected these proposals and said that although Shumsky had made some valid points, he "poorly understands Ukrainianization,"[86] and that in practice his line would result in a forced Ukrainianization of the Russian proletariat, which would violate Communist principles. Stalin saw the Khvyliovy case as evidence of a dangerous tendency among Ukrainian artists.[87] This letter was read by interested parties (Shumsky also knew of its contents) before the June plenum.[88]

Shumsky continued to press his demand for more native Ukrainians in leadership positions. Since Bolshevik leaders were, for the most part, either Russians or russified Ukrainians, such a demand was not welcomed.[89] On the other hand, Kaganovich, Skrypnyk and others agreed in principle with Shumsky, but accused him of using the criterion of ethnic origin rather than national identity.[90]

Once it was clear that Shumsky would not compromise, the Politburo accepted his original request for a transfer out of Soviet Ukraine. After the motion was passed Shumsky asked that deputy members of the central committee be allowed to speak. Karlo Maksymovych, deputy member of the central committee of the CPWU, then took the floor and outlined his party's reasons for abstaining from the vote.[91] In a careful statement he assured the plenum of his complete agreement with the policies of the CP(B)U, and its national policy in particular.[92] He had doubts, however, about the decision regarding Shumsky. From the charge against him it was difficult to see the difference between Shumsky's position and the central committee line. Therefore, the final decision seemed incommensurate with the charges. Maksymovych then enumerated the services Shumsky had rendered to the CPWU. He had favourably influenced the party in the following matters: in overcoming the Trotskyite and Zinovievite deviations, in fighting pressures from right and ultra-left elements in the CPP, in fighting the residue of national bolshevism in the party ranks and in the organizational and ideological integration of the CPWU and CPP. Maksymovych also recalled Shumsky's long-standing opposition to Ukrainian nationalism. The removal of a man of this calibre from Ukraine, he said, would be misunderstood "on both sides of the border" and even within the CPWU, though the party's central committee would support the CP(B)U's decision "completely and unreservedly"[93] and would "effectively repulse any attacks on the party."[94] Maksymovych's statement did not alter the decision of the central committee, but his words were disturbing, since he spoke in the name of the entire West Ukrainian party.

At a 26 March meeting of the Comintern's Polish-Baltic Landessekretariat, the CPWU representative, Roman Kuzma (Turiansky), protested statements made about Shumsky by the director of the Secretariat, V. Mickevičius-Kapsukas.[95]

Thus signs of a growing discord were evident. The central committee of the CP(B)U posed a question to its fraternal West Ukrainian party: "Does the CC CPWU stand behind... Maksymovych's statement or not?"[96] Since no answer was forthcoming a special plenum was called in which Skrypnyk (O. Mykolos), representing both the Comintern and the CP(B)U, would report on the Shumsky affair.

Notes

1. *Ukraina. Statystychnyi spravochnyk* (Kharkiv, 1925), 13, table 6.
2. In 1928, for example, during a period of intensive Ukrainianization, 1.3 million Ukrainians continued to give Russian as their mother tongue. Skrypnyk, Speech at the Third CPWU Congress, CA KC PZPR, 165/1–3, 5: 13.
3. V. Zatonsky, "Pro pidsumky ukrainizatsii. Z dopovidi na chervnevomu plenumi TsK KPbU, 1926," in *Budivnytstvo Radianskoi Ukrainy*, 7.
4. *Ibid.*, 10.
5. *Ibid.*, 7.
6. The subject is explored further in J. Radziejowski, "Ruch narodowy i rewolucyjny na Ukrainie w okresie działalności Centralnej Rady (marzec 1917–kwiecień 1918," *Studia z dziejów ZSRR i Europy Środkowej* 9 (1973).
7. V. I. Lenin, "The Constituent Assembly Elections and the Dictatorship of the Proletariat," *Collected Works*, 45 vols. (Moscow, 1960–70), 30: 270.
8. See, for example, Lenin, "It Is Undemocratic, Citizen Kerensky!" *ibid.*, 24: 568–9; "The Ukraine," *ibid.*, 25: 91–2; "The Ukraine and the Defeat of the Ruling Parties of Russia," *ibid.*, 25: 99–101.
9. S. Korolivsky, M. Rubach, N. Suprunenko, *Pobeda sovetskoi vlasti na Ukraine* (Moscow, 1967), 231, 233, 267, 269; M. I. Kulichenko, "Taktika

bolshevistskoi partii v sviazi s osobennostiami razvitiia sotsialisticheskoi revoliutsii na Ukraine," *Voprosy istorii KPSS*, no. 10 (1967): 103–8. M. Rafes, *Dva goda revoliutsii na Ukraine* (Moscow, 1920), 45.

10. On 17 November 1917 the Ukrainian social democrat Mykola Porsh telephoned Stalin, who was then peoples' commissar for nationalities, and requested recognition of the Central Rada, but this was refused. Rafes, *Dva goda*, 62.
11. In the summer of 1917, when the Central Rada governed Ukraine, in the elections to the local dumy the Ukrainian parties together took 20 per cent of the votes in Kiev, 10 per cent each in Katerynoslav and Zhytomyr and 4 per cent in Odessa. The results were similar in other towns. See *Entsyklopediia Ukrainoznavstva*, 1, part 3: 505.
12. Nazarenko, *Ocherki*, 247–8; M. Popov, *Ocherk istoriii Vsesoiuznoi kommunisticheskoi partii bolshevikov* (Moscow-Leningrad, 1927), 183–6.
13. In an unrecorded statement at the December conference of the RCP(B) in 1919, Lenin showed that the failure of the Bolsheviks in the civil war was due to their errors in the national and peasant questions. For information on this statement see Popov, *Ocherk*, 247. Similar statements are found in Lenin's article "The Constituent Assembly Elections and the Dictatorship of the Proletariat." It should be noted that Lenin did not always combine the principle of nationalization with support for the Kievan Communists in their desire for organizational independence.
14. V. Zatonsky, "Materialy do ukrainskoho natsionalnoho pytannia," *Bilshovyk Ukrainy*, no. 6 (1927): 12.
15. A Soviet historian states that "the largest petty-bourgeois party at that time [February 1920] was that of the Borotbists, which numbered around fifteen thousand members." See P. Bachynsky, "U borotbi za zdiisnennia leninskoi natsionalnoi polityki," *Ukrainskyi istorychnyi zhurnal*, no. 6 (1968): 40. For comparison: in March 1919 the CP(B)U had 16,364 members, and in March 1920—25,247. See *Ezhegodnik Kominterna. Spravochnaia kniga po istorii mezhdunarodnogo rabochego, politicheskogo i professionalnogo dvizheniia. Statistika vsekh stran mira za 1923* (Petrograd, 1923), 447, cited in B. Dmytryshyn, "National and Social Composition of the Membership of the Communist Party (Bolshevik) of the Ukraine," *Journal of Central European Affairs*, no. 3 (October 1957): 246.
16. Zatonsky, "Pro pidsumky ukrainizatsii," 11.
17. One should keep in mind that in the two years after the civil war, party membership among Ukrainians in comparison with other nationalities was fairly low. They made up less than 6 per cent of the total membership of the RCP(B) in 1920, although they formed 20 per cent of the Soviet population according to the 1926 census. See *Sotsialnyi i natsionalnyi sostav VKP(b). Itogi vsesoiuznoi partiinoi perepisi 1927 g.* (Moscow, 1928).
18. In 1923 Ravich-Cherkassky published a historical work in which he stated that the CP(B)U arose from the fusion of two currents in the workers' movement: a Russian one (the RCP[B]) and a Ukrainian one (the USDWP). See M. Ravich-Cherkassky, *Istoriia Kommunisticheskoi partii (bolshevikov)*

Ukrainy (Kharkiv, 1923), 6. This statement, which was criticized at the time, was an exaggeration since a merger of the two parties never took place and USDWP members did not play a major role in the life of the CP(B)U. It is true, however, that the left wing of the USDWP, especially the Borotbists, strengthened the ranks of the CP(B)U and brought it closer to the Ukrainian masses.

19. Zatonsky took a more moderate position within the Ukrainian movement and on that account Skrypnyk found it necessary to disagree with him publicly on several occasions. They differed in their attitude toward the CPWU leadership (the Vasylkivists) whom Zatonsky distrusted from the beginning. Among the Vasylkivists, in particular, Zatonsky was considered a declared "Luxemburgist." The fact that he was a native Ukrainian and a clever speaker with an excellent command of his native tongue only made matters worse. But Zatonsky was not totally anti-national. During the civil war, and in the five-year period after it, when there were arguments for and against Ukrainianization, Zatonsky always supported the national movement. Like Skrypnyk, he defended from the first the autonomous rights of the Soviet republics, criticized Russian great power chauvinism at all-Union party forums, including Stalin's ultra-centralist encroachments and felt that to have overlooked the national question in Ukraine during the civil war was a "colossal error." See, for example, his statements in *Desiatyi sezd RKP(b) mart 1921. Stenograficheskii otchet* (Moscow, 1963), 201–6.
20. Khristian Rakovsky, born in 1873 in Bulgaria to a family of the landed gentry, later a Romanian citizen, participated in the socialist movement in many European countries. He was a delegate to the founding congress of the Communist International. During the civil war in Ukraine he was a member of the CP(B)U central committee. From 1919 to 1923 he was head of the Council of Peoples' Commissars in Soviet Ukraine and was afterward a Soviet diplomat. Later he became a leading member of the Trotskyist opposition. In 1927 he was expelled from the party for oppositionist activities and exiled to Astrakhan. Among the exiled oppositionists he led a group of "intransigents" who, unlike other Trotskyists after 1929, remained in exile after the decision to industrialize the country. In March 1938 he was sentenced to twenty years in prison at a Moscow trial.
21. The quotation is from the report of the CP(B)U representative to the Third CPWU Congress, Ie. Hirchak. See Third CPWU Congress: Minutes, CA KC PZPR, 165/I–3, 5: 25.
22. *Ibid.*
23. Nazarenko, *Ocherki*, 298.
24. *Kommunisticheskaia partiia Ukrainy v rezoliutsiiakh i resheniiakh sezdov i konferentsii* (Kiev, 1959), 73.
25. *Ibid.* In the original—*rusotiapy*, a popular term used as a synonym for Russian nationalism, but of a mild, unconscious variety.
26. *KPZR w rezolucjach i uchwałach zjazdów, konferencji i posiedzeń plenarnych KC*, pt. 1 (Warsaw, 1956), 586–656.
27. Before 1917 Lenin, like Marx, Engels and Kautsky, was in favour of national

assimilation if it was spontaneous and not coerced. He considered the absorption of smaller peoples by larger peoples a progressive process and condemned those who opposed the natural assimilation of their own people (for example in his polemic with Iurkevych, a left Ukrainian social democrat). See Lenin, "Critical Remarks on the National Question," *Collected Works*, 20: 30–2. On this basis of this position Lenin condemned all proposals made at the time of a federal system for the future post-revolutionary Russia and supported a centralized state with limited autonomy for some national minorities. (For a summary of Lenin's views on this question, see E. Tadevosian, "V. I. Lenin o gosudarstvennoi federatsii," *Voprosy istorii KPSS*, no. 2 (1961): 43–59.) For the same reasons Lenin opposed programmes calling for the development of "national culture" as nationalistic and called instead for an "international culture." Lenin, "Critical Remarks," 20: 23–8. Lenin began to change his programme on the national question in 1917 and especially in 1919 during the civil war in Ukraine.

28. Recalling the rise of the Ukrainian state, Zatonsky said: "Our party set itself the task of organizing Ukraine as Soviet Ukraine, but disregarded the distrust of the majority (let us be truthful) of the working class and initially even part of the peasantry." Zatonsky, "Pro pidsumky ukrainizatsii," 13.
29. Dmitrii Lebed (1893–?), a railway worker in Katerynoslav and member of the RSDWP, was from 1905 in the Bolshevik faction and during the revolution in the local Bolshevik organization. In 1920 he became secretary of the CP(B)U Central Committee and in 1924 a member of the bureau of state control. After 1926 he was sent to Moscow where he performed similar functions (in the party's Central Control Commission and in state control). Lebed later published a pamphlet on this question: *Sovetskaia Ukraina i natsionalnyi vopros za piat let* (Kharkiv, 1924), 32 pp.
30. From the report of the CP(B)U representative at the Third CPWU Congress, Ie. Hirchak. See Third CPWU Congress: Minutes, 26.
31. *Ibid.*
32. A. Khvylia, *Proty ukrainskoho i rosiiskoho natsionalizmu* (Kharkiv, 1926), 33.
33. V. Ter-Vaganian, a well known activist and later a member of the Trotskyist opposition, was among those who criticized the nationalist aspirations of the republics. Several years later he published a book in which he stated, as Lenin once had, that the slogan calling for the development of national cultures contradicted the development of an international culture and therefore fostered nationalist and reactionary elements. V. A. Vaganian, *O natsionalnoi kulture* (Moscow-Leningrad, 1927), 192.
34. At the Eleventh Congress of the RCP(B), March-April 1922, Skrypnyk stated that the Bolshevik party could not continue to represent the aims of oppressed peoples of the world without a corresponding domestic nationalities policy. "We can observe a very definite phenomenon as regards both Ukraine and other Soviet republics, namely the desire to liquidate their statehood which was won by the efforts of the workers and peasants of each country.

The question of liquidating the worker-peasant statehood of Ukraine is also being posed here." *XI sezd RKP(B). Stenograficheskii otchet* (Moscow, 1961), 73–5.

35. S. Kosior, *Wyniki i najbliższe zadania polityki narodowej na Ukrainie. Referat na listopadowym plenum KC KPbU* (Moscow, 1933), 77.
36. M. Skrypnyk, "Natsionalne pytannia i Chervona Armiia," *Statti i promovy*, vol. 2; *Natsionalne pytannia* (Kharkiv, 1929), 44.
37. M. Skrypnyk, "Natsionalnyi vopros v programme Kominterna," *ibid.*, 37.
38. Thus, for example, after Skrypnyk's above-mentioned remarks at the Ninth Congress the first secretary of the CP(B)U Central Committee, Dmytro Manuilsky, found it necessary to note that his comrade was stating his own view and not that of the CP(B)U delegation. *XI sezd RKP(B)*, 115.
39. *KPZR w rezolucjach*, 816–27.
40. This congress took place under the influence of Lenin's "Testament," in which he strongly opposed Stalin's centralist tendencies and defended the opposing tendencies of the Georgian Communists. At the same time Lenin cautioned against Russian chauvinism, which had not been eradicated even at the highest levels of the state apparatus. He suggested a far-reaching decentralization or the complete independence of the national republics from Moscow except in matters of war and foreign relations. Lenin wanted to avert a situation in which "the 'freedom to secede from the [Soviet] Union' [i.e., the right of self-determination] ... will be a mere scrap of paper, unable to defend the non-Russians from the onslaught of ... the Great Russian chauvinist." Lenin relied on the authority of the party, cautiously applied, to counterbalance the negative consequences (mainly economic) of the proposed system. Lenin, "The Question of Nationalities or 'Autonomization'," *Collected Works*, 36: 606.
41. Popov, *Ocherk*, 304, 321.
42. Zatonsky, "Pro pidsumky ukrainizatsii," 13.
43. "Kaganovich ... took decisive steps toward Ukrainianization." I. Majstrenko, *Borotbism*, 335. V. Holubnychy [Holub] makes the same statement in *Konspektyvnyi narys istorii KPbU* (Munich, 1957), 53. The Soviet historian P. Bachynsky says that Ukrainianization began to develop unhindered in 1925. Bachynsky, "U borotbi."
44. *Komunistychna partiia Ukrainy v rezoliutsiiakh i rishenniakh zizdiv, konferentsii i plenumiv TsK* (Kiev, 1976), 1: 567.
45. Khvylia's report, Third CPWU Congress: Minutes, CA KC PZPR, 165/I–3, 1.
46. Popov, *Ocherk*, 321.
47. W. Pobóg-Malinowski, *Najnowsza historia polityczna Polski*, 2: 535. Many emigrants from Eastern Galicia held important positions in Soviet Ukraine. Matvii Iavorsky, director of the Institute of Marxism-Leninism in Kharkiv and a leading Ukrainian historian who was removed after 1930 for nationalism, came from Eastern Galicia. During this same period Mykhailo Hrushevsky, the prominent historian and former president of the Central

Rada in Kiev, returned from the West and continued his work. He was head of the Institute of History of the Ukrainian Academy of Sciences. In 1931 his work was severely criticized and he was expelled from Ukraine. He died in 1934.

48. Khvylia, *Proty ukrainskoho i rosiiskoho natsionalizmu*, 25.
49. *Ibid.*, 45.
50. See, for example, *Pravda*, no. 136 (1925) for information on people living in Kharkiv who were forced against their will to subscribe to the Ukrainian press.
51. The writer Fedor Gladkov once remarked while in Ukraine: "Why return to the pre-Petrine era, why galvanize the Ukrainian language which has been brought to nothing (*pokrylsia prakhom*)? All this only hinders the development of socialist construction.... Ukrainian writers want to compete with Russian writers, but this is only aping." Quoted in *Kultura*, no. 2–6 (1929): 22.
52. Iu. Larin, "Ob izvrashcheniiakh pri provedenii natsionalnoi politiki (pechataetsia v poriadke obsuzhdeniia)," *Bolshevik*, no. 22–4 (31 December 1926) and no. 1 (January 1927).
53. *Ibid.*, 55. This matter came up again at the Fifteenth Congress of the all-Union CP(B) (December 1927). During the congress Skrypnyk attacked Larin for his article, accusing him of Russian nationalism. Larin defended himself effectively and thanks to his wit and oratory won the applause of the audience. Summarizing the proceedings, Bukharin admitted that Larin was right on several minor points, but said that on the whole, given the seriousness of the national question in Ukraine, his article was too negative. See *XV sezd VKP(B). Stenograficheskii otchet* (Moscow, 1927), 716–19, 781–3, 882.
54. There is little biographical data on Mykola Khvyliovy, though in his short life (1 December 1893–13 May 1933) he managed to accomplish much. He took part in the uprising of the Ukrainian SRs against the Skoropadsky regime and later fought in the Red Army as a political officer. After the war he won recognition as the author of stories in which he depicted the complexity of the political situation in Ukraine during the civil war, and the passion and cruelty of both sides. The stories revealed him as an ardent Communist, and a fearless analyst both of the contradictions of his time and the mysteries of human consciousness. He was also an outstanding critic and polemicist. He co-operated with many former Borotbists, like Mykhailo Ialovy, co-founder of the CPEG, who were close to him ideologically. He came under suspicion and after long talks with the party control commission he was accused of nationalism and Trotskyism, recanted and returned to literary work. Several years later he committed suicide. See *Budivnytstvo Radianskoi Ukrainy*, 114, 199–201; M. Popov [Lovytsky], Speech at the Third CPWU Congress, CA KC PZPR, 165/I-3, 1: 21; P.U. Shygymata, "Fakty do biohrafii M. Khvyliovoho," *Vpered*, no. 11 (1955): 5–6; Iu. Lavrinenko, *Rozstriliane vidrodzhennia. Antolohiia 1917–1933* (Paris, 1959), 393–406.
55. M. Khvyliovy, "Apolohety pysaryzmu (Do problemy kulturnoi revoliutsii),"

Kultura i pobut, no. 9–13 (1926). Extracts of this work appear in Lavrinenko, *Rozstriliane vidrodzhennia*, 821–9.

56. *Ibid.*, 827–8.
57. Quoted from the unpublished article, "Ukraina chy Malorosia," in A. Khvylia, *Vid ukhylu u prirvu*, (Kharkiv, 1928); also quoted in Iu. Lavrinenko, *Rozstriliane vidrodzhennia*, 830.
58. Quoted in Ie. Hirchak, *Shumskizm i rozlam v KPZU* (Kharkiv, 1928), 111–12.
59. *Ibid.*, 119.
60. Zatonsky, "Pro pidsumky ukrainizatsii," 24.
61. *Budivnytstvo Radianskoi Ukrainy*, 28.
62. The "Ukrainian enlightenment" was the name given to a programme that wanted to limit Ukrainian cultural activity to the dissemination of existing achievements rather than artistic exploration. Khvyliovy bitterly opposed this theory and the party also rejected it.
63. *Budivnytstvo Radianskoi Ukrainy*, 28.
64. Hirchak, *Shumskizm i rozlam v KPZU*, 12–13.
65. *Budivnytstvo Radianskoi Ukrainy*, 31–40, 54–7.
66. *Ibid.*, 44.
67. The historian of the CP(B)U, Popov, who represented the views of the party leadership, wrote in his well-known work, which first appeared in 1927: "We must not blur the fundamental fact that until recently, and basically even today, our party was and remains a party of a Russian or Russified proletariat." Popov, *Ocherk istorii KPbU*, 11.
68. *Ibid.*, 43.
69. This sort of accusation against Shumsky at the May meeting of the Politburo elicited from him the following statement: "There has been nothing in my life except the struggle for the class and national liberation of the working class together with the peasantry. I have known no other traditions but that one and since 1909 I have not deviated from it one iota. I reject nothing of my past since I think I fought as a Bolshevik Leninist ought to fight in the conditions of Ukrainian reality, although at that time I did not belong to Lenin's party. I do not reject this past, on the contrary, I am proud of it." See Ie. Hirchak, *Shumskizm*, 121.
70. Andrii Khvylia, a former Borotbist, was director of the CP(B)U press section, a publicist and opponent of Shumsky, who often took part in the struggle against him in the press.
71. *Budivnytstvo Radianskoi Ukrainy*, 47.
72. *Ibid.*, 54.
73. *Ibid.*, 61.
74. *Ibid.*
75. *Ibid.*
76. *Ibid.*, 64.
77. Hirchak, *Shumskizm*, 124–5.

78. O. Shumsky, "Ideolohichna borotba v ukrainskomu kulturnomu protsesi," *Bilshovyk Ukrainy*, no. 2 (1927): 11–24.
79. M. Skrypnyk, "Khvyliovyzm chy shumskyzm," *Statti i promovy*, 2: 146–64.
80. M. Skrypnyk, "Natsionalistychnyi ukhyl v KPZU," in *Dzherela ta prychyny rozlamu v KPZU* (Kharkiv, 1928), 76.
81. Skrypnyk at the Third CPWU Congress, CA KC PZPR, 165/I–3, 2: 87.
82. Majstrenko, *Borot'bism* (published English version), 217.
83. Related orally by M. Tesliuk, a former member of the CPWU Central Committee, who was present at their conversation. Lviv, September 1967.
84. J. V. Stalin, "To Comrade Kaganovich and Other Members of the Political Bureau of the Central Committee, Ukrainian CP(B)," *Works*, 13 vols. (Moscow, 1952–5), 8: 157–63.
85. *Ibid.*, 158.
86. *Ibid.*, 160.
87. *Ibid.*, 161.
88. Skrypnyk, "Natsionalistychnyi ukhyl," 18.
89. At the June plenum there was a typical quarrel between Skrypnyk and K. Gulia because the latter had not learned to speak Ukrainian despite his promises to do so. *Budivnytstvo Radianskoi Ukrainy*, 33.
90. *Ibid.*, 140.
91. Skrypnyk, "Natsionalistychnyi ukhyl," 25.
92. "Zaiava tov. Maksymovycha na plenumi TsK KPbU," *Nasha pravda*, no. 1–2 (1928): 92–3.
93. *Ibid.*
94. *Ibid.*
95. "Rezoliutsiia VII Poshyrennoho Plenumu TsK KPZU pryiniata po zlozhenniu tov. Turianskym informatsii shcho do ioho vystupu na Liandessekretariiati KI," *Nasha pravda*, no. 1–2 (1928): 93.
96. From a letter (in Ukrainian) from the CP(B)U Central Committee to the CPWU Central Committee (undated) on the question of Maksymovych's remarks at the March plenum, signed by Klymenko. Arkhiv Institutu istorii partii TsK KPU, f. 233, op. 1, od. zb. 76, 24.

Chapter Six

Factional Struggle and Split, 1927–8

The April Plenum of the CC CPWU

From the beginning of the debate in Soviet Ukraine, the CPWU observed it carefully but remained silent. The party press printed only Skrypnyk's mildly critical article on Khvyliovy which was written at the beginning of the dispute,[1] and the conflict with Shumsky was not reported at all.

At the fall meeting of the Politburo in Kharkiv, which followed the CP(B)U's June plenum, Vasylkiv declared his party's unconditional support for the political line of the Communist Party in Soviet Ukraine.[2] This declaration was not reported in the CPWU press and remained unknown to the party membership. In those times of rigid ideological discipline such silence, together with Maksymovych's position and Turiansky's performance in the Comintern, could hardly go unnoticed. Also a CP(B)U Central Committee inquiry about the matter went unanswered.[3] Maksymovych, moreover, had caused displeasure at the CP(B)U plenum by emphasizing Shumsky's role in aiding the CPWU, and minimizing that of Skrypnyk. The matter was referred to a special plenary session of the CPWU Central Committee on 9–10 April 1927 in Gdańsk.[4] Skrypnyk represented the Comintern and the CP(B)U under the pseudonym "Mykolas." He submitted many documents to the meeting, including a letter from his party, minutes of meetings, correspondence between the Politburo and Shumsky, and a letter from Khvylia and an unnamed comrade charging that Shumsky had persecuted them for ideological reasons. Edward Próchniak (pseudonym Weber) and Jan Lubieniecki (pseudonym Rylski) both of whom belonged to the majority faction, represented the CPP Central Committee.

Skrypnyk opened the discussion by claiming that there were three routes for "fascism's" offensive in Western Ukraine: first, seeking out and organizing elements conciliatory toward the Polish authorities; second, discrediting the Ukrainian Soviet Republic, the CP(B)U, its national policy and achievements in Ukrainianization; and third, orientation on its own forces. The second route, according to Skrypnyk, was the strongest and safest, but the CPWU had instead concentrated its struggle against the first. This was no accident. In recent years when the struggle over the national question in Soviet Ukraine had erupted in a series of disputes on issues such as literature, the Khvyliovy affair and the liquidation of the Ukrainian Communist Party,[5] the CPWU did not speak out, or explain these matters to its membership or discuss them at plenums and conferences. When the CPWU representatives finally did comment, it was to defend Shumsky.[6] Skrypnyk claimed that Shumsky not only supported Khvyliovy, but gave him ideological direction. During the period of the most intense debate with Khvyliovy, the commissar of education continued to give financial support to his publishing enterprise, Vaplite. Shumsky voted for the June resolution (1926) only after his two amendments to the draft resolution had been defeated, and the views he expressed in the press opposed the resolution.

Shumsky broke with Khvyliovy only after two months of discussion with the central committee, which was unwilling to lose Shumsky. Skrypnyk thought that Shumsky was hampered by his political past: the Borotbists were not a proletarian party and the Bolshevik ideology was alien to them. He recalled that in 1921, after the civil war, the Borotbists had threatened an uprising. Skrypnyk felt that the Borotbist leader had retained remnants of his former ideology (although these did not always represent a wrong line in the CP[B]U). In the difficult situation of 1926, Skrypnyk noted, Shumsky had taken an incorrect position. Such matters were common to the history of the workers' movement and in the CPWU it had occasionally been necessary to break with people who had served the movement well in the past (for example, representatives of the so-called "CWPP tendency" expelled by the Vasylkivists in previous years). Shumsky was no longer capable of guiding the process of Ukrainianization and therefore should step down. But, said Skrypnyk, the West Ukrainian party did not see this or that reactionaries were trying to use the Shumsky affair for an attack on Soviet Ukraine. The greatest enemy of the CPWU was internal: national Bolshevism. It was necessary to fight it daily, Skrypnyk stated.[7] Maksymovych's position was no error, but part of a definite opposing line. Finally Skrypnyk asked the participants to decide: "Are you with Maksymovych and Shumsky or with the CP(B)U? With Bolshevism or with national Bolshevism."

In response to Skrypnyk's speech, the CPWU members took the floor (led by Maksymovych himself) and defended Maksymovych and Shumsky. They stated that although Skrypnyk's analysis of the situation in Western Ukraine was correct, as was the national policy of the CP(B)U, his evaluation of Shumsky and Maksymovych was mistaken. The former, according to the CPWU speakers, differed from the CP(B)U Central Committee only on a tactical question and could not be equated with Khvyliovy who was indeed guilty of nationalism. Maksymovych's doubts about the appropriateness of removing Shumsky from Ukraine did not represent a separate political line. Vasylkiv commented that in Kaganovich's speech at the plenum of the CC CP(B)U, "he emphasized unanimity on the national question. Basically we all agree with the position taken in the resolutions of the CP(B)U and condemn Khvyliovy. But how can we explain [in the press] the removal of Shumsky when we are unable to discern his national Bolshevist ideas and cannot reveal them to the party masses.... When we are shown these deviations we will struggle against them without regard to the reaction in the petty-bourgeois camps, but what are we to do in the absence of specific deviations? The convulsions in this area are alienating our allies, the middle and poor peasantry, who are sensitive to such matters."[8]

Edward Próchniak (Weber) of the CC CPP had a difficult task at the plenum. As already noted, he represented the majority faction in the CPP, which was on friendly terms with the CPWU. He began his speech by pointing out that the CPWU clearly understood the situation in its own territory and was quite aware of its tasks and obligations. Recently "the CPP has been closer than ever to the CPWU.... We will co-operate in correcting our organizational errors, but if one takes the work of the CPWU as a whole, there is nothing there that one might call national Bolshevism."[9] Nevertheless, Próchniak took a different view of the Shumsky affair. He felt that a single letter from the party leadership in Kharkiv showing that early in the dispute Shumsky had not broken with Khvyliovy would have been sufficient to confirm the accusations against the former. Yet Skrypnyk had provided many documents, and thus Shumsky's deviation could not be doubted, though he had not really taken a separate political line. Jan Lubieniecki, the other CPP representative at the plenum, took a similar view.[10] With some reservations, Natan Shapiro (Sukhy) and Pinkus Minc (who took the pseudonym "Brener" at this plenum) also took Skrypnyk's side.[11]

There were unpleasant incidents during the debate. Maksymovych thought that Skrypnyk suspected him of having contacts with the Polish *Defenzywa* (the secret police) (Skrypnyk had recalled that the day after the CP[B]U plenum the police knew about the Western party representative's speech). This matter was smoothed over, but it is evidence of the tense atmosphere of the proceedings. Some participants criticized statements in some of the documents read at the plenum which implied that the CPWU had emerged from the ranks of its "fraternal Eastern party," which they perceived as an attempt to belittle the independent development of the CPWU and its regional distinctiveness.[12]

Voting began at the end of the second day. After a long debate, the plenum accepted Skrypnyk's demand for a roll-call vote on Maksymovych's statements at the CP(B)U Central Committee. Members of the CPWU Central Committee and their alternates, Illia Kaliatynsky (Havzner), Bartolomii Kopach (Kovalsky), P. Lyshega (Tasma), Maksymovych (Hak), Stasiak (Taras), Osyp Skrypa (Vronsky), Tesliuk (Ernest), Turiansky, Vasylkiv and Volynets (Iarema), all voted for Maksymovych; Sukhy and Brener ("Aleksander"-P. Minc) and the two CPP representatives voted for Skrypnyk's resolution condemning Maksymovych.[13]

A resolution was also accepted which stated that Skrypnyk's analysis of the situation in Western Ukraine and of the tasks of the CPWU emanating from it were correct, that the CP(B)U's policy in all matters was also correct as were Maksymovych's reservations, which only referred to a particular organizational sanction and could not be considered disagreement with the policies of the CP(B)U.[14] The resolution was passed with the same composition of votes for and against, except that Próchniak and Lubieniecki abstained this time. Also, the resolution approved Turiansky's polemics in the Comintern with Mickevičius-Kapsukas over the Shumsky affair.[15] Another session of the plenum, called a few days later at Skrypnyk's insistence, decided only to send a delegate to the Comintern to explain the plenum's position. It concluded that, on the basis of the material received, "the CPWU Central Committee sees no nationalist deviations in Comrade Shumsky" and that statements made by Maksymovych did not contradict the national policy of the CC CP(B)U.[16]

On 5–7 April, a few days before the above mentioned plenum, the Seventh Conference of the CPWU took place. The conference did not discuss the national problem,[17] but its resolutions, which were sent to Kharkiv only in June, contained many elements of Skrypnyk's speech at the Gdańsk plenum (added after the conference had taken place), including a fragment on the national question.[18] The resolutions described Piłsudski's policy toward Ukrainians, the campaign against Soviet Ukraine and the attempts by Polish "fascism" to discredit the national policy of the CP(B)U, all of which agreed with Skrypnyk's assessment at the plenum.[19] One resolution called Khvyliovy's position a "deviation" and suggested that he was being dragged in the wake of Ukrainian nationalism. It charged that "Polish fascism is searching for non-existent cracks within the CP(B)U ... in order to discredit its national policy."[20] However, the resolution neither criticized Shumsky and Maksymovych, nor reiterated Skrypnyk's comments.[21]

The CP(B)U and the Problem of the CPWU

The refusal of the Western party to approve certain aspects of Soviet policy and its defeat of a Comintern resolution (Skrypnyk, we recall, represented the Comintern) were rare and worrisome events in the Communist camp. Further reaction from both the CPP and CP(B)U, which were most affected, was unavoidable.

The CP(B)U Politburo devoted a special meeting to the affair on 14 May 1927 in Kharkiv. In the opening report, Skrypnyk reviewed past relations between the fraternal parties and outlined the resolutions of the recent plenum.[22] The ensuing discussion severely condemned Shumsky and Maksymovych, and accused the latter of being the tool of a concerted political intrigue. Zatonsky, the first to speak, proposed that the meeting should again discuss the Shumsky affair since it was taking on new aspects. At this point Shumsky left the meeting. Zatonsky called after him sarcastically, "Just look, as soon as I take the floor Shumsky flees."[23] In a second speech Zatonsky said that an ideological "pogrom" would encompass not only the leadership, but also the rank and file of the CPWU, citing the situation in Selrob as evidence of this. He advocated a purge of the most harmful elements and an infusion of new blood.[24] At the CPWU plenum, Zatonsky noted, only two persons—both Jews—had voted for the Comintern resolution, which was evidence of a nationalist nest within that party. Hryhorii Petrovsky,[25] another outstanding activist, maintained that Shumsky, with the support of Maksymovych, a doubtful Communist and an immature and uncertain Bolshevik, had done great harm to the party at a time when the international situation was at its most complex.[26] After Shumsky was recalled, Petrovsky said, "the nationalist activities ... of the petty-bourgeois strata grouped around him diminished.[27] According to Oleksander Shlikhter,[28] the CP(B)U had made the mistake of delaying the struggle against "the poisonous spreading mushroom of nationalism."[29] Therefore, for Shumsky "there can be no place among us ... [We must be] ruthless in purging our own ranks." It was already difficult to fight "the one bona fide Ukrainian in the Central Committee," Shlikhter said ironically.[30] Shlikhter also pointed to the Academy of Sciences in Kiev, where nationalism had taken root. (At this point Zatonsky interjected that it would be unjust to accuse the Academy of Sciences of deviation from the Communist ideology, since no such ideology had existed there in the first place.)[31] As for Western Ukraine, stated Shlikhter, the CP(B)U had mistakenly allowed Maksymovych to direct political work in that area. It was now clear that Maksymovych had a harmful influence over the CPWU.[32] This accusation was indirectly aimed at Skrypnyk, who reacted angrily. Before he could speak, however, Vlas Chubar reminded Shlikhter that a large segment of Ukrainian society did not share the Communist ideology or accepted it only in part. The party was thus obliged to be tolerant and understanding. As for the Academy of Sciences, it was not a question of "they" against "us," since they were not enemies.[33] Moreover, concerning the Shumsky affair, the central committee had correctly delayed organizational sanctions in order to discuss the matter to find a correct line. "Shumsky," Chubar continued, "used another method. At the central committee plenum [of the CP(B)U] he tried to lay the blame on the General Secretary and [thus] passed from errors of principle to political intrigue." As for Maksymovych, Chubar said that the majority present did not know his background. He was one of the founders of the CPWU, not ideologically alien and had remained useful until he committed errors. Chubar agreed that Maksymovych should not have been promoted so quickly to positions of leadership.[34]

Next Skrypnyk took the floor. After Kaganovich[35] he was the most influential party leader and was responsible for co-operation with the CPWU. He stated that the members of the Politburo agreed on the nature of the conflict but not on the causes, cure and the role of Soviet Ukraine in the whole affair.[36] He explained to Shlikhter that the CPWU was not an affiliate of the Communist Party of Ukraine and its leaders could not simply be removed. "Our [i.e. the CP(B)U's] resolutions cannot be directives for the CPWU."[37] It was possible, however, for the CP(B)U to exercize influence both through the Comintern and, most important, ideologically. But a direct intervention, declared Skrypnyk, would be disruptive. In the past, when the CPP had erred, the CPWU had often been right, and that, Skrypnyk emphasized, was due to help from the CP(B)U. The CP(B)U's policies in influencing the Western party had been correct. "There are nationalists there and they must be searched out,"[38] Skrypnyk admitted, but matters could best be corrected by criticism, joint councils and "bringing new forces into the Central Committee from the factories and work-shops." Skrypnyk also denied responsibility for Maksymovych's appointments (as an alternate) to the central committee and to the government's Commission of Foreign Affairs.[39]

An incident between Skrypnyk and Shlikhter shows how heated the discussion had become. The latter accused Skrypnyk of retaliating against him on Shumsky's behalf. Skrypnyk responded: "What sort of retaliation should I take for Shumsky? When Shumsky was unmasked in the Politburo, in the press, it was Skrypnyk . . . who proposed the resolution on this affair. Why then should Skrypnyk, who fights against Shumsky, now support him? Such suspicions are unnecessary and as harmful as accusations of diversion."[40] The bureau established a commission, consisting of Kaganovich, Skrypnyk and Zatonsky, to draw up a letter to the Comintern stating the essence of the conflict between the parties.[41]

The question of Shumsky and the CPWU was examined again by a plenum of the CP(B)U Central Committee in June 1927. In his report for the Politburo,[42] Skrypnyk declared that the nationalist deviation of the CPWU was no accident, and listed several causes: the origin of many members in the Galician USDP, known for its nationalism, or directly in the national liberation movement;[43] the party's predominantly non-worker social structure; the party's work among the Ukrainian petty bourgeoisie which had itself influenced the party; and the lack of a solid Leninist tradition.[44]

Nevertheless, Skrypnyk considered the past policy of the CPWU to have been correct. It was true, he said, that in the factional struggles from 1920–1 both sides had deviations. The CWPP, burdened on the one hand with the Luxemburgist tradition of the SDKPL, and on the other with the "nationalist" and even "imperialist" (sic) past of the PSP-left,[45] could not have a "correct Leninist line." The CPWU (CPEG) which emerged from the national movement became involved with the struggling Ukrainian peasantry and, in Skrypnyk's opinion, yielded to the nationalist or nationalist-peasant deviation.[46] But the Ukrainian struggle in Eastern Galicia in 1919 was anti-imperialist and thus progressive, so the CPWU's deviation was less threatening than that of the CWPP. The next five years for the CPP were full of crises and errors, whereas the CPWU came through those years without mistakes and even supported the admonishments of the Comintern against the errors of the Polish party.

Why, then, had the Ukrainian party now committed an error? Skrypnyk saw the main cause in the new economic and political situation in Western Ukraine, in the radical change in the national policy toward Ukrainians, and in the not altogether unsuccessful attempt to persuade a sector of Ukrainian society to co-operate with Poland.[47] While Skrypnyk felt that the problem could be resolved by discussion, he also emphasized the need for organizational changes: "I must say that in no case can the composition of the CPWU remain as it now is. The CPWU has learned not only discipline from our party, but also organizational politics."[48] Some members of the party's central committee would return, Skrypnyk said, but "the Maksymovyches will not return. They must be trained for other work."[49]

Next Skrypnyk enumerated the characteristics of both nationalist deviations in the Ukrainian Communist movement. The largest, the Russian deviation, had several characteristics:

1. an attempt to lessen the significance of Ukraine as an independent

state within the Soviet Union, and the interpretation of the establishment of the USSR as the liquidation of the separate republics;

2. the demand that the party take a neutral position on the development of Ukrainian culture, which was perceived as a lower, rural and inferior culture, whereas Russian culture was considered synonymous with proletarian culture, an all-union culture;
3. the view that Ukrainianization was artificially imposed from above and that the Ukrainian literary language was a "Galician" language incomprehensible to the masses;
4. the attempt to limit the process of Ukrainianization to the countryside;
5. the exaggerated publicity given to the mistakes made during Ukrainianization.[50]

Skrypnyk then examined the characteristics of the Ukrainian deviation:

1. an underestimation of the role and significance of the proletariat and the Communist party in solving the national question in Ukraine, or simply a lack of faith in the ability of the proletariat and its party to accomplish their historic mission. Hence the defeatism, disbelief in building socialism in the country, and systematic attempts to undermine faith in the party cadres;
2. the assertion that only those "of Ukrainian blood" should carry out Ukrainianization;
3. a bureaucratic approach to the assimilation of Ukrainian culture by a part of the proletariat in Ukraine, evident in the attempt to accomplish changes rapidly by administrative means, although these changes required an entire historical epoch;
4. the treatment of the CP(B)U as a party burdened with Russian nationalism, and the proliferation of rumours that Ukrainians in the party had been persecuted or removed from active work, that anyone who opposed Russian nationalist views was branded a renegade and traitor.[51]

Skrypnyk again recalled Khvyliovy's errors and described Shumsky as a barometer of "tendencies alien to us, nationalist trends which exist outside of the party."[52] He accused Shumsky of transferring the factional struggle to another party after suffering defeat in the ranks of his own.[53] The plenum decided to send a letter to the Comintern written in the spirit of Skrypnyk's speech.[54]

The CPP and the Ukrainian Question

The parent-organization, the CPP, did not enter the dispute immediately. There were several reasons for this. Members felt that the communists from Soviet Ukraine would solve the problem themselves. More important, the majority faction in the CPP did not wish to concern itself with the errors of one of its strongest sections (the CPWU unanimously supported the majority faction). The first resolution passed by the CPP criticized Maksymovych and the CPWU's position, but was mild and brief. It confirmed that the CPWU had committed errors and approved the position taken by Próchniak and Lubieniecki at the April plenum.[55] Matters came to a head only at the Fourth CPP Congress when the Ukrainian problem became a trump card for the "minority" in its struggle with the "majority."

An additional cause for concern were the increasing conflicts between the two wings of the recently created Selrob. Different traditions and mutual distrust complicated the task of consolidating the new organization. The April conflict immediately awakened old prejudices and intensified the conflict between the former members of Selsoiuz and the People's Will. Those of the People's Will demanded that their Selsoiuz comrades leave the Ukrainian Club in the Sejm where they sat together with UNDU. Selsoiuz, on the other hand, accused its opponents of organizational separatism, factionalism and breaking with the left bloc in the communal elections. The dispute in Selrob attracted the attention of the entire Communist camp which looked to its own ranks for the deeper causes of the conflict. Therefore, the lines on the Ukrainian question at the congress were more clearly defined than on many other issues.

The "minority" considered the CPWU programme right-wing and nationalist. It maintained that the error on the question of Soviet Ukraine typified CPWU thinking.[56] The deviation of the CPWU on its own terrain had two aspects: agrarian and national. In the former, the party had yielded to the pressure of the rich peasantry and neglected the class struggle in the Ukrainian countryside; hence the appeals to the entire countryside rather than to its poorer section. The "minority" cited a portion of a resolution from the Sixth CPWU Plenum calling for the parcelling out of large landholdings to the peasants "at a price established by them."[57] In places where land was acquired even by the poorer peasants (the Stanyslaviv region), the CPWU proposed the creation of committees to fight "against usurious prices."[58] In practice, this signified that the CPWU advised peasants who already had acquired land from parcellation to fight for lower prices without simultaneously abandoning the slogan "land to the peasants without compensation." This policy was linked with the resolution of the Fourth CPP Conference which stated that "in the event of 'agrarian reform' legislation the CPP must never limit itself to the slogan 'land without compensation,' but, unmasking the 'agrarian reform,' it must, inside and outside the Sejm, organize the peasant masses to fight for land through the implementation of the agrarian law."[59]

Moreover, the most recent (seventh) conference of the CPWU, in the spirit of the Fourth CPP Conference, had announced that "in the struggle for general political demands, such as a solution to the school problem, the struggle against national oppression, terror, etc., the party considers it possible to activate the entire countryside in opposition to the bourgeoisie, the large landowners and the fascist government."[60]

Neither the existence of an earlier CPP resolution on the agrarian question nor the fact that the resolutions of the Ukrainian party had been approved by the CC CPP prevented the "minority" from attacking the agrarian policy, for which it did not feel responsible. This line of attack was effective in the debate and was expressed later in the congress resolution. It also served for a long time as evidence that the deviation of the Ukrainian party was no accident. In reality the differences on this question mattered little to the CPWU, which readily voted with the other delegates to condemn its own position,[61] and did not commit this "error" again.

The "minority" saw the CPWU's relationship with Selrob as a key problem. The party had, ostensibly, not opposed the nationalist tenets of Selrob, and had made no attempt to persuade Selrob members to abandon the Ukrainian Club in the Sejm. Consequently, a "united national front" instead of a class front had been created. The "minority" accused Selrob of separating itself from Communists, avoiding revolutionary action and appealing to the entire countryside, including the kulaks. Not only was this newly created party (in contrast to the Belorussian Hramada)[62] not a class group, but at times it was even "pro-fascist," as evident in a resolution proposed by Serhii Kozytsky, a member of the party's central committee, condemning the "reactionary encroachments of Muscovite centralism."[63] The "minority" felt that the erroneous policy of Selrob (connected only with former members of Selsoiuz) had been deliberately unopposed by the CPWU, whose leaders in 1920–1 "were dragged in the wake" of the nationalist petty bourgeoisie.

A new source of conflict arose when Stanisław Budzyński (Tradycja) and the CPWB leader, Iosif Lahinovich (Korchyk), declared that they considered the Polish-Ukrainian war and the subsequent armed struggle of the Ukrainians against the Polish state a conflict between nationalisms.[64] The implication of this thesis was that the position of the CPWU in previous years had been unequivocally nationalist as were the resolutions of the Second CWPP Congress which inclined toward that same position.

Korchyk also denounced the nationalism manifested in the current policies of the CPWU, declaring that "the error of the CPWU is your [the "majority's"] error. Comrade Warski was influenced by Polish nationalism ... and comrade Vasylkiv by the Ukrainian variety."[65] Korchyk even went so far as to say that Piłsudski owed his success in Western Ukraine to the CPWU.

The "majority" had a different point of view on almost every question: up to 1924 the Ukrainian bourgeoisie was not anti-Soviet, and, despite its hostility to the system, it was attracted to Soviet Ukraine as a national Ukrainian state. The brutal negation of all its national rights by the Polish government, which was putting into effect the programme of the Polish national democrats, forced the Ukrainian bourgeoisie into this position. Only recently, the "majority" maintained, had conditions arisen which moved that class toward a pro-Polish position. Nevertheless, the war waged against Poland by the WUPR in 1918–19 and the partisan struggle of the Ukrainians in the years 1920–2, though not led by the West Ukrainian left, were just and progressive struggles.[66]

On the question of Selrob, the "majority" recalled that the party had begun operations during a frontal attack by the Piłsudskiites, which combined concessions on national demands with a broad repression of revolutionary organizations (the liquidation of Hramada, for example). In Próchniak's opinion, the policy of bringing the entire countryside into the struggle against the large landowners and the regime, which had proven successful in the case of Hramada, was correct.[67]

Vasylkiv, who represented the CPWU Central Committee's "majority" at the congress, questioned the depiction of Selrob as an agent of fascism since, despite its vacillations, its policies were undoubtedly close to those of the Communist party and were pro-Soviet. Kozytsky's proposed resolution, he recalled, had not even been discussed by the central committee, so that not all the party's members could be accused of fascist tendencies. Even Kozytsky did not merit the appellation. Like many of his colleagues, he had not taken a Leninist position on the national question, but then Selrob was not, in fact, a Communist party. To call Selrob a fascist agency was to be guilty either of ultra-leftist tendencies or of attempting to make an allied organization an adjunct of the Communist party, which would be very harmful.[68] Vasylkiv ignored the question about Selrob remaining in the Ukrainian Club, perhaps because the accusation was not without some basis. The CPWU representative in Selrob, Kraikivsky, had tried unsuccessfully to persuade Selrob deputies to leave the club, in which UNDU members continually attacked leftist organizations and, more often, the USSR. Another delegate of "majority" persuasion at this juncture assured the meeting that the Selrob deputies intended to leave the Ukrainian Club, but awaited the opportune moment to do so in a manner that would be convincing for the masses.[69] The assessment of the agrarian economic situation also led to controversy. Vasylkiv, for example, thought that the new boom would benefit not only the rich, but also the middle peasants.[70] Żarski disagreed, stating that an increase in the number of parcelled estates would be advantageous only to the landed gentry.[71]

The one matter on which the Polish "majority" and "minority" were in agreement was the conflict between the CPWU and the CP(B)U. All the congress delegates (except for the few Ukrainians)[72] felt that the error of the CPWU was unquestionable and should be quickly corrected.[73] Consequently, the two chief CPWU representatives, Turiansky and Vasylkiv, declared in the name of their party that "comrade Shumsky showed signs of a deviation of nationalist content," by "insufficiently and belatedly dissociating himself from Khvyliovy's deviations"[74] as well as in certain statements listed in the resolutions of the CP(B)U. Their declaration also criticized Maksymovych and the position of the central committee at the April plenum in Gdańsk.[75]

In a separate declaration, "minority" representatives of the CPWU Central Committee, Sukhy and Aleksander, expressed satisfaction with the self-criticism of the party's two most outstanding leaders. They demanded the removal of Maksymovych from party work, expansion of the central committee by bringing in active workers from the party ranks, a fundamental reorganization of the Zakordot (which was Maksymovych's domain), a reorganization of the party press and upper levels of the central committee and a full and complete discussion of the nationalities question in the press.[76] In brief, the demands echoed those of the CP(B)U prior to the self-criticism by the party leaderhsip. But the CPWU leadership could hardly accept these conditions. They would have entailed a purge of the party, wrecking a well-integrated collective leadership and eradicating the hard-won autonomy that allowed the CPWU to pursue a relatively independent policy on its own terrain.

For some time, party members wondered whether the declaration of Turiansky and Vasylkiv was sincere, or simply a maneouvre to delay confrontation. The evidence supports the latter view. In a letter to Canadian Communists, written just after the split of 1928, Vasylkiv explained that "the 'Kaganovichites' purposely printed a black picture and used 'Shumskyism' as a screen[77] to hide their Russian jingoistic attack... in which we graciously aided them by giving in to their pressure and 'for the sake of blessed peace' signing a declaration on the 'nationalist deviation' in the summer of 1927, which you surely know about."[78] The letter indicates that the Vasylkivists had made a compromise that need not necessarily have ended in a split. Skrypnyk (even before the Fourth Congress) accurately described their position: "The present position of the CPWU Central Committee [members] can be characterized as a certain reconciliation with the line of the Comintern and the CP(B)U short of making it their own line in terms of either thought or action."[79]

The congress brought few advantages for the Vasylkivists. The final resolution on the Ukrainian question contained a large number of minority theses. Moreover, not only were all the "errors" of Selrob noted and the CPWU blamed for not opposing these mistakes, but the resolution criticized the CPP Central Committee because it "carried out a policy of not interfering in CPWU disputes and gave too much autonomy to that party."[80]

The Ukrainian Commission of the Comintern's Executive Committee, August 1927

Although the CPWU had sent a delegate to the Comintern concerning the Ukrainian question, and the CP(B)U had appealed to the same body in April and May, there was no response until August 1927. Possibly the Comintern was awaiting the results of the Fourth CPP Congress. The Ukrainian Commission of the Comintern's Executive Committee met in August and adopted a resolution on the affair on 3 September. According to the Soviet historian Ie. Halushko, a group composed of Stefan Królikowski (Bartoszewicz), Khristian Kabakchiev, Hermann Remmele, Andrei Ivanov, Volodymyr Popel (Iurchenko), Maggi and Osip Piatnitsky investigated the conflict.[81] Representatives of the parties in attendance were Vasylkiv and Turiansky (CPWU "majority"), Sukhy and Aleksander (CPWU "minority"), Lahinovich (CPWB), and Skrypnyk and Khvylia (CP[B]U Central Committee).[82] Halushko reports that the CPWU was severely criticized but that only the "minority" demanded the removal of the party's leadership.[83] From the materials of a second Ukrainian commission and from discussions at the eighth party plenum (October 1927) it is clear that the August commission presented the CPWU Central Committee with certain conditions. These included the removal of Maksymovych from the central committee and the replacement of Turiansky by Vasylkiv as the party's representative to the Comintern. Turiansky was to occupy Vasylkiv's position in Gdańsk.[84] This was later revealed to be an attempt to limit Vasylkiv's influence on the party. But the conditions did not mention bringing new members into the CPWU Central Committee as demanded by the CC CP(B)U and the "minority" in the CC CPWU.

The commission proposed to consolidate Selrob around the editorial board of *Nashe slovo*, which was mistakenly thought to be uninvolved in the factional struggle. It also informed the CPWU Central Committee's "minority" that it had made a mistake in denying the necessity of bringing the entire countryside into the revolutionary struggle. As at the Fourth

Congress, Vasylkiv and Turiansky admitted their errors and gave assurances that they would correct them.[85]

In October the Comintern issued an official statement about the affair. In accordance with the views of the CPP majority, the statement noted the evolution of the Ukrainian bourgeoisie from a position of struggle with the Polish government to one of co-operation, a tendency that had penetrated to the "upper strata of the middle peasantry."[86] The description of the problem of Russian and Ukrainian nationalism in Ukraine reflected the resolutions of the CP(B)U. Finally the statement declared that "a large degree of pressure and influence of petty-bourgeois, nationalist elements on the CPWU Central Committee is noticeable. This was the source of the CPWU Central Committee majority's great political error." At the same time the statement stressed that "all errors [of the CPWU] could obviously be corrected."[87] It recommended a press campaign to explain the errors and to popularize the resolutions of the CP(B)U, CPP and Comintern but did not outline any organizational changes.

The period of dissension and debate appeared to be over. Whether sincerely or not, the CPWU leaders had given up their defence of Shumsky, admitted that his position was erroneous and nationalist and that they had been wrong to defend him. Possibly they intended to continue their own line and evade the unacceptable demands. When the masses directed by the CPWU leadership slipped from its control, however, it was unable to conceal the outcry and protest. This was particularly true of Selrob and its membership.

Factional Struggle and the Split in Selrob

Selrob played an important role in the history of the crisis in the CPWU. This is understandable in view of the two opposing traditions of that organization, the majority of whose members were not prepared to subordinate the national question to the interests of the socialist revolution, a requirement of Communist ideology at the time. In fact, it was the national policy in Soviet Ukraine that had attracted the former Selsoiuz members to co-operation with the Communists. The open and firm recognition of the Ukrainian nation and its rights by the leadership in Moscow and hence by Russians reconciled former People's Will members to Ukrainian ethnicity. Relations between the two factions—never good—grew worse in direct proportion to the increased national conflict in the Ukrainian Communist movement. Moreover the union was never fully completed, since each faction operated in its own terrain and maintained its own newspapers. Both factions followed events in the Communist movement closely and sought support in one or another of its circles.

The formal head of Selrob was Panteleimon Kraikivsky, delegated to that post by the CPWU Central Committee (he used the pseudonym "Herasym"). From July 1927, his reports to the CPWU Central Committee describe a state of chaos and factional struggle over which he had no control. At times he was in despair. It was, perhaps, in such a state that he wrote, "Selsoiuz is as alien to us as the People's Will. . . . It would be hard to say which of them is the more trashy."[88] He informed the CPWU leadership that meetings descended to a mutual exchange of abuse and profanity "as at a bazaar."[89] A similar picture emerges from the police records.[90]

But Kraikivsky exaggerated when he accused the leading members of Selrob of careerism and lack of ideology. In fact, the form in which dissatisfaction and factional struggle was manifested was typical of the unsophisticated rural intelligentsia that made up the organization. Moreover, Kraikivsky did not consider the effect of the Shumsky affair on his charges. Another CPWU member explained that Kraikivsky lacked authority over the membership because both factions "are convinced that everything can be attained behind the back of the party [i.e. the CPWU] . . . they speculate on alleged dissension between the party and X, and the possibility of taking care of certain matters over the party's head, via the shortest road through Rome,[91] confirms them in that conviction."[92] Kraikivsky's letters clarify this. He often refers to a certain "Iurko" who constantly went over "Herasym's" head to make contact with Selrob members who supported Valnytsky's group. The mysterious "Iurko" is never identified by name. From police records, the CPWU archives, the press and the memoirs of former activists it is clear that he was Jerzy Sochacki, a member of the CPP Central Committee and deputy to the Sejm in Warsaw. Though he had no formal authority, with the support of former People's Will members he gradually acquired control over a part of the Selrob membership. In one of his letters, Herasym, who refers to this repeatedly, stated that "Comrade Iurko has crossed our path and as a result Selrob is not really in our hands."[93]

During this period, Sochacki was friendly with Valnytsky,[94] who was closer to him than other Selrob leaders because of his general and political experience. But this was not the deciding factor in Sochacki's choice of this particular group. More significant was that Valnytsky's was the only organized group in the Ukrainian camp on whose support the CPP could rely in the event of open conflict with the Vasylkivists. Thus the group was seen as a channel for CPP influence in the Ukrainian revolutionary camp. Kraikivsky conferred with Sochacki, but failed to convince him that Valnytsky and several activists close to him should resign from the leadership of the party, and that the newspaper *Volia naroda* should be liquidated as a remnant of "Russophilism." Sochacki favoured Valnytsky for future party leader and demanded that his newspaper be retained, at least temporarily.[95]

Within Selrob itself there were several reasons for internal struggle. The Selsoiuz faction carried out several actions that ran counter to Comintern policy and gave the People's Will group an opportunity to criticize it: it sent a delegate (Stepan Makivka) to a conference of the socialist parties of the national minorities of Poland; it also dispatched delegates (Serhii Kozytsky and I. Pasternak) to a church conference devoted to the problems of Ukrainianizing the liturgy of the Orthodox church in Western Ukraine; it signed a joint protest with the PSP against the new press bill; and Kozytsky's draft resolution mentioned above.[96]

Moreover the People's Will faction, in agreement with the CPP, had long demanded that Selrob deputies should leave the Ukrainian Club. In the summer of 1927 conflicts within the new organization led to the suspension of central committee members, Valnytsky, Mykhailo Zaiats and Kuzma Pelekhaty.[97] The People's Will faction was concerned because the inclusion of Andrii Bratun on the central committee upset the three-three balance in favour of the Selsoiuz faction. They were also anxious about the Selrob Central Committee 's adoption of a resolution (proposed by the CPWU Central Committee) calling for *Volia naroda* (immediately) and *Nashe zhyttia* (shortly) to cease publication as remnants of the past. The resolution ordered the People's Will faction to turn over the party office (and files with addresses of subscribers to *Volia naroda*, membership list, etc.) to the editors of the newly-created newspaper, *Nashe slovo* (former Selsoiuz members and Kraikivsky).[98] The People's Will had formerly run the office because the party's headquarters were in Lviv. During its administration, the People's Will had not allowed rival factions to use the office. Valnytsky and his comrades responded on 11 September 1927 by publishing a declaration of their break with the former Selsoiuz members, using the reasons already mentioned.[99]

The most important demands of the People's Will faction were, in fact, met. On 9 September, thus before the split, the Selrob deputies resigned from the Ukrainian Club and created a Selrob Club.[100] Moreover, the CPWU leadership criticized the participation of the Selrob's delegate in the church congress.[101] The steps taken by the Selrob Central Committee against the People's Will faction might have been seen as discriminatory and might even have hastened Valnytsky's decision to split. But Valnytsky could not have made this decision without the support of CPP circles for the People's Will's organizational and ideological independence within Selrob.

The day after the formal break, Kraikivsky wrote that "the split in Selrob is the result of Iurko's policy, his interference in all the affairs of the party and the line which he promotes there. Essentially it is not the party [CPWU], but Iurko who has gained control in Selrob, subordinating both the People's Will and Selsoiuz, and he has drawn people to himself even from the regions."[102] Thus Kraikivsky felt that the split was an indirect result of Sochacki's factional activity. Certainly, Kraikivsky exaggerated Sochacki's domination of the Selsoiuz faction, which opposed unanimously the "secessionists" in Selrob and later defended the CPWU Central Committee in its quarrel with the CP(B)U. Some members of the faction maintained this position to the end, thereby signing their own political death warrants.

From 18 October 1927 the People's Will published a weekly called *Sel-Rob*, and referred to itself as Selrob-Left and to its opponents as Selrob-Right.[103] From the beginning the vast majority of the party joined Selrob-Right, although the Left dominated a large number of organizations in Lviv *województwo* and then in Ternopil *województwo* as well as in the Stolin and Drahichyn regions of Polissia. The remaining centres—the one that encompassed nearly all the Stanyslaviv region, the powerful Volhynian organization,[104] and the strong organization and propaganda centre in the Chełm region with the popular paper, *Nashe zhyttia*—supported the Right. Nevertheless Selrob-Left came out of the split considerably stronger than it had been before the union with Selsoiuz. It claimed to represent the line of the Comintern and the CPP, and also enjoyed the support of the PSP-Left. It had emerged as a party at a conference held 16 and 17 October,[105] and gained influence, especially in Polissia, at local conferences where its delegates opposed representatives of the Right.[106] Both sides called for reunion, each stating its own conditions, but the Right attacked the "three generals without an army" (Valnytsky, Pelekhaty and Zaiats), branding them the instigators of the split.

On 18 December a conference of Selrob-Right considered the following three resolutions:

1. that the faction should not reunite with the Left (Kozytsky)
2. that it should reunite with the Left rank and file, but not the Left leaders (Kraikivsky)
3. that it should call a joint congress of both wings to overcome the split (Mykhailo Durdella)

The conference adopted Kozytsky's resolution.[107] Soon, however, there were new calls for reunion on the condition that the opposition accept total blame and remove the three leaders mentioned above. The discussions of the split, however, were far from candid. Each side was making tactical moves against the other and the chief problem, that of Shumskyism, was not dealt with at all. Although both factions formally disapproved of Shumsky, the Selsoiuz faction never condemned him.

As the dispute between the CPWU and the CPP deepened, the Right's organ, *Nashe slovo*, became more aggressive and launched a merciless attack on *Volia naroda*, in which it accused the latter of rabid anti-Ukrainianism and Russian nationalism of a monarchist variety. This was untrue of Valnytsky's group, even before it co-operated with the Communists; it had previously gravitated toward an SR ideology.

The events within Selrob complicated an already difficult situation in the Communist party. In the same period the CPWU leaders discovered that, besides Sochacki, Iurii Kotsiubynsky had also been in contact with Valnytsky.[108] Although Kotsiubynsky had persuaded the Left leader to condemn publicly his own part in the split, he also influenced Valnytsky's critical attitude toward the CPWU Central Committee.[109] The Ukrainian party also learned of long-standing contacts between the Soviet diplomatic mission and the Petrushevych group, which was sympathetic toward the Soviet Union and which a few months earlier had broken with UNDU to form a separate Ukrainian Labour Party.[110] The Vasylkivists were concerned that Sochacki's and particularly Kotsiubynsky's actions were attempts to limit their activities and undermine the CPWU's authority and political strategy. They felt that Valnytsky, who was openly contemptuous of the CPWU's leadership role, could not go unpunished and thus did not attempt to check the excessive attacks of *Nashe slovo* on Selrob-Left. This in turn worried the minority of the CPWU and CPP who had nothing to fear from the real or imagined pro-Russian stance of the People's Will, since it had no anti-Soviet basis.

In their first memo to the CPP and CP(B)U, CPWU members Sukhy and Aleksander claimed that meetings were being held behind their backs[111] and that the recommendations of the Comintern on correcting the error were not being carried out. At regional conferences in Lviv and Stryi the membership was not informed of the Shumsky affair, the events of the Fourth Congress, or the recommendations of the Ukrainian Commission.[112] Thus Sukhy and Aleksander demanded that a plenum be called to explain these matters.

The Eighth CPWU Plenum

The plenum that Sukhy and Aleksander called for took place in October 1927.[113] The CPP Central Committee was represented by Lubieniecki (Rylski), Jan Paszyn (Czarny) and for part of the time by G. Henrykowski (Henryk) and Kazimierz Cichowski (Teofil).[114] Królikowski also took an active part in the later discussions.[115] The CP(B)U was represented by Vasyl Sirko and Volodymyr Popel (Iurchenko)[116] whom the Kharkiv central intended to co-opt to the Politburo. Since both were Galician Ukrainians, and former members of the CPWU who were well known to the party, this was expected to be a straightforward process.[117] As a member of the CP(B)U, Sirko had worked in the Zakordot and became head after Maksymovych was removed. Thus he had maintained constant contact with West Ukrainian affairs.

There were about forty persons present at the plenum, of which thirty-three had the right to vote. The majority of the latter were from the central committee and regions. From the beginning the plenum was divided in two. The "minority" and the CPP representatives complained that they had not been informed ahead of time of the plenum's purpose or the dates of its convocation, and thus had had no part in the preparations and no time to draft resolutions.[118] These accusations were rebutted by the "majority." V. Popel-Iurchenko later described the hostile atmosphere: "I tried to convince Vasylkiv and others that they were acting incorrectly, that they were slandering Sukhy and Aleksander and isolating themselves."[119] But, he added, "Sukhy and Aleksander defended the line of the Polish CC minority at the plenum" which he also considered an erroneous move.[120]

During the proceedings Sukhy and Aleksander accused their own central committee of avoiding self-criticism on the Shumsky question and of moulding both Shumsky's real and imagined acts into a "nationalist deviation." They accused the committee of being too weak in its anti-war position, while the Poles were threatening war against the USSR.[121] In accordance with the decision of the Comintern, the "minority" demanded that Maksymovych be excluded from the central committee and that Vasylkiv replace Turiansky in Moscow.[122]

In the ideological sphere the debate centred on three problems: the split in Selrob, the opposition in the CPWU Central Committee and the degree to which Shumskyism was erroneous and harmful. The opposition and the CPP maintained that by taking the nationalist position of Selsoiuz the Ukrainian Central Committee was responsible for the split.[123] They said that *Nashe slovo* (organ of Selrob-Right) and *Svitlo* (unofficial organ of the CPWU for Ukrainian peasants) used nationalist arguments to counter the views of the People's Will.[124] They attacked Kraikivsky with particular vehemence since he was responsible by virtue of his position for the ideological stance of Selrob-Right. They also accused Kraikivsky of not attending the plenum to avoid having to vote formally for a resolution condemning Shumsky.[125] From others, like Kaliatynsky, they demanded a retraction of an earlier defence of Shumsky and defamatory statements about the president of Soviet Ukraine, Petrovsky.[126]

The Vasylkivists put forward a resolution declaring that they desired the unity of the rank and file of Selrob but that Valnytsky and Zaiats were irredeemable. This was accepted, despite the bitter objections of the opposition. The Vasylkivists succeeded because their followers, who had an overwhelming majority of the votes, remained staunchly loyal.[127] They also adopted a resolution condemning the factionalism of Sukhy and Aleksander.[128] The latter was removed from the Secretariat. Maksymovych, despite the Comintern's decision, remained on the central committee and was removed only from the Politburo. The plenum placed Sirko on the central committee, but ignored the CP(B)U's advice that Iurchenko be appointed to the Politburo and elected him only as an alternate.[129] On the Shumsky affair, the plenum admitted that his error consisted in not breaking with Khvyliovy sooner and ultimately stemmed from a lack of information.[130] In general, events at the plenum only heightened the tension. New opposition memos accused CP(B)U delegates of siding with the Vasylkivists at the Eighth Plenum.[131] Turiansky sent letters on behalf of the CPWU Central Committee defending CPWU actions and attacking those of others.[132]

Subsequently (in November 1927), Kraikivsky opposed his own central committee for what he considered its conciliatory policy on the Shumsky question, demanded a return to the party's April position and open criticism of the "erroneous policies of the CP(B)U and CPP."[133] The Vasylkivists revealed this only after the split.

The Second Plenum of the CPP Central Committee was devoted to Ukrainian affairs. Besides the members of the central committee, all delegates to the Ukrainian plenum, including Królikowski, Vasylkiv, Aleksander and Sukhy, were present. The plenum elected a Ukrainian Commission to draft the final resolution, which consisted of Królikowski, Lahinovich, Sukhy, Vasylkiv and Paszyn.[134] Representatives of the "majority" (Lubieniecki and Królikowski) and the "minority" (Henrykowski, Paszyn, Lahinovich) proposed their own resolutions, but the differences were minor and a joint resolution was agreed upon by all except Vasylkiv.[135]

All in attendance at the plenum agreed that the essence of Shumskyism and the party's mistake in this matter had been misapprehended at the Ukrainian plenum. The latter had played down the party's guilt and had not followed the resolutions of the Comintern. Participants at the Second Plenum also agreed that the April error had been profoundly detrimental to CPWU activity. The Second Plenum admitted that the party had been incapable of defending the CP(B)U and Soviet government against assault from the capitalist world and that its silence during the most critical period had disoriented the masses. The judgment of the Polish plenum was no less harsh on the question of the Selrob. "While condemning the split affected by the leaders of the former People's Will," the resolution stated, "it must also be said that the CPWU majority is responsible for it.... The CPWU majority is still pursuing the same policy."[136] The plenum criticized the CPWU's failure to react to the arguments of *Nashe slovo* and many other errors of the Ukrainians at their eighth plenum. It annulled the resolution condemning Sukhy and Aleksander for factionalism and again ordered the Ukrainians to remove Maksymovych. Vasylkiv considered the decisions of the CPP Central Committee unjust, but said that his party would submit to them.[137]

The CP(B)U's Discussion on the CPWU

The course of the CPWU's October plenum worried the CP(B)U no less than the CPP. On 25 November the Politburo met again in Kharkiv to hear reports of the parties present at the plenum and to discuss the affair. Królikowski represented the CPP at the meeting. The reports on the CPWU plenum, given by Sirko and Popel-Iurchenko, were indecisive and incomplete. On each subject they usually began by condemning certain actions of the Vasylkivists and ended by attributing their mistakes to the minority in the CPWU or CPP Central Committee. Both speakers, and particularly Iurchenko, insisted that they had tried to dissuade the leadership from repressive measures against the minority but that Aleksander and Sukhy had provoked the majority to implement such measures. Only on the question of Selrob did Sirko and Iurchenko openly side with the CPWU majority. They considered Valnytsky and Zaiats unsuitable for leadership of the organization, and felt that their return would mean the moral victory of a non-Communist party over a Communist one, an unsatisfactory outcome.[138]

Stefan Królikowski (Bartoszewicz) was the next to speak and he did not hide his indignation at the Vasylkivists. He reported on the decisions of the Polish plenum concerning the conflict, and recalled that the Comintern had recommended the consolidation of Selrob around a group outside the factional struggle. This could not be the editors of *Nashe slovo*, however, whom the Comintern had had in mind, because they wholeheartedly supported Selrob-Right in the factional conflict.[139] While Królikowski admitted that Valnytsky had not completely assimilated Leninist views on the national question, he did not think that that necessitated his removal. He noted that Valnytsky's political adversaries in Selrob had also failed to understand that question. Królikowski gave a protracted criticism of the position of the CPWU leaders. "I asked Vasylkiv not to make matters worse" (by putting forward a resolution condemning Sukhy and Aleksander), he said, "but it was like talking to a wall."[140] Since that group had long ignored the recommendations of the CPP and Comintern, it was necessary to "break their monopoly" in the party.

The Comintern executive committee's representative, Dmytro Manuilsky, gave the most severe criticism of the Vasylkivists. He declared that the present dilemma in the West Ukrainian movement was no accident. Whoever knew the demoralizing atmosphere of Galician parliamentarianism, Manuilsky said, the utterly unprincipled social democracy of the region, would easily understand the environment in which the Ukrainian party had grown and, hence, the origins of the nationalist influence on that party. Because the proletariat was very small in Eastern Galicia, the CPWU easily succumbed to petty-bourgeois influences. "At the last congress [the Fourth CPP Congress] we arrived at a compromise and left the old leadership in power.... It is now clear to me that the Comintern made an error and was brazenly deceived."[141] The disease of Shumskyism, Manuilsky thought, was most evident in the CPWU's attitude toward the split in Selrob. That this "national group" regarded the problem of Russophilism today to be the same as it was during tsarist days and then raised the issue in its "struggle with Moscow" was evidence of its nationalist disease. Addressing Sirko and Iurchenko, Manuilsky asked "Are you aware that you have fallen into their [the nationalists'] embraces, that you are with them?... The best internationalist elements, Sukhy and Aleksander, are being baited in the CPWU...a strong campaign is being initiated against them.... Do you understand that you have adopted a resolution against the people who are carrying out the Comintern line...in all this there is a genuine, base anti-Semitism."[142] Despite his recognition of Sukhy and Aleksander, the Comintern representative did not agree with Królikowski that they could become the leadership nucleus of their party. In fact, though he demanded the exclusion of Vasylkiv, Turiansky and others, Manuilsky did not indicate who should take control of the party.

The next speaker, Andrii Khvylia, though that the Eighth CPWU Plenum's greatest error was its failure to exclude Maksymovych from the central committee. He also stated that as long as Vasylkiv and Turiansky remained at the head of the party the situation in the CPWU would not improve.[143] Khvylia considered Comintern policy on the CPWU correct, cautious and temperate, and thought it gave the party the opportunity to correct its errors. As a former Borotbist, Khvylia did not trust Valnytsky and his followers. He considered Valnytsky's practice of going over the heads of the Ukrainian Central Committee to the CPP leadership intolerable and demanded the gradual limitation of Valnytsky's power and eventually his complete removal. Khvylia agreed with Manuilsky that Sukhy and Aleksander could not be party leaders because they were unfamiliar with national and agrarian problems.

Skrypnyk urged the "immediate implementation of the resolutions to remove Vasylkiv and Turiansky." He disagreed with the view that Russophilism had lost its reactionary character: only a year and a half had passed since Valnytsky had first recognized the Ukrainian people, he noted, but Russophilism had existed for decades and "people there remember its content, and its leaders."[144] He criticized the "minority" of the Polish Central Committee, which contained elements of nationalism. Domski, a member of the "minority," Skrypnyk declared inaccurately, had taken a nationalist position when the Red Army marched on Warsaw (1920).[145] Another member of the minority, Lahinovich, commented (at the Fourth CPP Congress) that the side of the "Polish bourgeoisie" was historically justified in the Polish-Ukrainian war of 1919. "How could he say something like that?," Skrypnyk asked indignantly. "Something should be done about that Polish Central Committee" (the "minority" faction).[146]

Mykola Popov, a political activist and outstanding historian, demanded the straightforward removal of Vasylkiv and Turiansky.[147] Vlas Chubar concurred that "we can expect nothing good" from Vasylkiv, Turiansky and Maksymovych.[148] He reminded the meeting, however, that these three should be removed only by the CPP or, preferably, by the Comintern. He agreed essentially with Manuilsky that the crisis in the CPWU was a logical consequence of the line it had developed and not merely a result of the present situation. On the question of Selrob he agreed with the majority of the Politburo, against Skrypnyk and Khvylia, that the CPWU leadership rather than the People's Will faction was to blame for the split. "The situation there forced the People's Will people to flee before they were driven out.... Kotsiubynsky warned us that a split was imminent and that the CPWU Central Committee was doing nothing to prevent it." Chubar felt that the term "Russophilism" should not be used at all. The People's Will opposed fascism (i.e. the existing government in Poland) and that was the essential thing. Skrypnyk interjected that the People's Will had "a Black Hundreds tail." Chubar countered that this was in the past and that it should not be dragged into the current conflict.

Lazar Kaganovich agreed with Chubar's assessment of Russophilism,[149] and that the past history of the People's Will revealed its sympathy for Moscow. He pointed out that any reorganization of the party leadership in Western Ukraine would have to be carried out cautiously since Vasylkiv, Maksymovych and others had direct contact with the CPWU masses, and the CP(B)U had influence only through them. It was essential that the organizational changes did not destroy the party. While Kaganovich agreed that the ruling troika—Vasylkiv, Maksymovych and Turiansky—should be removed, he did not agree with Manuilsky's view that the deviation in the CPWU resulted from its ideological development. He defended Skrypnyk's view that new conditions had arisen in Poland that made things difficult for a revolutionary party. He answered Manuilsky's argument that the "unproletarian" state of the CPWU was caused by a weak working class base in the country by pointing out that petty-bourgeois deviations also occurred where the working class was strong, as, for example, in Czechoslovakia. More appealing to Kaganovich was the thesis that such things could easily happen in a young party. He defended Sirko and Iurchenko, declaring that after conversations with them he believed that they sincerely accepted the resolutions of the CP(B)U and that they should be allowed to remain in the party. Their failure, according to Kaganovich, lay not in their political position, but in their stand against Vasylkiv and Turiansky at the plenum, which had proved too much for them. Iurchenko, he said, was innocent, and Sirko had only to dissociate himself from the events at the plenum. Sirko declared that he had already done so, whereupon Kaganovich replied that everything was then in order. Finally, Kaganovich rejected Królikowski's proposal that the CP(B)U Central Committee should stop financing the West Ukrainian party independently of the CPP, since such aid should be considered part of the Comintern's subsidy for the CPWU.

Zatonsky, like Manuilsky, maintained that the CPWU had never overcome its nationalism. He thought the solution lay in radical organizational changes. Discussing his assessment of the CP(B)U delegates, he told Kaganovich, "Sirko went there as our delegate and returned as an advocate of the CPWU. Perhaps he shouldn't be removed, but this should be pointed out to him."[150]

In a second speech, Manuilsky moderated his criticism of Sirko and Iurchenko and pointed out to the CP(B)U leaders that they had chosen the wrong people for such an important mission. Iurchenko, he said, was politically weak and Sirko had not yet, "even here," broken with "the anti-Russophilism" campaign. When Kaganovich objected that Sirko had protested his loyalty at the plenum, Manuilsky replied that Sirko had defended the CPWU majority. "One cannot entrust vacillating people with such important tasks. The executive committee has the right to demand at least that much from the CP(B)U Central Committee." Manuilsky firmly rebuffed Skrypnyk's attempts to turn the discussion toward the Polish Central Committee and Lahinovich. He told Skrypnyk that only minor differences divided them on the national question and that he would welcome an understanding of their position on the part of the CP(B)U Central Committee. Evidently, Manuilsky and Zatonsky had made a declaration to the Politburo (it is not clear exactly when or to which Politburo) that the deviation in the CPWU was a result of the policies carried out by Skrypnyk. After examining the matter the Politburo rejected this accusation.[151]

The other participants contributed nothing new to the proceedings. Ivan Kulyk was alone in supporting Skrypnyk's assessment of the People's Will. From the material cited above one can see that it was only on the question of the People's Will that some of the participants (Skrypnyk, Khvylia and Kulyk) differed. The participants agreed unanimously that Turiansky and Vasylkiv be removed and Maksymovych excluded. The CP(B)U referred this decision to the Comintern.

The Second Ukrainian Commission of the Comintern Executive Committee

On 17 December 1927, at the request of the CP(B)U Central Committee, the Commission of the political secretariat of the Comintern executive committee met. The committee members were: Leon Purman (probably chairman), Otto Kuusinen, Skrypnyk and (listed as "present" in the minutes) Popov.[152] Possibly others were present, but not included in the minutes.

After a long discussion the commission reached agreement on the full text of a resolution except for a point on organizational means of correction, which was referred to the executive committee of the Comintern. The agreed upon part of the resolution stated that the leaders of the CPWU had not grasped the meaning of the Comintern's resolution or shown a "sufficiently sincere desire" to implement it. They had done nothing to implement the directives of the CPP concerning the split in Selrob and had ignored the suggestions of the CP(B)U Politburo. Thus they were in opposition to the Comintern political lines on these matters. The commission recommended the immediate unification of the two Selrob groups on the basis of ideological principles. This was to be undertaken without masking "the nationalism of some former Selsoiuz members by eagerly expounding on the former anti-Ukrainianism of certain Peoples' Will members."[153] It accused the CPWU of using the struggle against an antiquated Russophilism to hide its own passiveness while certain circles displayed a growing hostility toward Moscow and the Russian proletariat.

The resolution reiterated the Comintern's recommendations on the organizational question and forbade the CPWU Central Committee to "persecute the 'minority' or remove it from work." At the same time the commission did not accept the proposals of the minority since "this would lead to the effective liquidation of the present Central Committee." The resolution further called for the exclusion of Maksymovych from the CPWU and ordered him as a member of the CP(B)U to refrain from contact with the leaders of the West Ukrainian party.[154]

The drafting of part of the resolution led to disagreement. Purman and Kuusinen proposed the following wording: "The chief blame for not implementing the directives of the Comintern belongs to Vasylkiv and Turiansky. The Political Secretariat is making one final attempt to retain these comrades in leadership positions... while simultaneously recommending that Vasylkiv remain in Moscow as the CPWU representative attached to the CPP representation."[155] At first the CP(B)U delegates demanded the complete removal of Vasylkiv and Turiansky, but when this demand was rejected,[156] proposed the following compromise: "Remove Vasylkiv from work not only in the CPWU Politburo... but also in the CPP representation in Moscow. Let Turiansky remain as a representative, but give him a final warning."[157] Purman, with Kuusinen's support, rejected this proposal. The final text of the Political Secretariat's resolution was adopted on 24 December 1927 with the amendment of Purman and Kuusinen cited above,[158] thus Vasylkiv and Turiansky remained in the leadership despite the demands of the CP(B)U.

The Split

It is not our intention to give a detailed account of the further vicissitudes of the factional struggles. Suffice it to say that they developed almost openly. District committees were fought over and drawn into the struggle. The Drohobych, Ternopil and Przemyśl regions and the central committee of the Union of Communist Youth of Western Ukraine sided with the minority at an early stage.[159] In December the minority held a meeting of its followers in Gdańsk which was no less factional from the legal point of view than those of the majority at the Eighth Plenum.[160]

There was virtually no chance of restoring unity. In organizational matters, such as relations with Selrob-Left and the exclusion of Maksymovych, the Vasylkivists maintained their position and ignored the decision of the CPP and Comintern. The Secretariat of the CPP Central Committee tried to take the entire matter into its own hands. It adopted a resolution calling for a provisional executive of the CPWU Central Committee "composed of one representative of the CPP Central Committee, one of the CPWU Central Committee majority and one of the minority. The CPP representative has the right to refer all contentious questions to the CPP Secretariat for final resolution."[161] The resolution forbade the creation of new organizations and promised that many organizations recently formed, mostly by the "minority," would undergo verification. The same document announced a forthcoming national conference of the CPWU.[162] Somewhat later, the date of the conference (also called the Ninth Party Plenum) was set for January 1928. On 13 January, when most of the delegates were already assembled in Gdańsk, the CPP Secretariat postponed the meeting for two days, first, because two delegates had not arrived and second, in order to verify credentials. But the leadership of the CPWU-"Majority" went ahead with the meeting on the assumption that many of its followers would have trouble with credentials. A few days later those who had accepted the CPP postponement began their proceedings.[163]

Thus two conferences were in process at the same time, that of the "majority" and the official one of the "minority." At their meeting the

Vasylkivists vented their accumulated grievances, especially on the creation of a provisional executive. The CPP leaders denounced the Vasylkivist meeting and tried unsuccessfully to persuade its participants to join the official conference. Only a few activists, including central committee member Bartolomii Kopach, left the factional meeting. Vasylkiv arrived from Moscow, shortly after writing an indignant letter to the CPWU Central Committee criticizing his colleagues for not implementing the recommendations of the Comintern.[164] Initially he appeared at the CPP Conference in Gdańsk, but it soon became apparent that he was speaking as an "advocate of the splinter conference," though his views were more moderate than those of some of his followers.

The official conference was chaired by Aleksander Danieluk (Stefański).[165] His report repeated the accusations against the Vasylkivists. He also revealed that in unofficial conversations the Vasylkivists had told Danieluk that Ukraine was being harmed economically "by Moscow," as was evident from the "budget policy." Danieluk concluded that such statements were in opposition to official resolutions and to the policy of the CP(B)U. He said that the Vasylkivists had moved politically with lightning speed from Communism to nationalism, though many did not realize that they were becoming "a tool in enemy hands" and embarking on a path of "open struggle with the USSR and Soviet power." Vasylkiv responded to Danieluk as follows: "On the question of the People's Will our differences consist in the fact that we consider them a petty-bourgeois group of speculators, *smenovekhovtsy*, while you see them as revolutionaries with deviations."[166] Maksymovych, Vasylkiv said, had not been removed because "we made a mistake together and together we composed declarations. The blame was mutual." "The accusation that we want to reform the CP(B)U line," Vasylkiv admitted, "does not frighten us. From what comrade Stefański [Danieluk] has said it would follow that the CPWU should not take an interest in the affairs of Soviet Ukraine, that it should [merely] 'stand on the alert.' We do not feel that our task consists in merely reprinting statistical information on Soviet Ukraine, but that we must examine matters from a general Ukrainian point of view."[167]

Sochacki, Sukhy, Wysocki (Kazimierz Cichowski), Zatorski (?), Rudolf (Andrii Stetsko), Jerzy (Ozjasz Szechter), Kowalski (Kopach) and others all criticized their old comrade. Kopach said that he had believed to the last that Vasylkiv would overcome the crisis, but now clearly saw the falseness of his position. Sochacki stated that the Comintern had long intended to relieve Vasylkiv of work in Western Ukraine and he had remained in his position only because of the intervention of the CPP Central Committee.[168]

The Secretariat of the CPP Central Committee decided to suspend the CPWU leadership.[169] The resolution noted correctly that the "Ukrainian deviation" in the Communist movement occurred in a period of increased Ukrainianization in the towns and development of Ukrainian culture and industry in Soviet Ukraine,[170] that "Ukrainian nationalism [central and right parties in Poland] has gone over to the anti-Soviet camp,"[171] which had not occurred before. The resolution expressed certainty that "the [Ukrainian] comrades were consciously and with premeditation preparing a split."[172] Beyond this, despite the great conviction with which it was written, the resolution introduced no new arguments.

The Eighth CPWU Conference

The Vasylkivist Conference was held on 13–16 January 1928. During the proceedings it was named the Eighth CPWU Conference. Turiansky acted as chairman until Vasylkiv arrived and devoted most of his opening speech to a criticism of the CP(B)U leadership.[173] Together with Vasylkiv he was co-author of the conference resolutions, which were published as a pamphlet.[174] Its first twenty pages analysed the international and Polish situations, and pointed out that the Ukrainian question was being settled in the interest of imperialist countries. The resolutions repeated the Communist assertions about the Ukrainian problem in Poland: the "partial stabilization of capitalism" and Piłsudski's policies had fostered a decline in the leftist orientation of the masses and initiated a current of collaboration with the government in many Ukrainian parties. But the pamphlet did not include the CPWU among these parties, although the CPP and CP(B)U had accused the West Ukrainian party of yielding to nationalist pressure and the opportunism of the Ukrainian petty bourgeoisie.

The fourth chapter of the pamphlet concerned the national question in Soviet Ukraine. It attributed the growth of both Ukrainian and Russian nationalism in the country to the policy of NEP.[175] Although nationalism was neither a working class nor a party phenomenon it strongly influenced both. Great power chauvinism was evident, according to the resolution, in "attempts to treat other peoples as an object of colonialism." The chauvinists, propagating the superiority of their own culture, could not reconcile themselves to the existence of separate national Soviet republics, followed the development of Ukrainian and Belorussian proletarian culture with strong distaste and tried to maintain the dominant position of Russian culture.[176] The authors of the resolution found that these attitudes influenced both the working class and the party and were expressed in:

1. the bureaucratic deformation of the process of Ukrainianization which limited it to the narrow aim of rapprochement with the peasants or treated it as merely a trump card in the struggle for the sympathy of the Ukrainian masses: "If we don't carry out Ukrainianization, Piłsudski will."[177]

2. the denial of the need to Ukrainianize the urban proletariat (Lebed's view);
3. seeking out the "culture of the dominant class" in every national culture;
4. driving away the best Ukrainian forces on the pretext of national deviation (Shumsky, Hrynko);[178]
5. attempts to diminish the significance of Ukraine in the Soviet system and to limit its rights to the sphere of national-cultural autonomy.[179]

As proof of the influence of these attitudes, the resolution cited the following facts: the demand that the Leningrad Academy of Sciences be turned into an all-Union academy; the proposal of Larin, Enukidze[180] and Lunacharsky that the schools in Kuban use the local dialect rather than standard literary Ukrainian as the language of instruction; Demian Bedny's pamphlet against the Ukrainianization of the Odessa opera;[181] Vaganian's book *On national culture*.[182] These facts, however, were not the result of CP(B)U policy, and some were the results of opposition to that policy (Larin and Vaganian). Therefore, the resolution dealt with the problem of the "CP(B)U–Kaganovich leadership" separately. The views of the leadership were supposedly stated in an article by Zatonsky. The article, which we will return to, raised the issue of CP(B)U members who had come from other parties in order, according to the resolution, to impugn their justified criticism by referring to their past activities.

In the area of practical policy, though the Kaganovich leadership had branded the views of Lebed, Rakovsky and Zinoviev of several years earlier erroneous, it had not "in time and with sufficient energy" opposed the present harmful tendencies. Thus, it had responded too late to Larin's arguments, it had not opposed firmly the attempts to hinder the tempo of Ukrainianization nor had it impeded the centralization that threatened the cultural and economic development of Ukraine. This was true of both the party and the state apparatus.[183]

The pamphlet devoted less space to the problem of Ukrainian nationalism, though its existence was admitted. It was perceived as a result of the economic recovery of the kulaks and their influence on the rural teachers and, indirectly, the urban Ukrainian intelligentsia. Several writers of the older generation, including the historian Hrushevsky and his journal, *Ukraina*,[184] were named as typical of that orientation. The pamphlet claimed that these circles desired the secession of Ukraine from the Soviet Union with the help of foreign intervention. A moderate version of this tendency was reflected in Khvyliovy's views. The conference considered Shumsky's prescription to be the only viable cure for this illness and gave the following description of Shumskyism: "Essentially Shumskyism ensures the leading role of the proletariat in the process of national construction, effective struggle against the pressure of both Russian and Ukrainian nationalism and continued socialist construction. It is therefore in accordance with Leninism on the national question and it is wrong to brand Shumskyism as a national deviation."[185]

The resolution strongly attacked the "nationalist-opportunist deviation in the CPP," as revealed in:

1. the Polish Central Committee's approval of proposals of autonomy for the *Kresy*, especially Leński's arguments that the autonomy programme was more acceptable to the mass following of the PSP;
2. the theses and conclusions of Bronowicz's (Bruno's) book, *Stefana Żeromskiego tragedia pomyłek*;[186]
3. Lahinovich's statement at the Fourth CPP Congress and statements by Konrad (Sochacki) and Mirko (Zdziarski) that Shumskyism originated in the years 1920–3;
4. the fact that the CPP did not condemn nationalist deviations in the Belorussian Hramada (attempts to form a bloc with UNDU and the Zionists);
5. support for former members of the People's Will.[187]

The resolutions also criticized the Czechoslovak CP for its slogan of autonomy for Transcarpathian Ukraine and its support of local Russophiles,[188] and the Romanian CP for neglecting work in Bukovyna.[189]

Since many of these problems had already been exposed by the CP(B)U, the CPP did not find the accusations convincing. Also, the CPWU had described some events inaccurately and exaggerated others. It was well known that the national question received greater emphasis in the CPWU than in the CPP, so that charging the CPP with Polish nationalism must have aroused suspicions that the Vasylkivists were more concerned with their own selfish interests than with correcting an erroneous line in the Communist movement. But the main elements of the resolution dealt with problems of the factional struggle, the harm done to the CPWU majority, the economic status of Soviet Ukraine, the defence of Shumskyism, and criticism of the erroneous policy of the CP(B)U on the Ukrainian question, which was basically disagreement with Volodymyr Zatonsky's interpretation of recent Ukrainian history.

In the CPWU and, with less success, in his own party there was an attempt to portray Zatonsky as an ideological antagonist of Shumsky.[190]

There was much truth in this. Zatonsky, undoubtedly one of the most outstanding members of the central committee, had his own opinion on the Ukrainian question, which was more moderate than either Shumsky or Skrypnyk. He was hardly the "evil spirit" of the Ukrainian question or an ideologue of the "Kaganovich group." At this time, though events in the CPWU weakened his authority, Skrypnyk remained a very important activist and was the author of many ideological party documents. But Zatonsky's views were perhaps more representative of the central committee. He had never belonged to the Ukrainian Luxemburgists as had Kviring, Piatakov and Bosh, nor had he ever been accused of nationalism in his own party, like Skrypnyk. Basically Zatonsky was a typical Communist from the years of revolution and civil war. His article,[191] which upset the Vasylkivists, was a slightly revised version of his report to the June plenum (1926) whose main points we already know. Zatonsky saw some merit in the distaste shown by the working class of Ukraine toward the Ukrainian question. The worker in Ukraine was not chauvinistic, but "indifferent to the national question"[192] and opposed to national separatism. The Ukrainian worker's view that Russian culture was above all a revolutionary culture had assured the unity of the Donets, Katerynoslav and "even" Kiev proletariat (the percentage of Ukrainians among the workers of Kiev was always larger) with that of Petrograd, Moscow and Ivanovo, but the price of that unity was a cultural gap between workers and peasants in Ukraine.[193]

Zatonsky emphasized that, besides the primary effect of Russification, capitalist development also fostered the growth of Ukrainian culture. The wealthy peasantry emerged as well as the nucleus of the urban bourgeoisie typified by ideologues of the intelligentsia, including Ukrainian marxists (USDPL). The latter "paved the way for the Ukrainian bourgeoisie as Struve had done in Russia for the Russian bourgeoisie."[194] Zatonsky showed that despite their apparent radicalism, both the Ukrainian populists[195] and mensheviks (USDPL) had prepared the advent of fledgling Ukrainian capitalism. He also thought that Khvyliovy displayed elements of Struvism under the cloak of Marxism. For him the chief carriers of nationalism were the petty bourgeoisie and the rich peasantry. The peasants, though, not only maintained the national culture, but by their very nature were predisposed to the "nationalist deviation," just as the proletariat was susceptible to internationalism.[196]

Zatonsky's treatment of the proletarian and Bolshevik position on the Ukrainian question was more sympathetic, though critical. He did not delve for the source of the error, but reiterated his position that it resulted not from nationalism, but rather from indifference to the national question, and from the fact that, "absorbed in a great struggle the worker overlooked this [link] as the chief means... of uniting the Ukrainian working class and peasantry."[197]

The Vasylkivists opposed this interpretation, first in the resolution of the Eighth Conference[198] and later in a special article by their chief publicist, Turiansky.[199] The article was devoted primarily to expanding upon the position of the Eighth Conference, i.e. a defence of Shumskyism and polemics against Shumsky's opponents. Using quotations from Kaganovich's speeches and from CP(B)U conference and congress proceedings, Turiansky demonstrated a gap between the rapid development of Ukrainian culture and the relatively slow pace of Ukrainianization as undertaken by the leadership apparatus: "We must recognize that the pace of Ukrainianization in the party and state apparatus in the towns and especially in the trade unions must be accelerated, otherwise we will always face the danger that the Ukrainian cultural process will be separated...from the proletariat and the party."[200] Andrii Khvylia, director of the CP(B)U propaganda section, declared that "either we will lead the entire cultural-economic process of the emergence of a Ukrainian culture, a Ukrainian economy...and the process will be proletarian in content, or, if we do not succeed, it will drown us, there will be a nationalist deluge...and the desires of the Ukrainian fascists under Dontsov will achieve their logical and full fruition."[201] Turiansky agreed with Shumsky that Ukrainianization was not necessary simply to communicate with the peasantry. For that it would be enough to Ukrainianize the apparatus that served the countryside. It was a question of something much broader. "We are concerned," wrote Turiansky, "with the creation of a Ukrainian proletarian culture that is socialist in content. Without that there is no proletarian leadership of the countryside and the Ukrainian peasant masses, and no socialist construction. Only an organic, and not bureaucratic, union of the proletariat with the Ukrainian countryside will enable it to lead [effectively]. This is the only road to the victory of socialism and the proletariat over the attempts of the Ukrainian bourgeoisie (the Hrushevskys) to direct the development of Ukrainian culture with the support of the peasant."[202]

Turiansky argued with Zatonsky about the Russian proletariat. Just because it was less susceptible to nationalism than, say, the Austrian, that did not at all mean that the Russian proletariat was free of nationalist sentiment. The Russian mensheviks in Ukraine had their base among that part of the proletariat which was not "absorbed in the great [class] struggle" that ostensibly caused the Ukrainian question to be "overlooked," yet they also had done nothing in this matter. "Pure" proletarians who were free of nationalism did not exist "in nature."[203] Turiansky said that the non-Bolshevik Ukrainian leftist groups had survived because the Bolsheviks in Ukraine did not advance the national question. If the revolutionary movement in Ukraine had to go through a Piatakov phase,[204] a Lebed phase and the Luxemburgism of the Kiev organization, Turiansky said, then phenomena such as Borotbism were also inevitable. The acceptance of the Borotbists into the Bolshevik party did not constitute merely a numerical increase in the organization, but a qualitative change in the CP(B)U. Turiansky also charged that Zatonsky's position on the Ukrainian question coincided with that of Rosa Luxemburg.[205]

Despite these unquestionably substantial problems, there is much in Turiansky's article that is petty. This is also true of other Shumskyist documents. The slightest slip of the tongue would give rise to suspicions of Russian nationalism. For example, when a participant spoke of "the southern part of our country," Turiansky suspected him of purposely avoiding the name "Ukraine" or of denying its national rights. There was a great deal of national sensitivity.

Notes

1. M. Skrypnyk, "Do teorii borotby dvokh kultur," *Nasha pravda*, no. 6–7 (1926): 16–36.
2. Letter of the CC CP(B)U to CC CPWU, 24.
3. J. Czeszejko-Sochacki [Bratkowski], *Na drogach nacjonalizmu*, 22.
4. Seventh Expanded Plenum of the CC CPWU: Minutes, CA KC PZPR, 165/I–3, t. 13.
5. On the UCP see note 60 to chapter 1.
6. Seventh Expanded Plenum of the CC CPWU, 1–3.
7. *Ibid.*, 4.
8. *Ibid.*, 10.
9. *Ibid.*, 11.
10. *Ibid.*, 15.
11. *Ibid.*, 14. There is no mention of what Sukhy said in the minutes, but it is easy to deduce the gist of his statement from what others had to say.
12. Seventh Expanded Plenum of the CC CPWU: Minutes, Vasylkiv, 9, and Huber (?), 13.
13. *Ibid.*, 21. There were three additional members of the central committee who supported the majority.
14. *Ibid.*, 23. The text of the resolution with minor abridgements was published in: *Przeciw rozbijaczom i zdrajcom—za Międzynarodôwką Komunistyczną. Dokumenty i materiały w sprawie rozbicia KPZU* (Lviv, 1928), 9–10.
15. Seventh Expanded Plenum of the CC CPWU, 22.
16. *Przeciw rozbijaczom*, 10.
17. Skrypnyk made the same accusation against Vasylkiv at the plenum in Gdańsk. See Seventh Expanded Plenum of the CC CPWU, 26.
18. Skrypnyk, Speech at plenum, 7 June 1927, 60. He stated that a large part of the conference resolutions were edited after the Gdańsk plenum.

19. *VII Konferentsiia KPZU (rezoliutsii)* (Lviv, 1927), 12–15.
20. *Ibid.*, 16.
21. Skrypnyk, Speech at plenum, 7 June 1927, 68.
22. Stenographic proceedings (incomplete) of the meetings of the Politburo of the CC CP(B)U on the situation in the CPWU, 14 May-25 November 1927, PA IIP TsK KPU, f.1, op. 69, od. zb. 11, pp. 1–3.
23. *Ibid.*, 10.
24. *Ibid.*, 13.
25. Hryhorii Petrovsky (1871–1958) was a veteran Russian Social-Democrat who became a Bolshevik in 1901 and represented the party in the Fourth Duma. After the revolution he was a member of the CP(B)U Politburo and president of the Central Executive Committee of Soviets in Ukraine.
26. Stenographic proceedings ... of the Politburo of the CC CP(B)U, 10. Piłsudski's assumption of power was seen as a direct threat of an attack by Poland on the USSR, hence the repeated references to the exceptionally tense international situation.
27. *Ibid.*, 12.
28. Oleksander Shlikhter (1868–1940) came from a German family of tradesmen living in Ukraine. He participated in the revolutionary movement from 1891 to 1903 in the Bolshevik faction and was the author of several economic and journalistic works.
29. Stenographic proceedings ... of the Politburo of the CC CP(B)U, 16.
30. *Ibid.*, 15.
31. At this time Hrushevsky was head of the Institute of History of the Academy of Sciences and the chief literary researcher was Serhii Iefremov, formerly an important member of the Central Rada.
32. Stenographic proceedings ... of the Politburo of the CC CP(B)U, 14.
33. *Ibid.*, 20.
34. *Ibid.*, 18.
35. In the discussion Skrypnyk found it necessary to emphasize his agreement with Kaganovich. The historian must note that Kaganovich's position at this conference, as at many others devoted to the CPWU, was clearly closer to Skrypnyk's views than to those of his adversaries in the Politburo. At this conference both protested Serbychenko's charge that in the "CPWU everybody is a nationalist" and persuaded him to withdraw his remark.
36. Stenographic proceedings ... of the Politburo of the CC CP(B)U, 24.
37. *Ibid.*, 26.
38. *Ibid.*, 27.
39. *Ibid.*, 31.
40. *Ibid.*
41. *Ibid.*, 28.
42. Skrypnyk, Speech, 7 June 1927, 3–77.
43. *Ibid.*, 70.

44. These theses were very clearly stated in a letter to the Comintern's executive committee. See "Rezolucja plenum KC KP(b)U w sprawie kierunku polityki narodowościowej," in *Przeciw rozbijaczom i zdrajcom*, 29. The letter was edited on the basis of Skrypnyk's report.
45. Skrypnyk, Speech, 7 June 1927, 72.
46. *Ibid.*, 70.
47. *Ibid.*
48. *Ibid.*, 73.
49. *Ibid.*, 75.
50. *Ibid.*, 8–9.
51. *Ibid.*, 73.
52. *Ibid.*, 75.
53. *Ibid.*, 24. Later, affinities with Trotskyism were perceived in Shumsky's views (the supposed petty-bourgeois inspiration of both political tendencies). At one session of the Politburo, Khvyliovy stated that Trotsky's views had made a great impression on him, but Shumsky made no such statements.
54. The resolution of the plenum of the CP(B)U Central Committee. *Przeciw robijaczom i zdrajcom*, 23–32.
55. *Ibid.*, 33–4. The resolution of the CPP Central Committee in connection with Maksymovych's remarks at the CP(B)U plenum.
56. Szłomka (Salomon Miller), CPWB representative, Fourth Congress of the CPP: Minutes of sessions, CA KC PZPR, 158/I–4, t.2, w. 130.
57. *Nasha pravda*, no. 1–3 (1927): 135.
58. Turiansky's remarks at the Fourth CPP Congress, *Nasha pravda*, no. 3–8 (1928): 188.
59. *Uchwały IV Konferencji KPP* (Warsaw, 1926), 65.
60. *VII Konferentsiia KPZU* (Lviv, 1927), 19.
61. J. Czeszejko-Sochacki [Bratkowski], *Na drogach nacjonalizmu*, 36.
62. The Belorussian Peasant Workers' Hramada, a legal party of the Belorussian peasants under the auspices of the CPWB. It's main leader, Branislau Tarashkevich was a philologist, grammarian, poet and political activist. When the party was declared illegal (27 March 1927) it numbered some one hundred thousand members, a record in the history of pro-Communist peasant organizations in Europe.
63. Kozytsky proposed this resolution at a meeting of the Selrob Central Committee in connection with the Shumsky affair. The resolution was defeated.
64. See the following statements of minority members at the Fourth Congress. Minutes, CA KC PZPR, 158/I–4: Korchyk, 2: 59–66; Szłomka (Miller), 2: 130–4; Budzyński, 11: 116.
65. *Ibid.*, 2: 15, Korchyk (Lahinovich).
66. *Ibid.*, 4: 117, Próchniak; 11: 86, Krajewski.
67. Próchniak, as quoted at the Second Plenum of the CPP Central Committee. CA KC PZPR, 158/III, 24: 37.

68. Fourth Congress of the CPP: Minutes, 158/I–4, r 10, 114, Vasylkiv.
69. *Ibid.*, 2: 188, Zarewicz (Abram Cukerman).
70. *Ibid.*, 112–13, Vasylkiv.
71. *Ibid.*, 85, 138–39, Żarski.
72. Sukhy and P. Minc, the so-called "minority" in the CPWU, were also part of the CPWU delegation at the congress, but in the internal CPP factional disputes these two activists like the other CPWU members belonged to the "majority" up to the end of 1927.
73. See e.g., Stefański's (Danieluk's) report, Fourth Congress of the CPP: Minutes, 1: 104.
74. *Przeciw robijaczom i zdrajcom*, 35.
75. *Ibid.*, 37–40.
76. *Ibid.*, 41–2.
77. *Firma* in the preserved text. In the original the term probably used was *shyrma*, which means a cover or screen. The contents of the letter were in the possession of the Lviv police who translated it into Polish.
78. See CA MSW, inw. 127, 37: 116–19. The quotation comes from page 118. The last page and signature are lacking. The contents and certain details indicate that this is a letter from Vasylkiv to comrades in Canada. Popov (Lovytsky) mentioned such a letter at the Third CPWU Congress. Third Congress of the CPWU: Minutes, CA KC PZPR, 165/I–3, 1: 31.
79. Skrypnyk, Speech at plenum, 7 June 1927, 60.
80. *IV Zjazd KPP. Uchwały* (Warsaw, 1928), 11.
81. Halushko, *Narysy istorii*, 228.
82. The full composition of the commission was established according to Second Plenum of the CC CPP, CA KC PZPR, 158/III, 22: 48.
83. Halushko, *Narysy istorii*, 229.
84. Eighth Expanded Plenum of the CC CPWU, CA KC PZPR, 165/I–3, 15: 35.
85. *Ibid.*, 55.
86. "Voprosy diskussii v KPZU," *Kommunisticheskii Internatsional*, no. 43 (1927): 25.
87. *Ibid.*, 28.
88. *Ibid.*, 47. Herasym's (Kraikivsky's) letter of 26 July 1927.
89. *Ibid.*, 38. Herasym's (Kraikivsky's) letter of 12 July 1927.
90. "Selrob-Jedność," police report, 54.
91. "X" and "Rome" probably refer to the CPP Central Committee and the CP(B)U Central Committee.
92. Letter to the CPWU Central Committee, 24 June 1927, on the situation in Selrob, signed "Iakym" (unresolved pseudonym). PA IIP TsK KPU, f. 233, op. 1, od. zb. 84, 19.
93. Herasym's letter of 26 July 1927, PA IIP TsK KPU, f. 233, op. 1, od. zb. 80, 48.
94. Memoirs of Hoshovsky recorded 7 June 1962, CA KC PZPR, 6.

95. Herasym's letter of 26 July and 14 June, PA IIP TsK KPU, 16.
96. *Nashe zhyttia*, no. 4, 20 and 52 (1927).
97. *Nashe slovo*, no. 3 (1928): 3. According to other sources they were suspended as members of the party but not as members of the central committee.
98. The first issue of *Nashe slovo*, later the organ of the "Right," appeared on 29 May 1927.
99. *Volia naroda*, no. 349 (1927).
100. M. Feliński, *Klub Ukraiński a parlament Rzeczypospolitej Polskiej 1919–1927* (Warsaw, 1928), 330.
101. See the report of the Ministry of Internal Affairs on the national minorities for September 1927, AAN, 961 (MSW), 138.
102. Herasym's letter of 12 October 1927, PA IIP TsK KPU, f. 33, op. 1, od. zb. 94, 49.
103. The Shumskyists of the CPWU and Selrob did not, of course, refer to themselves as the "Right" nor did they consider their opponents the "Left." The author has decided to use these designations since they are widely accepted by politicians and historians of all tendencies.
104. *Sprawy Narodowościowe*, no. 5–6 (1927): 541–2. According to other sources there were also leftist centres in the Stanyslaviv region. See *Pid praporom zhovtnia*, 324.
105. *Nashe zhyttia*, no. 44 (1927): 2.
106. This occurred at the local conference in Drahichyn where Valnytsky won a majority of the delegates over Makivka. *Nashe slovo*, no. 1 (1928): 2.
107. *Sel-Rob*, no. 16 (1928): 4; and Czeszejko-Sochacki [Bratkowski], *Na drogach nacjonalizmu*, 55.
108. Iurii Kotsiubynsky, was the son of Mykhailo Kotsiubynsky, an outstanding Ukrainian writer. Iurii joined the Bolshevik party in 1913 and became an active revolutionary in Ukraine. In 1927–30 he worked in the Soviet embassy in Warsaw.
109. Letter of Vasyl Sirko to the party leadership in Kharkiv, dated 28 January 1928, requesting permission to resign. In October 1927, Sirko joined the Politburo of the CPWU on the recommendation of the CP(B)U Central Committee. AM CA KC PZPR, 1356/13/261, 3.
110. *Ibid.*, 5–6.
111. One such incident was a meeting of the CPWU Central Committee's Secretariat, which was held without Aleksander's knowledge (though he was a member) on 16 September. See the text which contains the decision of the CPP representative, Teofil (Kazimierz Cichowski), on this matter. AM CA KC PZPR, 1356/4, 260.
112. Letters from Sukhy and Aleksander, 17 September 1927, AM CA KC PZPR, 1358/8, 24: 26. Sochacki maintained that, because the CPWU leadership prevented numbers 6–9 of *Nasha pravda*, which contained the texts of the resolutions of the Fourth Congress and the resolutions of the CP(B)U, from reaching the country, a large number of members did not

even know of them. See Czeszejko-Sochacki [Bratkowski], *Na drogach nacjonalizmu*, 23.

113. Seventh Expanded Plenum of the CPWU, CA KC PZPR, 165/I–3, 15: 31–41. The first documents are dated 3 October and the last 14 October 1927. However, Sirko who was a participant stated that it lasted four days. (See Stenographic proceedings . . . of the Politburo of the CC CP(B)U, 32.) Clearly, many important declarations were formulated after the proceedings.
114. They made their declaration at the plenum or just after it.
115. Stenographic proceedings . . . of the Politburo of the CC CP(B)U, 38.
116. Halushko, *Narysy*, 235, n. 128. Halushko repeats the information of a Lviv police agent that Skrypnyk represented the CP(B)U at this plenum and at a later meeting of his party's Politburo was attacked for leaning toward the majority position. Neither the minutes of the Eighth Plenum of the CPWU Central Committee nor those of the later meetings of the CP(B)U Politburo confirm this. On the contrary, from those sources it is clear that Skrypnyk was not present at the plenum.
117. Sirko participated in the founding conference of the CPEG (1919) in Stanyslaviv.
118. Eighth Expanded Plenum of the CPWU, 25, 35.
119. Stenographic proceedings . . . of the Politburo of the CC CP(B)U, 43.
120. One should note that at this stage of the struggle the "majority" and "minority" of the CPP Central Committee were quite close in their view of the CPWU. The "majority" faction, worried by the intensity of the dispute with the CP(B)U, was already attacking the Vasylkivists openly and differed from its factional opponent only in proposing more moderate solutions. This circumstance brought the increasingly "radical" minority of the CPWU (earlier oriented toward the CPP "majority") ever closer to the "minority" of the Polish party.
121. Eighth Expanded Plenum of the CPWU, 42. The "anti-war" action of the party was intended among other things to counteract the Western press campaign on Shumsky's condemnation (it was supposed that this was propaganda preliminary to major pronouncements). The Vasylkivists were very constrained in this matter and could not act as their opponents in the CPWU would have liked.
122. *Ibid.*, 35.
123. *Ibid.* Jan Lubieniecki (Rylski) cited statements, or even a resolution of the Ukrainian Central Committee, to the effect that because of the split, "Selrob [had] rid itself of organically alien elements," i.e. the People's Will Faction.
124. *Ibid.*, 45.
125. Letter of Vasyl Sirko, 28 January 1928, *ibid.*, 6. Presumably this was correct.
126. Kaliatynsky is said to have spread the story that the president of Ukraine, Petrovsky, did not know Ukrainian.
127. The oppositionist minority (not counting guests) got 5–6 votes each.
128. Eighth Expanded Plenum of the CPWU, 53–7; printed in *Nasha pravda*, no. 1–2 (1928): 94–7.

129. Stenographic proceedings...of the Politburo of the CC CP(B)U, 49, Skrypnyk.
130. The resolutions of the Eighth Plenum were not published in their entirety and are probably not extant.
131. Letter of the CPWU Central Committee minority to the Politburo of the CP(B)U, *Nasha pravda*, no. 1–2 (1928): 101. To be exact, Sirko and Iurchenko voted together with the opposition against the resolution on the factional activity of Sukhy and Aleksander. On other matters their position was usually vague.
132. *Nasha pravda*, no. 1–2 (1928): 97–105.
133. "Zaiava Vushera [Kraikivsky] do Politbiuro TsK KPZU," *Nasha pravda*, no. 1–2 (1928): 94.
134. Second Plenum of the CC CPP, CA KC PZPR, 158/II, 22: 3.
135. Resolution of the Second Plenum of the CC CPP: On the matter of the decisions of the Eighth CC CPWU Plenum, AM CA KC PZPR, 1356/4/271–277.
136. *Ibid.*, unpaginated.
137. Second Plenum of the CC CPP, 6.
138. Stenographic proceedings...of the Politburo of the CC CP(B)U, 32–6.
139. *Ibid.*, 37.
140. *Ibid.*, 39.
141. *Ibid.*, 44.
142. *Ibid.*, 45. When Sirko remarked in his report that the factional division of the CPWU Central Committee had "unfortunately proceeded along national lines," Manuilsky retorted sarcastically: "The Jews are in opposition." Sirko tried helplessly to explain, "I don't want to call anyone a Jew, but," etc.
143. *Ibid.*, 46–9.
144. *Ibid.*, 49.
145. In 1920 when Domski was in Berlin he persuaded the German Communists to adopt a resolution warning against the imposition of revolution from without and demanded that the attacking Red Army stop at the ethnic Polish border. After 1926 he belonged to neither the majority nor the minority, but propagated his own views. In the Soviet Union he supported Zinoviev's opposition.
146. Skrypnyk's information was not accurate. At the Fourth CPP Congress, Lahinovich stated that the Polish-Ukrainian war of 1919 was "a war between two nationalisms." The matter was closed at the Fifteenth Congress of the all-Union Communist Party (Bolshevik) where Skrypnyk repeated his accusation against "a certain comrade from the Polish party" as proof that there were nationalist elements in the CPP. Bukharin replied immediately that this was not a Polish, but a Belorussian comrade and, summarizing the proceedings, said that Skrypnyk's statements were both inaccurate and tactless. *Piatnadtsatyi Sezd VKPb. XII 1927* (Moscow, 1961), 1: 720–1, 822.
147. Stenographic proceedings...of the Politburo of the CC CP(B)U, 53.

148. *Ibid.*, 55.
149. *Ibid.*, 58–60, 70–1.
150. *Ibid.*, 62.
151. *Ibid.*, 64, 69, 74.
152. Material of the Political Secretariat of the Comintern on the CPWU, AM CA KC PZPR, 1356/8, 37–48.
153. *Ibid.*
154. *Ibid.*, 42.
155. *Ibid.*, 41.
156. Third CPWU Congress: Minutes, CA KC PZPR, 165/I–3, 2: 79. Skrypnyk's statement at the congress.
157. Material of the Political Secretariat of the Comintern on the KPZU, 43.
158. The text in Ukrainian was issued as a supplement to Ie. Hirchak, *Shumskyzm i rozlam v KPZU* (Kharkiv, 1928), 216–17. It differs slightly from the original Russian typescript.
159. A. Danieluk [E. Stefański], "Od komunizmu—do bagna drobnomieszczańskiego nacjonalizmu," *Walka Klas*, no. 1–3 (1928): 29.
160. Related by O. Szechter, a conference participant. Memoirs recorded 3 January 1963, CA KC PZPR.
161. The decision of the CPP Secretariat on Ukrainian affairs, AM CA KC PZPR 1356/4/269, undated, not earlier than 12 December 1927.
162. *Ibid.*, 217.
163. Materials (incomplete) of the "pro-CPP" Conference, CA KC PZPR, 158/III, 25: 1–19.
164. Czeszejko-Sochacki [Bratkowski], *Na drogach nacjonalizmu*, 24.
165. Stefański (Danieluk), CA KC PZPR, 158/III, 25: 4–5.
166. Vasylkiv's statement at the "pro-CPP" Conference, CA KC PZPR, 158/II, 25: 12.
167. *Ibid.*, 13.
168. *Ibid.*, 14. The last such interventions probably took place at the Sixth Congress of the CPP. Later, only Leon Purman, an alternate member of the CPP Central Committee, but also an influential member of the Comintern, tried to hinder the "organizational efforts" of some Comintern members.
169. *Przeciw rozbijaczom*, 75. The resolution of the CPWU conference was adopted unanimously, 16 January 1928.
170. *Ibid.*, 74.
171. *Ibid.*, 67.
172. *Ibid.*, 74.
173. *Ibid.*, 5.
174. *Postanovy VIII Konferentsii KPZU* (Lviv, 1928), 72.
175. *Ibid.*, 27.
176. For a similar statement, see the resolutions of the Twelfth Congress of the RCP(B) (1923).
177. *Postanovy VIII Konferentsii KPZU* (Lviv, 1928), 29.

178. Hryhorii Hrynko, vice-premier and head of the Planning Commission of Soviet Ukraine, was transferred to Moscow in 1926 where he held the positions of vice-chairman of the Planning Commission of the Soviet Union, deputy commissar of agriculture and commissar of finance. In 1938 he was sentenced to death in the Bukharin trial. Hrynko did not support Shumsky in 1926, and his transferral to Moscow was not politically motivated, though it took place after Shumsky had wanted him named premier of Ukraine.
179. *Postanovy VIII Konferentsii KPZU*, 29.
180. There is a lack of data on this.
181. Bedny—a popular poet and veteran Bolshevik.
182. *Postanovy VIII Konferentsii KPZU*, 32.
183. The problem mentioned in the resolution aroused the interest of a wide circle of Ukrainian communists. A few months later the Kharkiv economist, Mykhailo Volobuiev, discussed it in the party press. "Do problemy ukrainskoi ekonomiky," *Bilshovyk Ukrainy*, no. 2–3 (1928), reprinted in *Dokumenty ukrainskoho komunizmu* (New York, 1962). The main thesis of the Ukrainian economist was that after the revolution the economy of old Russia had ceased to exist as a unified whole and became a co-operative system of economically separate Soviet national republics, each representing an economic whole. Without this the new socialist countries would not be able to form a socialist economic system without devastating their own economies. The need for a complex approach, however, was not perceived by many leaders, for whom the Soviet economy was not particularly different from the economy of old Russia. Disregard for the complex economic structure of the Soviet republics was evident in the faulty establishment of economic regions and in economic planning (pages 191–2, 1962 edition). Volobuiev also demonstrated that, despite its high development of heavy industry, pre-revolutionary Ukraine was backward and colonial and had a weaker native light industry than Russia. (He made comparisons in absolute figures without regard for size of population or territory.) He demanded that this disparity be overcome. He considered that Soviet Ukraine had been hurt economically by plans to rebuild sugar factories in ethnic Russia, or even iron foundries in Siberia (Kuznetsk) rather than in Ukraine at a lower cost (page 221). He also criticized the higher contribution of Ukraine to the all-Soviet budget which meant, in his estimation, that in 1924–5, one-third of the revenue of the Ukrainian republic was used outside its borders. Volobuiev's article was branded in the press as economic Shumskyism.
184. *Postanovy VIII Konferentsii KPZU*, 31.
185. *Ibid.*, 67.
186. This book, written by an outstanding member of the CPP, was an attempt to show Polish intellectuals of leftist pro-independence traditions the limits of their *szlachta* patriotism. In the factional struggle the book was branded as an example of national bolshevism.
187. *Ibid.*, 36–40.
188. The feeling of being Russian was considerably more widespread among Transcarpathian Ukrainians than among those of Eastern Galicia.

189. *Postanovy VIII Konferentsii KPZU*, 40. The Vasylkivists thought that, despite the present interest in the national minorities question, a number of European Comintern sections did not have a correct line on it. The Romanian, Yugoslavian, Czech and Polish parties, for example, either completely misunderstood the problem (Communist Party of Romania and Communist Party of Czechoslovakia) or misinterpreted Lenin's thoughts on this question (CPP). "Our Romanian party, for example, to this day does not see that the slogan of national autonomy [for Bessarabia] is an alien slogan... [the party] gives no attention to the Ukrainian question [in Bukovyna]." See *Die ukrainische Nationalfrage* (Lviv, 1928), 3–4. Thus, from the Romanian Communists they demanded a declaration of Bessarabia's right to secede and join Soviet Ukraine. The Romanian party did not accept this demand for several years.
190. *Budivnytstvo*, 124. Solodub, a defender of Shumsky at the June Plenum of the CP(B)U, made a statement to this effect.
191. V. Zatonsky, "Materialy do ukrainskoho natsionalnoho pytannia," *Bilshovyk Ukrainy*, no. 6 (1927): 9–32.
192. *Ibid.*, 16.
193. *Ibid.*, 11.
194. *Ibid.*, 10.
195. *Ibid.*, 11. It might be correct to say "Ukrainian SRs," but the SRs (the political successors of the *narodniki*) in Ukraine broke with their Russian comrades only after 1917 and Zatonsky was also concerned with the earlier period.
196. *Ibid.*, 18–19.
197. *Ibid.*, 12.
198. *Postanovy VIII Konferentsii KPZU*, 33–4.
199. R. Kuzma [Lazarkevych], "Cherez pryzmu marksivskoi krytyky," *Kultura*, no. 7–8 (1928): 7–54.
200. This is probably an excerpt from the report of the CP(B)U Central Committee at the Tenth Party Congress (20–29 November 1927). The quotation is unverified.
201. A. Khvylia, *Iasnoiu dorohoiu* (Kharkiv, 1927), quotation unverified.
202. Kuzma [Lazarkevych], "Cherez pryzmu," 29.
203. *Ibid.*
204. Georgii Piatakov, a Bolshevik since 1910, was the leader of the influential Kiev organization in Ukraine, co-founder of the CP(B)U, and its actual leader up to 1921. He was a Luxemburgist on the national question. For more on the Kievan Bolsheviks during the revolution, see J. Radziejowski, "Ruch narodowy i rewolucyjny na Ukrainie."
205. The statement by Rosa Luxemburg in question: "Ukrainian nationalism in Russia was something quite different from, let us say, Czech, Polish, or Finnish nationalism, in that the former was a mere whim, a folly of a few dozen petit bourgeois intellectuals, without the slightest roots in the economic, political, or psychological relationships of the country; it was

without any historical tradition, since Ukraine never formed a nation or government, was without any national culture, except for the reactionary romantic poems of Shevchenko.... And this ridiculous pose of a few university professors and students was inflated into a political force by Lenin and his comrades through their doctrinaire agitation concerning the 'right of self-determination including [secession], etc.'" Rosa Luxemburg, *The National Question: Selected Writings*, ed. H. B. Davis (New York and London, 1976), 298.

Chapter Seven

The CPWU and the Secessionists, 1928–9

Two Currents of the CPWU in the Pre-Election Period

Though the split was not yet irreparable, the approaching elections to the Sejm exacerbated the situation. During the two conferences in Gdańsk,[1] the Comintern's West European Bureau[2] had warned those responsible for the split that by refusing to submit to the Mandate Commission of the CPP Politburo they were violating the principles of party discipline and that any opposition to the CPP Central Committee would be treated as opposition to the Comintern.[3] Those with questionable credentials would be allowed to participate in the conference as guests. The Comintern gave them twenty-four hours to meet its conditions, with the right of appeal to a higher court. Even after this deadline a Comintern delegate made contact with the Vasylkivists and suggested that they should not openly oppose the CP(B)U and the CPP, that they should add three new members to the central committee on the strength of the resolutions of the December Ukrainian Commission, and that they should inform the Comintern of existing differences. For his part the delegate promised to persuade the CPP Central Committee to withdraw its decision to suspend members of the CPWU Central Committee; the Polish party agreed to this.[4] The Vasylkivists rejected these conditions and agreed only to co-ordinate electoral activity. Although willing to form an electoral coalition, they knew how acts of insubordination, much less open secession, were treated in the Comintern, and they knew there was little chance of forming "a united electoral front." More likely, the Shumskyist camp wanted to participate independently in the elections (this was particularly true of Selrob-Right). Because they had a considerable chance of success, the Shumskyists wanted an electoral contest with their factional rivals in order to prove their role in Western Ukraine and influence the Comintern. Selrob also hoped to strengthen its position in the legal political life of the country by winning seats in the Sejm.

The drive to win seats was reflected in the moral-political tone of the Shumskyist legal press, especially that of Selrob-Right, though occasionally even the weekly *Svitlo* (a newspaper for peasants, controlled by the CPWU) gave in to this tendency. Propaganda effort was focused on Selrob-Left, which was accused of anti-Ukrainianism and Russophilism (*katsapstvo*). Nearly the entire press of Selrob-Right devoted itself solely to this campaign against Selrob-Left. The tone of *Nashe slovo* became unusually brutal, full of tasteless epithets, abuse and incredible stories. The outbursts were often openly nationalistic.[5] This tone and the use of nationalist terminology severely damaged the reputation of the Shumskyist camp, especially among the working class.[6] The tone of the left, on the other hand, became increasingly composed, more understanding toward its opponents. The leftists often used the term "comrade," for example, and spoke well of Ivan Kalynovych, the late editor of *Nashe slovo*.[7] Within the Shumskyist faction of the CPWU, of course, the Selrob allies gravitated more toward nationalism. After the elections, they debated whether they should come out strongly against such nationalism,[8] but did not do so. Some privately blamed Vasylkiv for this. The more the splinter CPWU began to worry about its influence, the more tolerant it became toward its allies.

On 14 January 1928, without having reached an agreement with the Left, Selrob-Right handed the General Electoral Commission its slate of candidates.[9] The slate included, besides Selrob activists (Maksym Chuchmai and Stepan Makivka), the names of Stepan Volynets, secretary of the CPWU Central Committee since 1924, Panteleimon Kraikivsky and Petro Lyshega, also members of the central committee.[10] The list received position number eight on the ballot. In the Lviv region the CPWU-Shumskyists came out with their own slate at number thirty-six. On 18–19 January Selrob-Left held a conference of its representatives with the delegates of the Right and the PSP-Left to discuss a common electoral slate. Selrob-Right agreed to form a bloc on the condition that the Left publicly condemn its own splinter action and either retract its "slander of the workers' movement," or expel Valnytsky, Pelekhaty and Zaiats from the party. It rejected a counter-proposal for a joint declaration of self-criticism.

This unsuccessful attempt at rapprochement gave rise to new developments. Mykhailo Durdella was a Ukrainian Communist in America who had recently come to work in Western Ukraine. After he was suspended as a member of the central committee he left Selrob-Right and became the leader of a third movement, independent of both factions, with the ultimate aim of overcoming the split and reuniting the two sides. He called his organization Selrob-Unity, but concentrated his attacks solely on the Right, which he said opposed reunification.[11] Still, he was less hated by the Right than was Valnytsky, and the rank and file of the Right was wavering. He thus became the leader of a new and, in some sense, neutral movement.

The PSP-Left, Selrob-Left and Durdella's group formed an electoral bloc and put forward a slate of candidates that received position number nineteen under the name of Selrob-Unity. Selrob-Right, however, appealed to the Polish authorities and forced the bloc to give up this name.[12] The rightists declared that Selrob-Left was simply operating under the new name, which violated election law. Thus the bloc reassumed the name Selrob-Left, but used this denunciation by the Shumskyists as another argument in the factional struggle.

On 4 February, Vasylkiv and Turiansky sent a letter to the European Bureau of the Comintern on behalf of the Politburo. They proposed the following conditions for achieving unity:

1. The cessation of all actions against the so-called Shumskyists, since Shumsky was not guilty of nationalism;
2. Recognition that "the line of the CP(B)U Central Committee and the CPP Central Committee on the question of Selrob" is a capitulation to the nationalist deviation of the People's Will;
3. Annulment of all Comintern actions against the CPWU including the expulsion of Maksymovych from the central committee;
4. Initiation of a discussion of Shumskyism in the party to be summarized and closed by a party congress;
5. Co-ordination of a joint election effort with the central committee of the CPP (in the spirit of the Vasylkivist slate of 25 January) regardless of whether the other conditions for unity were accepted.[13]

This was more a call to arms than a proposal for rapprochement. Though the letter was sent after they already had a separate slate of candidates, the Vasylkivists might have attempted to normalize relations by not fielding their own candidates but, instead, urging their followers to vote for the official Communist slate as was done several months later in Volhynia. Such a tactic at a time when they were engaged in a struggle for what they considered a correct line made no sense.

Finally, in the latter half of February, the Ninth Plenum of the Comintern Executive stated that "the splinter group, by creating a separate party and by fielding its own slate of candidates, has either consciously or unconsciously submitted to the directives of Piłsudski, who is pursuing a policy of smashing the opposition in Poland ... has effected a split in Selrob and has begun to fight the Comintern on all fronts." The executive declared that the group's political platform consisted of nationalism, a campaign against the Soviet Union and Soviet Ukraine, a bloc with Ukrainian bourgeois democracy (*sic!*), and abandonment of the call for the confiscation of land (*sic!*), and had thus been transformed into a weapon of Polish imperialism, that mortal enemy not only of the proletariat, but of the entire Ukrainian people. "In view of this the Executive Committee of the Comintern, considering the actions of the splinter group to be an open betrayal of the proletarian revolution, has decided to expel this group from the Communist International." The executive committee summoned the Ukrainian proletariat and peasantry to struggle against this group of renegades.[14] Moreover it published the text of the proclamation in many languages and sent a copy to all members of the CPWU.[15]

Henceforth, the chief concern of the Communist press in Western Ukraine was to inform the electorate who represented the Comintern and who was a "traitor." Remarkably, the legal press of Selrob-Right did not report the expulsion of the CPWU leadership, but reported the entire conflict as a mere dispute with the Russophiles.

The Elections to the Sejm—Statistical Summary

The factional struggle before and during the elections was so intense that conspiratorial principles were sometimes forgotten, a circumstance the police availed themselves of to make many arrests. Each faction accused the other of dishonesty and deceit during the elections. Although it is difficult to identify distortions resulting from the actions of the police, a statistical analysis of the elections is possible, though difficult, since the police records contain information on invalidated votes cast for "subversive" parties. It is impossible, however, to establish the number of Ukrainian votes cast for Polish parties and the number of non-Ukrainian votes cast for Ukrainian parties. In the first case there could only be votes cast for the Non-Party Bloc for Co-operation with the Government. Given the national solidarity of West Ukrainians we can assume that these votes would be few, would be distinct from the general Ukrainian vote and thus have little importance. In the second case—the non-Ukrainian votes for Ukrainian parties—only the CPWU slate would figure largely. This was not, however, the chief representative of its camp and the number of votes cast for it (from 0.1 per cent to 2.0 per cent) precludes the possibility of significant error.

The statistical table on opposite page is based on the published[16] and unpublished material of the Ministry of Internal Affairs. It reflects in general outline the relative influence of political parties among Ukrainians during the elections of 4 May 1928 in Western Ukraine and adjacent areas. To the general total of Ukrainian votes the author has added the votes of the Russophiles and Old Ruthenians since the mass base of this movement was composed of Ukrainians who did not know Russian. Thus the movement did not develop on an ethnic principle—the native Russians in it were an insignificant minority—but on the basis of cultural-political sympathies.

The table does not show the total number of Ukrainian votes in the Chełm region and Polissia because slate number eighteen for the Bloc of National Minorities in these areas was ethnically mixed, whereas in Western Ukraine proper number eighteen was almost exclusively (Galicia) or predominantly (Volhynia) a Ukrainian slate.

As a result of the elections, the Shumskyists (Selrob-Right) elected three deputies from Volhynia (Stepan Volynets, Ivan Fedoruk and Adriian Seniuk) and one from Polissia (Maksym Chuchmai). The Left won one seat in the Lviv region (Valnytsky) and two in Polissia (Mykhailo Kham and Ivan Khrutsky, the latter being a Belorussian candidate). The very small number of seats won compared to the number of votes cast for the pro-Communist slate was due to the fragmentation caused by the split. The success of the Ukrainian Labour Party, which took 4 per cent of the vote in Galicia and won one seat in the Sejm, was also a result of the peculiar situation in the Communist movement, whereby this pro-Soviet and liberal group enjoyed the support of Soviet diplomacy.

The CPWU and Selrob-Left won an absolute victory over their rivals in Eastern Galicia only in Lviv; elsewhere the vote was divided evenly at thirty-one thousand each. On the other hand, it can be stated categorically that the efforts of Selrob-Right to portray its opponents as Russophiles failed. A large number of Ukrainian peasants voted for Selrob-Left. The decisive win for the Shumskyists in Volhynia arose from the disqualification of the Left slate (number nineteen) in Kovel (district number thirty-seven)[17] and, as described at the Third CPWU Congress, by a temporary loss of communication with the area.[18] In fact, this "temporary loss" lasted until 1930.[19] Moreover, the Shumskyist camp got a substantial number of non-Ukrainian votes from PSP-Left followers, for example in the Przemyśl region,[20] and owed its success in Polissia mainly to an ethnically mixed slate (a Belorussian candidate had first place on the slate).[21] Of those who would have voted for the invalidated Communist slate, thirteen proably ended up voting for the Shumskyists.[22] However, a significant number of Ukrainians in this area also supported Selrob-Left[23] (Durdella's group was not active here). In general both Communist

Notes

[1] If only a page number is given, the source used was a publication prepared by the Nationalities Division of the Ministry of Internal Affairs: *Mniejszości narodowe w wyborach do Sejmu i Senatu w r. 1928* (Warsaw, 1928).

[a] See K. Rzepecki and T. Rzepecki, *Sejm i Senat 1928–1933* (Poznań, 1928), 106.

[b] It was difficult to separate from the total of invalidated votes all the Ukrainian votes, especially invalidated votes for UNDU. But since the total number of votes for UNDU was large, the invalidated votes for this party do not substantially affect the relative numbers. Invalidated Ukrainian votes for the left-wing slates were, it appears, rather thoroughly documented by the Ministry of Internal Affairs; therefore their presentation in the table should be, in essence, exhaustive.

[c] According to M. Popov, about seven thousand votes were given to the invalidated slate 13 in Stryi as a form of demonstration. This is confirmed by no other source. See M. Popov [Lovytsky], "Dovetsky borotbu do kintsia," *Nasha pravda*, no. 4–5 (1928): 1.

[d] In Volhynia votes for the Bloc of National Minorities (slate 18) came overwhelmingly from Ukrainians as well as Jews and Germans. See *Mniejszości*, 254. Thus, to estimate the number of specifically Ukrainian votes, I reduced the total number of votes for slate 18 by 15.2 per cent. (According to religious statistics for 1931, the proportion of Ukrainians to Germans and Jews in Volhynia was 84.8:15.2.)

[e] Here Selrob-Right formed a block with Poalei-Zion-Left.

[f] Here Selrob-Left and PSP-Left voted for slate 39, "The Polish-Ukrainian Union of Workers and Peasants."

factions took second place behind UNDU among Ukrainians in Lviv, and in the Galician countryside fell back to third place behind UNDU and the USRP-USDP bloc.[24] In Volhynia the revolutionary left remained the strongest Ukrainian political current, though the influence of right-wing parties had begun to penetrate this Communist stronghold for the first time. On the average in Western Ukraine, one out of four or five Ukrainians and in Volhynia almost one in two Ukrainians voted for the Communist slate.

In terms of the factional struggle the results of the elections could not have pleased the Shumskyists. Their small victory—at the beginning of the dispute before their opponents had succeeded in mobilizing their supporters—was no guarantee of future success.

The Position of the Communist Camp on the Split

After the elections the Communists launched a frontal attack on the opposition. A new party leadership was formed for the CPWU. During the split Sochacki was head of the party. The CP(B)U delegated Adam Kaufman of the CPP as secretary of the central committee and sent Leon Kotowicz-Klonowicz (K. Winiarski) to work in the Secretariat. Mykola Popov (Lovytsky), a well-known historian and ideologue of the CP(B)U, was added to the Politburo. The role of Aleksander and particularly Sukhy grew after the split, but they were not given key positions. Of the central committee members only Bartolomii Kopach remained. Fedir Bei and Pavlo Ladan, who were out of the area at the time of the split, found themselves in the background. Of those Ukrainians who were in opposition to the Vasylkivists during the disputes of 1920–2 and took a pro-CPP position, only Myron Zaiachivsky (I. Kosar) and Hryhorii Ivanenko (Baraba) were permitted to remain in the party. The latter was leader of the CPWU for the next six years.

The split, its causes and the ideology of the secessionists occupied the attention of the Communist camp. In the CPP, the minority defended the view that the Vasylkivists had always been characterized by "a behaviour typical of nationalists, not of Communists—and this has permeated all their activity,"[25] or took the more extreme position that they had "subordinated Communism to nationalism...they reflected Ukrainian petty-bourgeois sentiments."[26] In brief, the Vasylkivists had always been nationalists, but had only now been unmasked. They had managed to hide their true colours for so long, the minority explained, because the Polish party was cut off from its Ukrainian comrades. The minority even hinted that part of the blame for the failure to expose the Vasylkivists belonged to "our Ukrainian comrades from the Soviet side,"[27] probably with Skrypnyk in mind.

The majority maintained that in the past, the secessionists represented Bolshevism or "tended toward Bolshevism"[28] and only under the influence of contemporary events had they reverted "to the position from which they had come to the revolutionary movement."[29] Leon Purman said that the Vasylkivists "came to us with demands in the national question, were educated in the CPP and the Comintern, subordinated themselves to Bolshevism and, despite resistance, submitted to re-education. But ultimately we were not able to assimilate them."[30] Purman stressed, however, that the mechanical solutions constantly proposed by the minority were not correct. If the party had managed to keep such people as Skrypa and Durdella within its ranks, it was in spite of the minority. Only in the final period when the Vasylkivists had resolved to separate, Purman said, was it necessary to act more energetically.

A similar difference of opinion emerged in the CP(B)U at the party plenum held on 12–16 March 1928. Zatonsky evidently applied his Struvist theory to the Vasylkivists and his listeners thought he was saying that the Vasylkivists had never been authentic Communists and that their defection should have been foreseen.[31] Other, perhaps less experienced activists were even harsher in their judgment of the affair. "In Western Ukraine," one said, "there is no Communist movement.... All this time the nationalist bourgeoisie has been dominant there, masking itself with Communist slogans.... The treason of the CPWU Central Committee merely brought to light what had always been present."[32]

Skrypnyk and Kaganovich opposed such views. Taking up the example of Struve, the general secretary of the CP(B)U stated that the author of the first Russian social democratic manifesto was sincere both in taking and abandoning a revolutionary position. His betrayal could not be explained by hypocrisy or by his political past any more than the common political past of Louis Frossard and Marcel Cachin could explain why the first betrayed revolutionary Marxism while the second remained faithful to it.[33] Skrypnyk espoused similar views. A few months later at the Third Congress of the CPWU, he attacked the view that the Vasylkivists were a crypto-Petliurite group: "If such an explanation is given we free ourselves of the need to seek other causes, and so we merely replace social relations...with banal subjective causes, with the particular traits of a group of persons. These explanations are simple, but their very simplicity—demanding no further social analysis of what has occurred and is occurring...proves that they are mistaken."[34]

The resolution accepted by the plenum of the central committee of the CP(B)U stated only in passing that the CPWU leaders had "under new conditions reverted to their nationalist past" and finally "had lost the correct line." This was an expression, though hardly firm and equivocal, of the views of Skrypnyk and Kaganovich.[35] Not everyone was convinced by this argument. In the Comintern Dmytro Manuilsky adopted the minority view of the CPP,[36] which became increasingly pervasive and was eventually completely victorious. This was due in part to the general ideological tendency of the period and in part to the effectiveness of the methods of political struggle then employed. Franciszek Grzelszczak put it quite frankly: In order to "kill that group politically," it was necessary not to concede that it was even 1 per cent correct. This, according to the minority faction, was the essence of Leninist tactics.

Among the Polish activists, Jerzy Sochacki made the most comprehensive analysis. He published a pamphlet in which he synthesized the views of the minority and the majority.[37] He recalled that at the beginning of the 1920s all Ukrainian society had revolted against the Polish occupation, and that disenchantment with the West and pro-Soviet sympathies prevailed. This was particularly true of the left-wing petty bourgeoisie. It was on the crest of this revolutionary tide that "the present group of secessionists came to the party."[38] Sochacki admitted that the "Vasylkiv-Turiansky group in large measure expressed the mood of the West Ukrainian countryside,"[39] thereby increasing its value in the eyes of the CPP and Comintern, which were eager to win such people for communism. He argued further that the Vasylkivists had never been true Communists and enumerated their many "sins": their joint boycott with the Ukrainian right of the 1922 elections and their simultaneous rejection of co-operation with the CWPP; the planning of a separatist uprising in Eastern Galicia; and their inability to win the support of the urban proletariat, though they were anxious to do so. The Vasylkivists, he noted, had defended their separatism with a "mafia-like" policy of breaking up those local organizations that threatened their monopoly over the population.

Sochacki's main point was that the Vasylkivists had subordinated the class struggle to the national question. For them the class struggle of the proletariat was only a means of mobilizing the masses to fight for national freedom.[40] To prove his point he cited the statement from the party press: "Ukrainian nationalism will die a natural death since there is no Ukrainian bourgeoisie."[41] The statement perceived the latter as the only class that would have an interest in the creation of a national state on a capitalist basis. Sochacki also made use of Vasylkiv's article, "Natsionalne vyzvolennia a ukrainske dribnomishchanstvo" (National Liberation and the Ukrainian Petty Bourgeoisie) mentioned above. He noted correctly that this article developed these same thoughts.[42] Clearly the CPWU had not perceived or had not appreciated class differences, and from the notion that there was no Ukrainian bourgeoisie, it had apparently concluded that the entire Ukrainian people was essentially revolutionary. Sochacki pointed out that the practical results of this theory could be seen in the desire for a "common national front," in the boycott of the 1922 elections to the Sejm, in the tolerance of Ukrainian nationalism,[43] in the appeals to the national feelings of the Ukrainian intelligentsia to mobilize them against capital, which in Western Ukraine was foreign capital, and in the use of such concepts as "national interest" and "national honour," which were alien to the revolutionary left. Sochacki also interpreted Vasylkiv's article,"KPZU i druhyi Zizd KPRP"[44] (The CPWU and the Second CWPP Congress), which demanded "political and organizational autonomy in local Ukrainian and Belorussian problems," as a specific application of the slogan "Ukraine for the Ukrainians," which found its practical expression in organizational separatism.

Sochacki's arguments deserve some comment. The existence or non-existence of a Ukrainian bourgeoisie would not be easy to establish statistically. In tsarist Russia there was no lack of industrialists of Ukrainian descent, like Mykhailo Tereshchenko, a member of the Provisional Government in Petrograd, but virtually none were active politically on behalf of Ukrainian interests and the majority did not consider themselves Ukrainians. Capitalists and large landowners were not represented among the creators of the Central Rada and Petliura's movement. To quote the activist, Domski, whose views were quite dissimilar to those of Vasylkiv: "In Ukraine and especially in Western Belorussia the Polish bourgeoisie does not permit the creation of possessing classes from among the native populace—the possessing classes, the bourgeoisie and large landowners there are to this day Polish."[45] Dłuski made similar statements.[46] This view was widespread among the Polish revolutionary left in the early 1920s. Zatonsky also said that capitalism was not native to Ukraine; in a speech at a Komsomol plenum in 1926 he declared that "there was, it is true, no Ukrainian bourgeoisie comparable to the Russian, Polish or Jewish bourgeoisie, but there was a place for it, which it could have taken in accordance with all the laws of political economy. There is still a place for it."[47]

Vasylkiv's position was not so different from those cited above. He did not maintain that Ukrainian nationalism would disappear altogether, but thought that the chief aim of that nationalism, an independent Ukrainian bourgeois state, was unrealizable owing to a lack of the social force necessary to bring it about.[48] His dominant theme was that in the new conditions only the proletariat could effectively lead the people in their struggle for liberation. Sochacki's claim that the CPWU leaders put national goals before social ones is not entirely convincing, especially after the May putsch. But in relation to the previous period the accusation is more credible. If, despite its subordination to social criteria, the national question was treated to some extent independently, and was moreover a factor in the mobilization of the masses to revolutionary action, then it was presumably necessary to appeal to the patriotic sentiments of the petty bourgeoisie and intelligentsia in their own language with arguments they could understand. Julian Brun, for example, did this in his book, *Stefana Żeromskiego tragedia pomyłek*. The limits of this policy were usually determined by the experience and traditions of the party leadership and the Comintern, both of which had always been convinced that the Vasylkivists were tainted with nationalism. In fact, the CPWU was visibly more national in its work, language and attitude than the CPP or the average Comintern section. Many in the CPP thought that there were nationalist elements in their Ukrainian comrades from the beginning of the West Ukrainian party's existence.[49] (This feeling began to wane after May 1926 during the period of close co-operation with the CPP majority.) Some Ukrainian members, however, also shared this view, chiefly Volhynians like Hryhorii Ivanenko and Nestor Khomyn who had been pushed into the background or out of the party during the Vasylkivist ascendancy. Thus in anti-Vasylkivist circles Sochacki's pamphlet met with approval. The general opinion was that the Vasylkivists had no answer for nine-tenths of the accusations made in it.

Among the Ukrainians who made extensive criticisms of Shumskyism were Ie. Hirchak in the CP(B)U and Serhii Vikul,[50] a member of the CPWU residing in Kharkiv and editor of the party press. Vikul perceived the cause of the CPWU leadership's lapse as the Drahomanovian ideology, which it had never fully succeeded in overcoming. For it was Drahomanov, Vikul recalled, who had advanced the concept of the non-capitalist character of the Ukrainian people and had concluded that Ukrainians, by nature, were inclined toward socialism. Drahomanov thought that if a Ukrainian was not a socialist it was because he had not thought the matter through or had not studied sufficiently. According to Vikul, the leadership of the CPWU had retained this view.[51]

The reaction to the split in the left-centre Russian emigre circles (Mensheviks, Bund and Russian SRs) was similar to that of those Communists who were more favourably disposed toward the Vasylkivists. They did not see the Vasylkivists as crypto-Petliurites, but rather as a group "brought to Communism on a national programme."[52]

The Vasylkivists were extremely sensitive about their political origins (the principal leaders had come from the IRSD) and reacted strongly to any belittlement of their international pedigree even on the part of Skrypnyk, to whom they were usually more deferential.[53] But there was much truth in the statements of Skrypnyk and others who stubbornly maintained that the Vasylkivists' origins lay in the national movement. This was evident not only from biographical facts (their service in Petrushevych's Galician Army, participation in the Polish-Ukrainian War and the USDP past of many members) but also in their moral-political stance and enormous sensitivity to the national question. The anti-Shumskyists made wide use of Lenin's pre-revolutionary thought, which stressed the ideological and organizational necessity of international unity in the workers' movement, while the Western Shumskyists ignored Lenin's earlier conclusions and appealed to his last letters[54] and the resolutions of the Tenth and Twelfth Congresses of the RCP(B), which stressed nationalization and meeting national demands.

Considering the Vasylkivists' organizational separatism, we should note that in comparison to the CPWB the Ukrainian party was undoubtedly more independent. Did this organizational distinctiveness exceed the statutory norm of party autonomy? In practice the Communist movement was centralist and, regardless of statutory definitions, deviations toward centralism were more tolerated than others. Thus the CPP leadership distrusted the relative autonomy of the CPWU regardless of existing statutory norms.

Another question posed by the supporters of the CPP is more difficult to answer. Why, they asked, did the split occur precisely at a time when Ukrainianization of the towns, the party and the state apparatus in Soviet Ukraine was making its greatest progress and the rapid development of Ukrainian culture was beyond question? The Vasylkivists pointed to such events as the expulsion of Ukrainian activists from the non-Bolshevik left, but these were far from the rule in the CP(B)U, as indicated by many facts, statistical data,[55] and even statements of Ukrainian emigre observers from the nationalist camp. The Vasylkivists themselves stated that the development of Ukrainian culture was outpacing Ukrainianization of the party and state. Also, the situation in previous years (1923–4) had been much worse. Why, then, did the split come in this period?

The Galician Ukrainians, including the Communists, were always more nationally oriented. Unlike their eastern and northern (Volhynian) compatriots they were not bilingual in Russian and Ukrainian and had never adopted Russian culture. They had learned Russian only in the course of their revolutionary activity and had never really mastered it. Some, arriving in the capital, Kharkiv, had some amusing difficulties making themselves understood.[56] More than other Ukrainians, they had, from the establishment of Soviet Ukraine, been predisposed to perceive Soviet Ukrainian reality through Shumsky's eyes. For them Ukrainianization was only the beginning of a difficult process which had to be defended and supported. The statements of Turiansky and Vasylkiv concealed far-reaching demands for nationalization and a quite different concept of the legal status of the Ukrainian republic than that which actually existed. Finally the appointment of Kaganovich as head of the CP(B)U at the beginning of Ukrainianization shook their faith in the party's sincerity to undertake the new course.

The factional struggle of the Vasylkivists produced their obstinacy, one-sidedness and excesses. It was responsible also for their fault-finding, suspiciousness, and extravagant criticism of Lunacharsky, Bedny and finally the CPP. The attitude of the Vasylkivists toward the Polish question is a separate problem. Theoretically the Ukrainian Communists agreed completely with the need to modernize the CPP's position on the national question and eradicate the last vestiges of the SDKPL ideology. In practice, however, the Vasylkivists feared the nationalization of the Polish party. At the Fourth Conference, we recall, Vasylkiv began by approving efforts to reformulate the Polish national question, but then thwarted all actions in this direction. He was unable to explain exactly what he meant by the phrase "defending the present independence of Poland." In fact, he denied the need for Polish Communists to defend the independence of their country prior to the socialist revolution. The Vasylkivists accused the Poles of nationalism, but never informed the Polish minority living in Western Ukraine what its future would be after the union of Western with Soviet Ukraine. They were immensely jealous of and disposed to comment negatively on any hint of Polish-Soviet rapprochement even in the areas of literature and art.[57] But one must not make judgments hastily: national-social relations in the *Kresy* were extremely complicated. On the one hand the Poles were the oppressors, while on the other their own national existence was threatened. This posed a difficult theoretical problem. The CPWU later tried to solve the matter, but invariably met with opposition from within the party and the censure of the unfortunate author of the solutions.[58]

The Third Congress of the CPWU and Post-Congress Disputes

From 21 June to 8 July 1928 the Third Congress of the CPWU was held in Soviet Ukraine. Delegates represented 629 party members. Before the split the party had numbered 1,743 members, not counting those in prison.[59] Popov, Skrypnyk, Hirchak and Khvylia represented the CP(B)U. Together with Sochacki, they gave the main reports on the political situation.

In his analysis of the political past of the Vasylkivists, Popov followed Sochacki's interpretation closely. He elaborated on Shumsky, and compared his views to those of Trotsky (petty-bourgeois ideological origins, the demand for "super industrialization," attacks on the party apparatus).[60] He also stated that the Vasylkivists had premeditated the split in the CPWU. As evidence of this Popov cited the removal of the editorial office of *Nasha pravda* to Berlin, a series of factional meetings and the fact that Shumsky had warned the editors of *Svitlo* of the coming split.[61] Popov did not mention similar moves by Sochacki and Kotsiubynsky or the December conference of the minority.

Skrypnyk did not indulge in polemics, but listed Vasylkiv's errors, declaring that they were a result of Vasylkiv's distrust and disparagement of the Polish party. Nonetheless, Vasylkiv had shown himself willing to listen to criticism and even to change his position. Suspecting that he might be held partially responsible for the position of the Vasylkivists, Skrypnyk assured the delegates that it had been "his duty to be the first to expose Shumsky"[62] and that he had condemned the secessionists in the CPWU with the utmost severity.[63] The conflict with the secessionists, Skrypnyk said, was essentially a dispute over whether the national policy in Soviet Ukraine required "revolution or reform."[64] There had been errors in implementing the policy, but criticism of these errors, in Skrypnyk's opinion, would not have led to a split. But the Shumskyists sought a total change in the party line, and only for tactical reasons did they acknowledge the achievements of the CP(B)U in the area of Ukrainianization. Skrypnyk defended Zatonsky's thesis that the Russian proletariat was generally free of chauvinism despite its errors on the Ukrainian question. In the Donbas region, for example, what was sometimes taken to be an anti-Ukrainian posture was really nothing more than an attachment to Russian culture. It was necessary to build Ukrainian culture, Skrypnyk insisted, not because it was Ukrainian, but because it was inseparable from the process of socialist construction in the country.[65]

All CP(B)U activists commented on the situation in Soviet Ukraine. They cited data on the rapidly growing number or predominance of Ukrainians at all levels of government, and statistics on the growing number of publications in Ukrainian. They denied charges that the foundation of Ukrainianization was "bureaucratic" and pointed out that such a problem could not be solved quickly. They admitted that the proletariat of the country remained Russian, but, as Hirchak explained, the national policy in the first days of Soviet power had not been undertaken "in a Leninist spirit." In 1920–1, and even in 1923–4 "very responsible workers" of Ukraine took a position, which would later be called a Russian "nationalist deviation."[66] "The party cured itself" of this problem "in the course of struggle," but Russian great power chauvinism remained a "great threat" which the party would have to overcome. The greatest falsehood advanced by the Shumskyists, the CP(B)U delegates maintained, was the accusation that the CP(B)U did not fight this threat resolutely, or that its leaders had themselves succumbed to Russian nationalism.[67]

Skrypnyk also took up a polemic with Volobuiev. He stated that the industrial potential of Ukraine was 20 per cent and its capital base was 25 per cent of that of the Soviet Union. Ukraine was better armed and was developing faster than the other republics because approximately

20 per cent of investments were being made there.[68] New sugar mills were being established not only in Russia (Volobuiev had written about this) but also in Kirghizia and Kazakhstan, where the raw material had long been produced. Yet Ukrainian nationalists and "Communists with a tinge of nationalism" like Volobuiev, the Shumskyists and Vasylkivists, complained that Ukraine was losing its monopoly in that area.[69]

A mood of implacable enmity toward the leaders of the splinter group prevailed at the congress. Those who wavered (Popel-Iurchenko and Sirko) were removed from work in the CPWU, and the CPP Central Committee majority was reminded that it "had dealt too gently with the leaders of the CPWU."[70] Other speakers, like Kopach, warned of increasing an atmosphere of suspicion in the party, citing CPWU member and follower of the CPP minority, Enzel Stup, as one who contributed to such an atmosphere.[71]

The news that Valnytsky had been accepted as a member of the Communist party elicited strong objections from the congress delegates.[72] Sochacki defended the decision and reminded the delegates that the new member had long collaborated with the party and assured them that this did not mean that Valnytsky would lead Selrob. The decision held in spite of the strong antipathy of the Ukrainian party membership toward the former "leader of the Russophiles."

The congress defined a general course of action intended to isolate the Vasylkivists politically and cut them off from the party masses. A programmatic innovation was a chapter of the resolution concerning "work among the national minorities in Western Ukraine,"[73] i.e., among Jewish and Polish workers. It contained a plan to attract the Polish workers by calling for the defence of Poland's independence, which was threatened by the country's growing subordination to foreign capital. The resolution stated that the CPWU, like the CPP, stood for "the independence of a workers' and peasants' Poland" and that it would work for such a Poland by struggling against the fascist government and through the socialist revolution.[74] Their treatment of this problem resembled that of the Fourth CPP Conference, but was more moderate in tone.[75] Otherwise, there were no significant changes in the CPWU programme, which retained the demand for annexation to Soviet Ukraine.

The following new party leaders were elected to the central committee: Adam (Kaufman), secretary; Andrij Cywiński (Piotr Zaleski), Emil (Rozenbusz), Hrabovy (Mykola Pavlyk), Herman (Enzel Stup), Klemens (Leon Kotowicz), Konrad (Jerzy Czeszejko-Sochacki), Kovalsky (Bartolomii Kopach), Kosar (Myron Zaiachivsky), Lovytsky (Mykola Popov), Mavtii (Iavorsky), Roman (V. Furer), Rudolf (Andrii Stetsko), Sukhy (Natan Shapiro), Zalevsky (Mykola Kulyk). Alternates were Borys (Durdella?), Hutsul (?), Ivaniv (?), Jerzy (Ozjasz Szechter), Kazik

(Chruściel?), Leonid (Oleksa Kozhan?), Orlovsky (Fedir Bei), Petro (Sozont Bukatchuk), Stryikis (?) and Vasyl (Jan Zarwa).[76]

The congress did not achieve complete unity. It unanimously condemned the secessionists, but even in the condemnation one could perceive certain differences in emphasis on national and political problems. The influence of the CP(B)U on the West Ukrainian party weakened, while that of the CPP increased. The latter party, however, continued to be beset by factional strife which precluded a united approach in policy. Therefore after the congress there soon arose divisions within the CPWU which, with some reservations, we might call factions. They were as follows:

1. In the first group were Adam Kaufman, the new secretary of the central committee, earlier a leader of the CPP organization in Lódź and member of the CPP majority; Leon Kotowicz Klonowicz, who had come from Kharkiv and sympathized with the CPP majority; and Roman Werfel (pseudonym, Gert), deputy secretary of the UCY WU Central Committee,[77] a follower of the CPP majority and participant in its factional conference.[78]
2. The second group included Bartolomii Kopach, a member of the central committee and up to the split in Gdańsk, a Vasylkivist; and Andrii Shakh (pseudonym Nechui), a member of the central committee. We may call its members Skrypnykists; like Skrypnyk they sympathized with the CPP majority and were prepared to support it in a factional struggle.
3. The third group included Enzel Stup (pseudonym Herman), of the central committee; Izrael Sapfir (pseudonym Dolek); Ivan Blakytny, who signed himself "B" and was a follower of the CPP minority.
4. This, the most numerous group, was led by J. Czeszejko-Sochacki and had no clear allegiances. It included central committee members and alternates, Matvii Iavorsky, Mykola Pavlyk, Emil Rozenbusz and Ozjasz Szechter.

Each of these groups had followers among the rank-and-file party members. The central committee received letters complaining of disunity and factional meetings but, being divided itself, did not respond effectively.[79]

Two events hastened the final confrontation. The minority faction took power in the CPP; and the CPWU leaders were arrested by the police and brought to trial, and there explicitly stated their attitude toward the national question. The success of the police was probably due to the CPWU's factional struggles with the Shumskyists during the 1928 elections. The arrests were made between 1928 and 1929. The trial of the so-called "little central committee" began in March 1929 at the *województwo* court in Lviv. There were twenty-one defendants, including the following members of the central committee: Kaufman, Stetsko, Shakh, Szechter, Pavlyk, Stup, Bruno Korman, Ievhen Kushko, Kopach, Wiktor Chruściel, Bukatchuk and Szymon Grün. For lack of evidence Kopach and Stetsko were released.[80] The defendants declared themselves communists by conviction, but denied that they were members of the party.

The prosecutor accused the defendants of being anti-Polish and of betraying their own nationality by their membership in the Communist party which, in his opinion, was incompatible with fulfillment of one's patriotic and civic duties. He cited, as his prime example, Adam Kaufman, the son of a rich Polish businessman and a lawyer by profession. Kaufman, the central figure in the trial, was unable to counter the prosecutor's arguments. He declared that as a young student he had fought for "a peoples' Poland" in 1918 and 1920 (the Polish-Soviet war) because he wanted to serve his country.[81] The wound he received in the battle of Radzymin was the best proof of that. But he no longer wanted to serve the kind of Poland that had been established; instead his thoughts were for the hundreds of thousands of workers who were driven by unemployment and poverty to leave their country for a life of misery in France and Germany, and the hundreds of thousands of workers' children dying of illness in damp basements. Such a situation, he said, was the fault of the possessing classes and it was against these classes that he wanted to fight. Thus he was a communist. Communism arose from the necessities of life. The most modern Polish writers, like Żeromski[82] and Kaden Bandrowski,[83] treated the problems of communism in their works. Two other defendants spoke in a similar tone. Bruno Korman recalled that German Communists were fighting against the construction of new warships, which would surely be used in a war against Poland. Wiktor Chruściel (a member of the PSP-Left) recalled his participation in the war for Lviv in 1918, but unlike his comrades, he was not able to formulate his thoughts lucidly.[84]

Under the influence of the centralist tendencies connected with the collectivization campaign that commenced in the Soviet Union at this time, the new "majority" leadership of the Polish party was ultra-leftist and strongly anti-nationalist. Thus the reaction of the CPWU leaders to the expressions of national feeling at the Lviv trial was decidedly negative. In a special appeal to all party members the central committee explained that the statements made by the three defendants were characterized by Polish nationalism. The defendants were appealing to "Polish interests, the struggle for Poland and even to Polishness in order to justify and explain [their] revolutionary activity." Also unacceptable to the CPWU leadership were the defendants' references to the "fascist" Kaden Bandrowski and the "bourgeois writer" Żeromski. German battleships were being built for war not against Poland, but against the Soviet Union. Moreover, to call the wars of 1918 and 1920 "wars for a peoples' Poland" was "infuriating,"[85] since even then the nationalistic nature of these wars was clear.

Clearly, these criticisms were unfair and lacking in substance. The defendants referred to their participation in these wars only to show their disinterested service to their country. Nevertheless, the verdict was harsh. While still in prison Adam Kaufman was expelled from the party. He attempted suicide (he slashed his wrists while his fellow prisoners were taking a walk) but was saved. The affair did not end there, however, since Kaufman had more followers in the party than he supposed.

In March 1930 a letter to Kaufman and unnamed comrades was smuggled into prison.[86] The letter contained information about internal party affairs and factional moves which, the letter stresses, "I was authorized by you" to undertake. "The last plenum has given us a decisive victory on the internal front," the letter continues, referring to the fact that at the plenum, which took place after the removal of the "majority" in the CPP, most of the majority's followers in the Ukrainian party had retained their positions. The letter said that the many obstacles on the "external front," would remain only for a few months and that it was essential "that A . . . m [Adam] pull himself together and wait. He has no need to fear, I won't bungle things or miss the opportunity." The postscript, written in Polish, repeats the contents of the letter in abbreviated form and adds "you must have strong nerves and be patient. If we are strong, and we surely will be, everything will turn out all right."[87] This letter fell into the hands not of the addressees, but of the *starosta* of the prison commune, who immediately recognized the factional content and sent it to the CPWU. An investigation revealed the author to be Kopach, who later confessed to this.

On 23 April 1930 there began a plenary session of the CPWU Central Committee. The theme of the plenum was ideological purity. The first secretary of the CPP and leader of the victorious minority faction, Julian Leński, gave one of the main reports and actively participated in discussions on membership matters. The targets of criticism were Kotowicz-Klonowicz, several persons whose identity has not been established (including a certain Eryk), Werfel, who was not present, and above all Kopach. The latter was accused of factional activity aimed at revising the party line, of having connections with the "right wing" of the CPP, and of unrepentant Shumskyism. The critics quoted his "nationalist" statement: "For non-Ukrainian comrades the Ukrainian problem is like the Chinese problem." There was a hunt for Kopach's followers, some of whom were named, but no one would admit to collaboration with Kopach, who was soon ostracized. Skrypnyk also condemned Kopach, although earlier, after the expulsion of the Vasylkivists, he had held long conversations with him and evidently saw him as a political hopeful. In his report Skrypnyk also stressed the undisputed leadership of the CPP over the CPWU and noted that the CP(B)U saw its role as merely advisory. He also declared support for the victorious minority faction of the CPP and its leader, Leński. Such declarations of loyalty to leaders or emphasis on their special role were not customary in either the CPWU or the CPP. Now they were introduced by the delegates from the CP(B)U.

The plenum barred Sukhy from participation, since he had accused Skrypnyk of nationalism. Sukhy was sent to a non-Ukrainian part of the Soviet Union. Several months later Kopach, Kotowicz-Klonowicz and "Eryk" were transferred to the CP(B)U for disagreeing with CPWU policy,[88] but were not expelled from the party. (It is an interesting detail that when Kotowicz-Klonowicz was in Kharkiv, he stayed with Skrypnyk while waiting for accommodation to be assigned to him.) Other followers of the majority faction of the CPP were transferred to subordinate positions.

In conclusion, while the Vasylkivists were suppressed, the national problem immediately re-emerged in milder forms. This, perhaps, is witness to the depth and vitality of national feelings in this region.

The Ninth Conference of the Oppositionist CPWU and the Congress of Selrob-Right

After the split, when passions had cooled somewhat, the Vasylkivists retreated from their more extreme positions and began to modify their views. The first issue of *Nasha pravda*, published shortly after the split, understandably attacked "the Kaganovich leadership group"[89] (in unpublished letters to the Comintern they attacked the entire central committee of the CP[B]U), but they went so far as to ascribe to it diabolical motives of sabotage.[90] In the next issue of the paper, both the tone and the arguments were milder.[91] Moreover, it contained reports of the Tenth Plenum held in the latter half of 1928,[92] at which speakers had criticized some of Vasylkiv's more drastic statements. He was attacked specifically for declaring erroneous "the basic line of the CP(B)U on the national question"[93] and for suggesting that instead of a Ukrainian state a mere narrow "cultural-national autonomy" was being built in Soviet Ukraine.[94] The same issue also carried further discussions with the CP(B)U activists (Skrypnyk, Khvylia, Zatonsky, Hirchak, Popov, Mykhailo Levytsky, Volodymyr Iurynets) and with Sochacki and Vikul.

In the Shumskyist ranks disenchantment with the oppositionists' stand grew more rapidly. On 10 April 1928 a Congress of Selrob-Right directed by Volynets and Chuchmai was held in Lviv. It adopted a resolution defending both Shumsky and the CP(B)U, which, it stated, was struggling with "Ukrainian reaction."[95] From the rather unclear police reports it seems that statements of many activists contained a tone of rapprochement with the CP(B)U. Selrob-Right wanted to minimize the Shumsky affair, but remained extremely hostile to the Peoples' Will.[96] Osyp Bukshovany, a popular peasant activist (and former advocate of "sabotagism"), proposed his own draft resolution critical of the Selrob-Right leadership, but this was rejected. To the dismay of the Vasylkivists, Bukshovany broke openly with the Shumskyists in late June and joined Selrob-Unity.[97] He then returned to his native Pokuttia to work energetically and effectively against the Vasylkivists on behalf of the CPWU.

The entire Chełm organization of Selrob-Right underwent a similar change. After the congress its leaders, Stepan Makivka and P. Shcherbak, began to lean toward the CPWU and established contact with Selrob-Unity. Immediately a struggle broke out with the Selrob-Right headquarters in Lviv over the local organization, but by May most of the Chełm organization was in favour of joining Selrob-Unity.[98]

In October the final, Ninth Conference of the CPWU (Vasylkivists) was held.[99] In the face of official liquidation the party attempted once more to draw a balance sheet of the recent tragic events, its own actions and those of its rivals. In comparison with the Eighth Conference and Tenth Plenum, it introduced two new matters: an explicit declaration that the country of the Soviets and its party faced the "danger of a right-wing opportunist deviation";[100] and a perceived connection between the occurrences they had criticized and the right-wing deviation in the all-Union Communist Party (Bukharin's opposition). The conference declared that the CP(B)U was responsible for the victorious socialist revolution in Ukraine and was now the chief factor in building the socialist system. This party and not—as "many of our comrades" mistakenly held—Shumsky, was following the correct line on the national question, despite past errors.[101] The CPWU was more hostile toward the Borotbists and UCP than in the past, but remained critical of Zatonsky's view of these parties.

The conference also discussed Ukrainian nationalism, and Volobuiev's ideas. It considered correct the latter's criticism of great power tendencies in economic policy and in the bureaucratic centralization of the economy. At the same time, it charged Volobuiev with mistaking Russian nationalist tendencies for the political line of the Communist Party, like Khvyliovy. Also, the economic protectionism that Volobuiev urged for Ukraine, according to the conference, contradicted the policy of the economic centralization of the Soviet Union.[102]

The resolution adopted by the conference repeated the criticism of the CPP for its "national bolshevism" and "right-wing deviations."[103] It also outlined the political origins of the CPWU founders to refute Skrypnyk's insistence on their political nationalism.[104] Finally, with reference to the decision of the Comintern, which recognized the "CPWU-Minority" (this name was used in the resolution), the conference announced the liquidation of its own organization and appealed to all its members to join the officially recognized CPWU.[105] The last part of the announcement, in contradiction to other statements, states that the lines of the CP(B)U and CPP were "basically" correct.

In October 1929 the leader of Selrob-Right in Volhynia and deputy to the Sejm, Adriian Seniuk, announced in the press his intention to return to Selrob-Unity.[106] He took with him a large part of the Volhynian organization. For several months *Nashe slovo* printed the names of those expelled, i.e., persons who had left the Shumskyist camp and returned to the ranks of the Left. The most outstanding activists of the CPWU appealed to the Secretariat of the central committee in this matter.[107] By the middle of 1929 most of the regional organizations of the CPWU and Selrob-Right had returned to the Comintern camp. *Nashe slovo* ceased publication and the small group of former Selrob-Right leaders effectively ended their political activities. The organization formally dissolved itself on 25 December 1929.[108]

In contrast, the Shumskyist CPWU was never dissolved in fact. The name "CPWU" was dropped, but the group itself continued, publishing the *Information Bulletin of the Former CPWU-Majority*. The group intended to influence the Communist movement from without, but differences within it soon put an end to its operations.

Differences of Opinion within the Opposition group: The End of the Split

From the beginning of the split there were differences among the Shumskyist leaders. Those between Vasylkiv on the one hand and Turiansky and Kraikivsky on the other increased with the passage of time.

At the beginning of the split the leaders of the expelled group sought allies among Communist circles in the USA and Canada. Gradually, however, as the implacable attitude of the Comintern toward the Shumskyists became evident, all Communist circles turned away from them. In their search for allies, the Shumskyists may have met with German Trotskyists in Berlin. The April issue of the press organ of the (Trotskyist) Urbahns group carried a "Letter from Poland,"[109] which, it was later discovered, was written by Turiansky.[110] The letter criticized the "Stalinist-Bukharinist policy of capitulation to the NEP bourgeoisie and [its] chauvinism" and the practice of the "Stalinist group in the Central Committee of the CP(B)U under the leadership of Kaganovich."[111] As in his other articles,[112] the author cautiously defended Khristian Rakovsky, a leader of the left opposition under attack in Soviet Ukraine for the "erroneous" statements he had made on the Ukrainian question as premier of the republic (1919–22). Turiansky stressed that Rakovsky had long since corrected his errors both in theory and practice, and that rather than looking to the past, it was necessary to fight the present danger of Russian chauvinism, which had been neglected to date.

Shumskyist sympathy for the Trotskyist opposition is logical and understandable since the CPWU considered the source of both nationalisms in Ukraine (Russian and Ukrainian) to be the New Economic Policy (NEP), which revitalized the urban bourgeoisie and the kulaks. Therefore, when the Soviet Union decided to liquidate NEP and a dispute with Bukharin erupted (the second half of 1928), Turiansky and the majority of his comrades welcomed the turn of events. They quoted Stalin on the struggle against the kulaks and wrote favourably about the Sixth Congress of the Comintern. They demanded from the official CPWU a more uncompromising stance against the PSP, USDP and ULP and criticized both this party and the CPP on the basis of the most recent Comintern guidelines. The Shumskyists, however, omitted the term "social fascism," which the Comintern had introduced to describe the social democrats. Gradually the Turiansky group retreated from its defence of Shumsky, pointing out his errors. It held that the CP(B)U had begun too late to perceive the gap between the development of Ukrainian culture and the pace of Ukrainianization and considered that its fraternal duty was to point out this threat.

Such was the evolution of the views of the majority of the group led by Turiansky, but Vasylkiv's views developed in quite a different direction. He did not see the source of the difficulties and lapses in the growth of the kulaks and the bourgeoisie.[113] Since the time of Muraviev[114] the bourgeoisie in Ukraine had been crushed and the kulaks pacified. Instead, the difficulties had arisen because of the "permanent" pro-Russian stance (*rusotiapstvo*) of the CP(B)U and the fact that the party sought nothing more than national autonomy.[115] Unlike Turiansky, Vasylkiv saw that the reason for national conflicts in Ukraine lay not in class differences, but in national contradictions within the revolutionary camp. At times he stated this explicitly: "The Borotbists, the UCP and later Shumsky attempted to oppose the CP(B)U not because the kulaks were gaining strength or because Hrushevsky had become active again . . . but because of the CP(B)U's entire national policy." This, he felt, was the essence of Zatonsky's or Radchenko's[116] "leftist" opposition. Its cause was not to be found in NEP or the kulaks, but in the pro-Russian sentiments of the proletariat of Katerynoslav and Donbas which "had an interest in limiting the [rights of] Ukraine as a republic."[117]

Vasylkiv insisted that national—and not international—causes were responsible for the split in the CPWU.[118] "No matter how much we stand on our toes," said Vasylkiv, we will never reach "an international level," because our opposition is and will remain a national opposition. To Turiansky's argument that Soviet Ukraine was nevertheless developing under the direction of the "pro-Russian" CP(B)U, Vasylkiv replied that the republic was making progress "in spite of its pro-Russianism, by the force of its momentum and the very logic of socialist construction."[119] He associated negative phenomena in the Communist movement with "Stalinist policy... from which we suffered and which is [now] being carried out in Germany."[120] In Germany, he said, there had emerged "the historically formed group of [Ernst] Thälmann [and] Heinz Neumann, which took the path of ultra-leftist Ruth-Fischerism."[121] Vasylkiv defended Brandler's group (the so-called right) in Germany which opposed Comintern policy because it was fighting for "democratic, Leninist centralism in the Comintern,"[122] and it opposed the "atmosphere... which hinders consolidation of revolutionary forces in the West."[123] In contrast to his comrades, Vasylkiv blamed the Comintern and the "ultra-leftist Zinoviev" rather than Brandler's group for the defeat of the revolution in Germany in 1923.[124] He also maintained that the analysis of the Sixth Comintern Congress did not justify the ultra-leftist tactics it recommended. "We will not destroy the trust of the masses in their social democratic leaders," he said, "with screams and invective."[125] According to Vasylkiv, the new directives of the Comintern that the united front should be established "only from below" were absurd. He thought that the resolutions of the recent Comintern congress evinced a growing tendency "to cover up" its problems. He also sympathized with Bukharin's followers, but did not comment on this question. Despite his outspokenness, Vasylkiv feared complete isolation and requested tolerance and understanding, but on 20 March 1929 he was expelled from his own group.

Vasylkiv then made a final attempt to return to the party. On 10 April 1929 he wrote in a letter to the CPWU leadership that:

> From the beginning of the split I had differences with some comrade—especially Turiansky and Dresher [Kraikivsky]—in my assessment of the situation in the USSR, and in my attitude toward the all-Union CP(B) Central Committee and the Comintern. Whereas these comrades sympathized with the conclusions formulated in the platform of the [Trotskyist] opposition and in Trotsky's articles and also agreed with this opposition on several other issues [the Anglo-Russian Committee, the Chinese Revolution, the construction of socialism in one country], I have held and still hold the position that the line of the all-Union CP(B) generally, and in the struggle against the Trotskyists in particular, is correct. The opposition that we displayed toward Trotskyism as members of the

> Comintern must be maintained; there can be no question of contact or rapprochement with the opposition. I perceived that the split had been caused by the CP(B)U's superficially autonomist stance and by its erroneous policy in W[estern] U[kraine], but the above-mentioned comrades went further. They believed that we had found ourselves [as a group] outside the Comintern because of the "opportunist" and—when the struggle against rightist deviation in the all-Union CP(B) occurred—"centrist," "zig-zag" policy of the all-Union CP(B) Central Committee and the Comintern, both in the USSR and toward individual Communist parties. I did not reveal these differences earlier because as long as these comrades and their sympathizers took no action (they even announced their basic support for the all-Union CP(B) Central Committee on questions of internal Soviet policy and the Comintern), I considered it possible to co-operate with them.
>
> Now that the rejection of our latest declaration by the Politburo of the CPWU has become almost certain, these comrades have decided to form an official oppositionist group and, instead of limiting themselves as hitherto to criticism of exclusively West Ukrainian matters, have decided to criticize the policy of the all-Union CP(B) and Comintern as centrist, declaring themselves in sympathy on a number of issues with the Trotskyist opposition. They intended to protest especially the expulsion of Trotsky [from the USSR]. My position, that in accordance with our recent memorandum we make every effort to liquidate the existing split, was treated as opportunism and an ideological attempt to dissolve the group.
>
> As I disagree completely with this position—and the majority of the group supports it—I consider it impossible for me to remain in the group.
>
> Having reported briefly on the merits of my dispute I request the Politburo's permission to apply for readmission to the party.[126]

Vasylkiv's request was denied, since he had failed to derive the present ideological position of the group from its previous errors, which, the party authorities announced, was a necessary condition for readmission to the Communist movement.[127]

Vasylkiv went to Lviv and turned himself in to the authorities to serve out the sentence received in the St. George trial. In prison he was at first accepted into the prison commune, but after this was condemned by the party committee in Lviv,[128] he spent most of his sentence in isolation, shunned by his former comrades and factional rivals. When he was released, probably in the latter half of 1930, he emigrated to the Soviet Union, settling in Kharkiv where he worked in the Ukrainian Publishing House. In 1932 he was arrested. A few years later his wife, Marinka, as she was known in the party, was also arrested. She had long lived in Kharkiv under Maksymovych's care and saw her husband irregularly, because of his "nomadic" life. There is no information on the fate of their two daughters.

Vasylkiv's revelations about the internal politics of the Turiansky-Dresher group forced the latter to clarify its relationship with the Trotskyist opposition. In its press it explained that on many issues it disagreed with Trotsky. The group did not accept, for example, Trotsky's view of the trade union problem in the Soviet Union or his theory of permanent revolution. It condemned the attempts of his followers to organize strikes in the USSR. No one from the group, it said, had ever suggested subscribing to the oppositionist platform. It considered it necessary, however, to carry on discussions with the Trotskyists and subject them to authentic marxist criticism. The group also opposed the anti-Semitism that the question of Trotsky's exile had sparked.[129] Later issues of the Turiansky group's press (*Informatsiinyi biuleten* and *Kultura*) did not mention Trotskyism, and referred to the Urbahns group only in passing, as an example of "leftist panicmongering."[130]

Before he ended his political activities, Turiansky published a series of reflective articles.[131] He strongly attacked the Bukharinist movement, in which he included Zatonsky for his statement that "the kulak is no threat." Also, he took the CP(B)U side on the national question. The cardinal error of the CPWU, he said, was that while struggling against Khvyliovy "we uncritically defended Shumsky."[132] Re-examining the history of the CP(B)U, he admitted that that party was correct in the dispute with the Borotbists and the UCP, though he recalled the Bolshevik party's errors in Ukraine. He said that the UCP and, to a lesser degree, the Borotbists had transferred their (justified) hostility toward the monopolistic power of the tsars to Soviet and proletarian centralism and partly to the Russian working class, thereby revealing their nationalism. Turiansky declared that it was essential to maintain centralism during the period of revolution and socialist construction.

Turiansky called the views of Shumsky and Vasylkiv a continuation of the old UCP nationalist inclination, with the difference that Shumsky revived an old nationalism for new conditions, while Vasylkiv had never abandoned his original nationalist position. Turiansky passionately attacked Vasylkiv. At times he seemd to view him as the main source of his (Turiansky's) own failure and the bitterness of his last years. In his articles, he declared that the most pressing problem of the party was that of settling accounts with Vasylkivism, without which the Communist movement would be unable to advance. He traced Vasylkiv's politics back to Bukharin, who had postulated a long period of capitalist stabilization for Europe during which, until the next world war, there would be no prospects for revolution. Turiansky interpreted Bukharin's theory to mean that it was necessary to normalize relations with capitalism both inside and outside the country. As a representative of this deviation, Vasylkiv strove to take advantage of the suspension of the class struggle to defend the "national domain" from the Russians and Poles.

In his reflections, Turiansky recalled earlier disputes in the narrow circle of Ukrainian Communists that were unknown to the wider party membership. In these disputes Vasylkiv had "[turned] his back on Warsaw." In 1922 Rosdolsky had accused Vasylkiv of taking a UCP position and of denying the need for a single Communist party within the borders of the Polish state. Turiansky also remembered parts of resolutions adopted on Vasylkiv's initiative which he considered "provincial," such as the identification of Shumskyism and Leninism, the unwillingness to advance common slogans with the CPP or denying the need to demand a workers' and peasants' government in 1925. Given these harsh accusations, Turiansky's final definition of Vasylkivism was unexpectedly mild. He described it as: "national sensitivity, distrust, in a word, national provincialism. It is the infantile disorder of the working class of a beaten people deprived of deeper revolutionary proletarian traditions."[133] Analogies between Shumsky and Vasylkiv on the one hand and "Struvists" or "fascists" of the Dontsov type on the other, which were already appearing in the Soviet press, Turiansky rejected as absurd.

On 2 June 1930 Turiansky sent a letter to the central committees of the CPWU and CPP in the name of his group. The letter said that the former oppositionists considered all the Comintern's resolutions on the Shumsky question and the split to be correct, and that they were ready to submit to every decision of the party.[134] Attached was a list of seventy of the lesser known activists requesting readmission to the party.[135]

Thereafter, the fates of the oppositionists differed. Turiansky was in the West until 1932, when he emigrated to Moscow and worked in the publishing house of Profintern. He was arrested in 1933. Of the more outstanding leaders of the West Ukrainian party, only Mykhailo Tesliuk—because of the personal intervention of Ivanenko—was readmitted to the CPWU as a rank-and-file member. In 1932 Tesliuk went to Dnipropetrovsk, where until 1933 he taught history at the Higher School of Pedagogy.[136] Later he also was arrested. After many years in a concentration camp and in exile, both Tesliuk and Popel-Iurchenko were accorded personal rehabilitation in 1956 and party rehabilitation in 1962. Popel died in Warsaw in 1963. Maksymovych lived in other areas of the Soviet Union after 1927 and spent the years 1930–3 in Astrakhan[137] prior to his arrest. Bukshovany, Sirko and Vikul were all arrested in 1933 in the Soviet Union.

Several dozen former CPWU leaders did not go to the Soviet Union. Kraikivsky is assumed to have perished at the hands of the UPA during the war.[138] Stepan Rudyk, former editor of *Kultura*, was a member of the Trotskyist opposition in Lviv during the 1930s. With Rosdolsky's help, he published an underground Ukrainian newspaper. In late August 1939 he was arrested in Lviv. The former editor of *Svitlo*, Ivan Khaba, also belonged to the Trotskyist opposition. In 1934 he was publicly accused by members of the CPWU of collaboration with the police and committed suicide. Adam Kaufman joined a Polish Trotskyist group, but emigrated to the United States after the war.

Of all the former CPWU leaders, only Stepan Volynets went over to the Ukrainian right. In the mid-1930s, according to CPP information, he joined Dmytro Paliiv's "Front of National Unity." During the war, he helped to organize a division of the SS-Galizien and became a member of its Military Command.[139] He died in the late 1960s in Canada. Information is lacking about the fate of many other CPWU members. Thus ended the existence of the group that created and led the Communist movement for almost ten years.

In 1962 Vasylkiv and almost all the West Ukrainian Shumskyists, but not Shumsky himself, were posthumously rehabilitated.

Notes

1. Here we must mention something that happened a few days or hours before the split and had an influence on subsequent events. Popel-Iurchenko, recently appointed to the CPWU Central Committee, arrived at the Gdańsk plenum from Kharkiv and, in the name of the CP(B)U Central Committee, handed over a sizable sum of money to his comrades. When the "usurper" conference began, though he had declared that the decision of the CPP to postpone the proceedings was wrong, he submitted and took part in the pro-CPP conference (see *Nasha pravda*, no. 1–2 (1928): 110–11). When it became clear that the split was a fait accompli Popel demanded the money back from Vasylkiv and his comrades, who apparently laughed at him. Thus the Vasylkivists were provided for financially for some time. When Popel returned to Kharkiv he was called before a special commission of the CP(B)U Central Committee. After much deliberation, charges that he consciously aided the Vasylkivists were dropped.
2. This organ of the Comintern executive committee is usually referred to by its German name, WEB (Westeuropäische Büro der Kommunistischen Internationale). It had its headquarters in Berlin and had authority over European Communist parties. During this period it was probably headed by Manuilsky.
3. Resolution of the West European Bureau of the Comintern, 16 January 1928, AM CA KC PZPR, 1356/4, 54.
4. Lovytsky's (Popov's) report to the Third Congress of the CPWU, Minutes, CA KC PZPR, 165/I–3, 1: 20.
5. Some leaders of Selrob-Left were accused of having murdered Jewish communists in the past. Another time Jewish names on the joint

Selrob-Left-PSP-Left electoral slate were ridiculed. *Nashe slovo*, no. 8, 10, 18 (1928).

6. Among others, the PSP-Left in Eastern Galicia attempted to mediate the dispute to reach an understanding on the elections, but the Shumskyists retorted that it should concern itself with Polish affairs and not meddle in Ukrainian problems.
7. *Selrob*, no. 10 (1927), obituary.
8. To the executive committee of the Communist International (copies to the CPWU CC and CPP CC), Memorandum of Turiansky's group, 30 December 1930. CA KC PZPR, uncatalogued.
9. *Warszawska Informacja Prasowa (WIP), Komunikat Specjalny*, no. 3/38 (1928): 64.
10. *Nashe slovo*, no. 15 (1928): 3.
11. "Proch z kyrynnykamy i intryganamy," *Nashe slovo*, no. 6 (1928): 2; and M. Durdella, *Za iednist Selroba* (leaflet), Lviv, 23 January 1928.
12. Czeszejko-Sochacki [Bratkowski], *Na drogach nacjonalizmu*, 56.
13. Declaration to the WEB, AM CA KC PZPR 1356/13/269.
14. Resolution of the Ninth Plenum of the Comintern EC. See *Kommunisticheskii Internatsional v dokumentakh 1919–1932* (Moscow-Leningrad, 1933), 767, and *Przeciw rozbijaczom*, 78.
15. *Ibid.*, 89–94 and *Pravda*, no. 41 (1928): 2; and "Plenums des EKKI. Ausschluss der Opposition aus der KP der Westukraine," *Internationale Presse-Korrespondenz*, no. 21 (1928): 421.
16. *Mniejszości narodowe w wyborach do Sejmu i Senatu w r. 1928* (Warsaw, 1928).
17. *Ibid.*, 254.
18. See "Protokoły III Zjazdu KPZU." Lovytsky (M. Popov). CA KC PZPR, 165/I–3, 1: 22.
19. Postolowski (Walter) at the Fourth CPWU Plenum, 23 April 1930, CA KC PZPR, 165/II–25, 7.
20. *Mniejszości*, 208.
21. This assumption is based on the following data: slate number nineteen won 21 per cent of all votes cast in Polissia (*Mniejszości*, 263) while the percentage of people there giving Ukrainian as their mother tongue was 4.8 per cent (J. Tomaszewski, *Z dziejôw Polesia* [Warsaw, 1963], 24.).
22. *Mniejszości*, 267.
23. In Kobryn district, where the percentage of Ukrainians was highest (19 per cent) they won 54.4 per cent of the vote. See *Mniejszości*, 263, and Tomaszewski, *Z dziejôw Polesia*, 24.
24. The USDP, which had only recently been revived, did not have much influence.
25. Minority statement of "Marczyk" (probably a corruption of "Marcin"—Franciszek Grzelszczak) in a discussion at a meeting of the Comintern's Polish-Baltic *Landessekretariat*, 8 March 1928, AM CA KC PZPR, 1013/1, 38.

26. Czarny (Jan Paszyn), Crisis in the CPWU (article written for *Zemlia i volia*), CA KC PZPR, 1356/4/4.
27. F. Grzelszczak's statement.
28. Stefański's report at a meeting of the Polish-Baltic *Landessekretariat*, 8 March 1928, AM CA KC PZPR, 1013/1, k. 38, page 32.
29. *Ibid.*
30. *Ibid.*, 78.
31. Skrypnyk's closing statement at the plenum (13 March 1928). *Budivnytstvo*, 246 and 248.
32. *Ibid.*, 240.
33. Kaganovich's statement at the same plenum. *Nasha pravda*, no. 4–5 (1928): 123–4.
34. Skrypnyk's statement at the Third CPWU Congress published under the title "Pidsumky borotby z natsionalistychnoiu zradoiu" in his *Statti i promovy*, part 2 (Kharkiv, 1928), 2: 84.
35. *Budivnytstvo*, 251–2.
36. Meeting of the Polish-Baltic *Landessekretariat, 63.*
37. *Czeszejko-Sochacki [Bratkowski], Na drogach nacjonalizmu*, 79.
38. *Ibid.*, 7.
39. *Ibid.*, 8.
40. *Ibid.*, 10.
41. *Ibid.*, 11. This is from an editorial in *Nova kultura* no. 2–3 (1923): 1–7, entitled "Smert natsionalizmovi." The quotation is from page 6.
42. Czeszejko-Sochacki [Bratkowski], *Na drogach nacjonalizmu*, 12.
43. *Ibid.*, 13.
44. See above, chapter 2.
45. Miłaszewicz's (Domski's) report to the Third CPP Congress, Minutes, 504.
46. Dłuski's speech, *II Zjazd KPRP*, 363.
47. Quoted in Vasylkiv, "Do dzherel i prychyn suchasnoho rozlamu v KPZU," *Nasha pravda*, no. 3–8 (1928): 75.
48. In the 1930s Ukrainian capital made significant progress in Eastern Galicia in the form of co-operatives, but even then remained at an incipient stage. See M. Kravets, *Narysy robitnychoho rukhu v Zakhidnii Ukraini 1921–1934* (Kiev, 1959), 13–14.
49. See, for example, Królikowski's statements. *II Zjazd KPRP*, 358–9.
50. Serhii Vikul, originally a member of the Ukrainian Social Democratic Workers' Party and of the Central Rada, later became a Communist and a leader of the CPWU.
51. S. Vikul, "Do korinnia natsionalizmu ta oportunizmu v KPZU" in *KP(b)U pro rozbyvachiv KPZU* (Lviv, 1928), 40–1.
52. Quoted in Kuzma [Lazarkevych], "Cherez pryzmu," 49.
53. As distinct from other "right-wing" leaders in Kharkiv, Skrypnyk was described as a "centrist."
54. See, for example, *Die ukrainische Nationalfrage*, 6. Lenin's "testament," though unpublished at the time, was known to the party membership.

55. For example, among secretaries of local party committees of the CP(B)U, Ukrainians were found in the following percentages: 1923—32 per cent; 1924—34 per cent; 1925—39 per cent; 1926—44 per cent. M. Popov [N. Łowicki], "Co to jest szumskizm?," *Walka Klas*, no. 1–3 (1928): 58.
56. Interview with V. Popel-Iurchenko.
57. The Soviet consul in Lviv was condemned for expressing an interest in Polish literature and for suggesting a Polish-Soviet rapprochement in that area. On another occasion, *Svitlo* (a weekly edited by the CPWU) "calmed" its readers by saying that a scheduled Polish-Soviet scholarly meeting was merely a "gesture," for "what cultural links could exist between Polish science, permeated as it is by medieval clericalism, and Soviet science?" *Svitlo*, no. 1–2 (1925): 6.
58. See, for example, the Kotowicz-Klonowicz affair described below.
59. Adam [Kaufman], "V spravi orhanizatsiinoi polityky KPZU," *Nasha pravda*, no. 4–5 (1928): 88.
60. Lovytsky's (Popov's) report, Minutes of the Third CPWU Congress, CA KC PZPR, 165/I–3, 1: 5–39.
61. *Ibid.*, 17.
62. Skrypnyk's report. *ibid.*, 2: 87.
63. *Ibid.*, 165/I–3, 5: 49.
64. *Ibid.*, 52.
65. *Ibid.*, 58.
66. *Ibid.*, 15/I–3, 5: 25. Hirchak.
67. *Ibid.*, 36. Khvylia.
68. *Ibid.*, 8. Skrypnyk's response to the delegates' questions.
69. *Ibid.*, 7–8.
70. *Ibid.*, 19. Lovytsky.
71. *Ibid.*, 29. Kovalsky (Kopach).
72. *Ibid.*, Hrabovy (Mykola Pavlyk), 9–11; Blakytny (Ivan Iavorsky), 96; Kovalsky (Kopach), 25.
73. *Uchwały III Zjazdu KPZU* (Lviv, 1929), 78–95.
74. *Ibid.*, 86.
75. The programme's position on the Polish question did not last long. When Leon Klonowicz-Kotowicz, its chief proponent in the CPWU, attempted a few months later to justify his thesis, he met strong criticism. L. Klonowicz-Kotowicz, [K. Viniarsky], "Natsionalni menshosty na Zakhidnii Ukraini i zavdannia KPZU," *Bilshovyk Ukrainy*, no. 17, 18, 19 (1928). He was asked the question: Since Poland is an imperialist state, that is, one that exploits and suppresses other peoples, how can it be considered an exploited and downtrodden victim? In 1930 Kotowicz was condemned as a Polish national deviationist and removed from work in Poland. *Nasha pravda*, no. 5–6 (1930): 166–8.
76. Minutes of the Third CPWU Congress, 165/I–3, t. 10. Among the persons mentioned above Piotr Zaleski (pseudonyms–Andrij Cywiński, Paweł Berg)

especially deserves attention, as a person little known to Polish and foreign historiography. He was born into a Polish family in 1901 not far from Polatsk. He spent the First World War as a teenager with his family in Ukraine (Donets basin). In 1919 he began his revolutionary activity. In 1927 he was chief editor of *Komsomolets Ukrainy*, organ of the Communist youth. In 1928–9 he was a member of the CPWU Central Committee. He spent the years 1930–3 in Polish prisons. In 1934 he became a member of the CPWU Politburo and leader of the party. In 1939 he was in Prague and emigrated to England before the Nazi invasion. He died in London in 1943.

77. In 1948–68, Roman Werfel was a prominent journalist and a member of the leadership of the Polish United Workers' Party.
78. A letter of "Gert" (Roman Werfel) to the CPWU Central Committee, March 1929, in response to charges of factional activity.
79. A letter from the director of the CPP Central Committee's Jewish Bureau dated 14 April 1929, signed Feliks (identity not established), to the Politburo of the CC CPWU, AM CA KC PZPR, 1356/11.
80. Bill of indictment of the District Prosecutor in Lviv, 26 February 1929, CA KC PZPR, 1356/9.
81. "Velykyi politychnyi protses u Lvovi" *Sel-Rob*, no. 126 (1929): 3–4.
82. Kaufman was clearly thinking of Żeromski's latest novel, *Przedwiośnie* (Early Spring) (1925), which caused a considerable stir in Polish society. The novel portrayed a Polish intellectual who, through his participation in the Polish-Soviet War of 1920, comes to know Soviet Russia and is caught up in the Communist movement.
83. Juliusz Kaden Bandrowski, a legionnaire and later a well known writer close to the Piłsudskiites. His work dealt with the demoralizing effect of power on the ruling Piłsudskiite elite and the exploitation of the workers. Simultaneously, he caricatured leftist opposition movements.
84. "Velykyi politychnyi protses."
85. Letter of the CC CPWU on the political attitude of the accused,"to all members of the CPWU," no date, AM CA KC PZPR, 1356/9.
86. Letter dated 25 January 1930, Lviv, signed "B," AM CA KC PZPR, 1356/9.
87. *Ibid.*
88. Letter from the CC CPWU to the CC CP(B)U, 24 October 1930, CA KC PZPR, 165/IV–21.
89. *Nasha pravda*, no. 1–2 (1928).
90. These exaggerated statements came primarily from Vasylkiv. For example, he said that "the Kaganovich leadership has created Shumskyism as a screen to hide the aggressiveness of its great power Russian chauvinism [and at the same time] to consolidate the position of its reverse side, Ukrainian nationalism." *Nasha pravda*, no. 1–2 (1928): 62.
91. One must remember that in mid-1928 Kaganovich was recalled from Ukraine and Stanislav Kosior took over as first secretary of the CP(B)U Central Committee.

92. "Rezoliutsiia X plenumu," *Nasha pravda*, no. 3–8 (1928): 6–31.
93. Vasylkiv's letter of self-criticism, pages 238 and 243.
94. "Rezoliutsiia X plenumu."
95. "Rezoliutsiia Zizdu," *Nashe slovo*, no. 32 (1928): 1.
96. Police report on the Selrob-Right Congress, CA MSW inw. 227, 36a: 417–22.
97. *Nashe slovo*, no. 43 (1928): 3.
98. Report on the nationalities in the Lublin region given at a *starostas*' conference in Tomaszów, 23 November 1928, CA MSW inw. 222, 36a: 399–402.
99. *Do vsikh partiinykh orhanizatsii, do vsikh chleniv Kommunistychnoi partii Zakhidnoi Ukrainy. Vidozva IX Konferentsii KPZU* (Lviv, 1928), 1–10.
100. *Ibid.*, 8. At this time the Soviets began a press campaign against the Bukharinites (the so-called right) without, however, giving the names of the leaders.
101. *Ibid.*, 4 and 9.
102. *Ibid.*, 4.
103. *Ibid.*, 7.
104. *Ibid.*, 8.
105. *Ibid.*, 10.
106. A. Seniuk, "Zaiava," *Selrob*, no. 69 (1928).
107. See, for example, Bilensky's application of 25 May 1928. He was a former Borotbist and had been a member of the party since 1920. AM CA KC PZPR, 1356/13/309.
108. *Kultura*, no. 10 (1930): 200.
109. Kuzma [S...ki], "Brief aus Polen," *Die Fahne des Kommunismus*, no. 16 (1928): 151–2.
110. Turiansky's authorship is confirmed in *Uchwała III Zjazdu KPZU* (Lviv, 1928), 34. It is also evident from Turiansky's distinctive interpretation of various phenomena.
111. Kuzma [S...ki], "Brief," 151.
112. R. Kuzma [Turiansky], "Metody kahanovychivskoi borotby proty 'shumskivskoi' KPZU," *Nasha pravda*, no. 1–2 (1928): 96.
113. *Informatsiinyi biuleten hrupy b. KPZU-bilshosty* (April 1929): 3.
114. Muraviev was a member of the Russian Left SRs and the commander of the Red Army division which took Kiev in January 1918. He was known for his appeal to the inhabitants of the city in which he ignored the Ukrainian question and for his repressive measures against Ukrainians. Several months later he perished attempting to organize an uprising against the Soviets on the Volga.
115. *Informatsiinyi biuleten* (April 1929): 4.
116. Radchenko was a member of the CP(B)U Central Committee and an opponent of Shumsky.
117. R. Kuzma [Lazarkevych], "Vasylkivshchyna iak zakhidnoukrainska modyfikatsiia ukapizmu," *Kultura*, no. 9 (1930): 12.

118. *Ibid.*, 17.
119. *Informatsiinyi biuleten* (April 1929): 6.
120. *Ibid.*, 7.
121. *Ibid.* Activists who led the left opposition in the Communist Party of Germany. As indicated, Vasylkiv believed that they had been inspired by Moscow.
122. *Informatsiinyi biuleten* (April 1929). Heinrich Brandler was removed from power in the CPG in 1924 and led the right opposition in the party. In 1928 he was elected first secretary of the central committee (in place of Thälmann), but the Comintern executive committee declared the election invalid. Stalin came to Thälmann's defence.
123. *Informatsiinyi biuleten* (April 1929).
124. *Ibid.* The views of Brandler and Thalheimer were defended, we remember, in *Nasha pravda* in 1924.
125. *Informatsiinyi biuleten* (April 1929): 7.
126. *Zemlia i volia*, no. 1 (1929): 10. *Zemlia i volia* was an official CPWU organ (initially it belonged to the splinter group).
127. "Rezoliutsiia TsK KPZU z 17 III 1929" (the text erroneously gives 1927), *Zemlia i volia*, no. 1 (1929): 11.
128. The district committee in Lviv branded Vasylkiv's admission to the prison commune an instance of right-wing deviationism. See the letter of the district committee of Lviv (undated), AM CA KC PZPR, 1356/8/271.
129. *Informatsiinyi biuleten* (April 1929): 6.
130. *Kultura*, no. 11–12 (1930): 14.
131. R. Kuzma [Lazarkevych], "Pro ukhyly v ukrainskim natsionalnim pytanni," *Kultura*, no. 7–11 (1929); "Vasylkivshchyna iak zakhidnoukrainska modyfikatsiia ukapizmu," *Kultura*, no. 7–12 (1930).
132. *Kultura*, no. 7–12 (1929): 54.
133. Kuzma [Lazarkevych], "Vasylkivshchyna," 11.
134. "To the CPWU Central Committee" (copy to the CPP Central Committee). The letter is dated 2 June 1930 and signed by Turiansky. AM CA KC PZPR, 1356/11/962.
135. *Ibid.*, 963.
136. Interview with M. Tesliuk, Lviv, 18 September 1967.
137. A. Hoshovsky, "Zasnovnyky i diiachi KPZU," *Ukrainskyi kalendar* (Warsaw, 1965), 190.
138. *Ibid.*, 191.
139. S. Volynets, "SS striletska dyviziia Halychyna" in *Kalendar. Za narod* (1944), 46.

Conclusion

In the conflict between the three Communist parties presented here, all sides appealed to Lenin. Despite their familiarity with Lenin's works, however, and their sincere admiration for him, their political differences on a series of issues gradually increased. For each side was guided not only by ideological principles, but also by the experience of its own social and national milieu.

For the CPP the point of departure was the interests of the Polish revolution, with reliance, above all, on the Polish working class. Its chief concern was to win the broadest possible support of that class and it attempted to remove all ideological and organizational hindrances to achieving that goal. The CPWU, led by the Vasylkivists, was a Communist party, but was strongly influenced by the revolutionary Ukrainian peasantry and the intensely national Ukrainian leftist intelligentsia. It tried hard to maintain and broaden its influence among these groups, fought for the independence of the party and pleaded the Ukrainian cause in the Comintern. The CPWU refused to support the struggle for more democratic methods of rule within the Comintern which the CPP waged at the end of 1923 and the beginning of 1924, though, as revealed later, Vasylkiv himself was more critical of these methods than was the CPP.

Within the CP(B)U the need to implement a broad Ukrainianization was fully acknowledged only in 1925, and even then it was carried out cautiously in order to retain the support of the towns, which had been the mainstay of Soviet power during the revolution and the civil war. Also, still fresh was the memory of the bloody war with Ukrainian nationalists. The party was fearful and suspicious of the West Ukrainian peasantry. It valued the latter's pro-Soviet attitude, but feared its outbursts of national extremism. These considerations had their reflection in the ideological sphere. Thus, the process of Ukrainianization was accompanied by certain theories, such as Zatonsky's interpretation of recent Ukrainian history, which was deeply alien to the West Ukrainian Communists, who saw it as proof of the existence of Russian nationalism in the CP(B)U ("permanent *rusotiapstvo*").

An essential element in the thought of the West Ukrainian Communists was the creation of a strong Ukrainian urban culture or, as they called it, a proletarian culture. Only such a culture, in their view, would enable the continuation and renewal of Ukrainian national life and sever permanently the ties between Ukrainian political thought and the backward rural tradition. They put this demand firmly to their Soviet comrades. It was on this basis that they criticized the bureaucratic methods of Ukrainianization and waged their courageous struggle against Russian nationalism. They did, however, exaggerate some aspects of CP(B)U policy, for example in their view that the political line of the CP(B)U in the years 1926–7 called for the expulsion from Soviet Ukraine "of the best Ukrainian Communist forces" (i.e., the Ukrainian leftist intelligentsia). They certainly lacked the proof for such a statement. It was rather a prophecy of what was to occur later under different political conditions. It was equally unfair to accuse the CPP of Polish nationalism, but the CPWU probably misunderstood its parent party's tactics. It was not, however, these exaggerations (they came most often from Vasylkiv) which were the decisive factor in the political death of the Vasylkivists. The growing centralism in Soviet political life and in the Comintern led inevitably to their dissolution. Several years later the existence of a party that differed politically from the average Comintern section was an impossibility. The lack of a left-wing party strongly connected with the Ukrainian cause, as the CPWU-Vasylkivists had been, warped the political structure of West Ukrainian society and played a major role in the subsequent fate of that people.

Bibliography

Archival Materials

A. Centralne Archiwum KC PZPR

1. CPWU
    - Minutes of the sessions of the Third Conference of the CPWB (1926)
2. CPP
    - Minutes of the sessions of the Third Congress
    - Minutes of the sessions of the Fourth Congress
    - Materials of the CC plenum, February 1926
    - Materials of the Second CC plenum, October 1927
3. CPWU
    - Minutes of the sessions of the Second Congress
    - Minutes of the sessions of the Third Congress
    - Materials of the CC plenum, June 1924
    - Materials of the CC plenum, November 1924
    - Materials of the Sixth Extraordinary Conference, December 1924
    - Materials of the CC plenum, June 1925
    - Materials of the CC plenum, August 1925
    - Materials of the CC plenum, February 1926
    - Materials of the CC plenum, March 1926
    - Expanded meeting of the CC, June 1926
    - Materials of the CC plenum, July 1926
    - Materials of the CC plenum, October 1926

Materials of the CC plenum, January 1927
Materials of the CC plenum, April 1927
Materials of the CC plenum, October 1927
Materials of the (pro-Comintern) CPWU meeting, January 1928
Monthly reports of the CC CPWU on the situation in Western Ukraine, 1923–6
Monthly and quarterly organizational reports of the CC CPWU, 1924–6
Letters, notes, reports of CPWU activists, memoranda, declarations, 1920–9
Letters of CPWU leadership bodies to the CC CPP, CC CP(B)U and ECCI, 1921–9
Resolutions and reports of meetings of district committees, 1924–7
Materials of the Political Secretariat of the ECCI concerning the CPWU, 1927
Minutes of the sessions of the Polish-Baltic *Ländersekretariat* of the ECCI, 1928
Archives of the lawyer Teodor Durach, Materials concerning the Volodymyr-Volynskyi trial
Minutes of the meetings of the Socialist Deputies' Faction of the Ukrainian Club, 1923–4
Memoirs and interviews (recorded in 1962) of A. Hoshovsky, T. Maryshchuk, O. Szechter, J. Zawadzki. Memoirs of Ostap Dłuski [Adolf Langer] and Leon Rozenman

B. *Archiwum Akt Nowych*
Reports of the ministry of internal affairs on national minorities, 1927

C. *Centralne Archiwum Ministerstwa Spraw Wewnętrznych w Warszawie*
Reports and papers of the security divisions of *Województwo* administrations: a) Volhynia, 1923–7; b) Lublin, 1924–8

D. *Centralne Archiwum Wojskowe w Warszawie*
Reports and intelligence concerning Communist influences on the soldiers of General J. Haller's army

E. *Partarkhiv Instytutu istorii partii TsK KPU (Kiev)*
1. Correspondence of the CC CPWU with the Foreign Bureau to Aid the Revolutionary Movement in Western Ukraine (Kharkiv)
2. Meetings of the Politburo of the CC CP(B)U in matters concerning the CPWU

3. Correspondence of CC CPWU members with the secretariat of the CC CPWU

F. *Arkhiv Instituta Marksizma-Leninizma pri TsK KPSS*
Minutes of the sessions of the ECCI Secretariat, 1926

Published Sources

Borotba trudiashchykh Volyni za vyzvolennia z-pid hnitu panskoi Polshchi i vozziednannia z Radianskoiu Ukrainoiu (1921–1928). Zbirnyk dokumentiv i materialiv. Part 1. Lutsk, 1957.

Budivnytstvo Radianskoi Ukrainy. Zbirnyk. Volume 1: *Za leninsku natsionalnu polityku.* Kharkiv, n.d.

XIV Sezd Vsesoiuznoi kommunisticheskoi partii (bolshevikov) 18–31 XII 1925. Stenograficheskii otchet. Moscow-Leningrad, 1926.

IV Konferencja Komunistycznej Partii Polski (24 XI-23 XII 1925). Protokoły obrad i uchwały. Parts 1 and 2. Warsaw, 1972.

IV Zjazd KPP. Uchwały. Warsaw, 1928.

Desiatyi Sezd RKPb, mart 1921. Stenograficheskii otchet. Moscow, 1963.

Dokumenty i materiały do historii stosunków polsko-radzieckich. Volume 4. Warsaw, 1965.

Do vsikh partiinykh orhanizatsii, do vsikh chleniv Komunistychnoi partii Zakhidnoi Ukrainy. Vidozva IX Konferentsii KPZU. Lviv, 1928.

II Zjazd Komunistycznej Partii Robotniczej Polski (19 IX- 2 X 1923). Protokoły obrad i uchwały. Warsaw, 1968.

Kommunisticheskaia partiia Ukrainy v rezoliutsiiakh i resheniiakh sezdov i konferentsii. Kiev, 1959.

KPP. Uchwał i rezolucje. Volume 1. Warsaw, 1959.

KPZR w rezolucjach i uchwałach zjazdów, konferencji i posiedzeń plenarnych Komitetu Centralnego. Part 1. Warsaw, 1956.

"Majowe wystąpienie Piłsudskiego i taktyka naszej partii." *Nowy Przegląd*, 1926 (reprint: Warsaw, 1961).

Mały Rocznik Statystyczny 1939. Warsaw, 1939.

Materiały Egzekutywy Międzynarodówki Komunistycznej w sprawie Polski. N.p., [1925].

XI Sezd RKPb. Stenograficheskii otchet. Moscow, 1961.

Piatnadtsatyi Sezd VKPb. Dekabr 1927 goda. Stenograficheskii otchet. Volume 1. Moscow, 1961.

Piatyi vsemirnyi Kongress Kommunisticheskogo Internatsionala. Stenograficheskii otchet. Part 2: *Prilozheniia.* Moscow, 1925.
Pid praporom Zhovtnia. Vplyv velykoi zhovtnevoi sotsialistychnoi revoliutsii na pidnesennia revoliutsiinoho rukhu v Zakhidnii Ukraine, 1917–1920. Dokumenty i materialy. Lviv, 1957.
Pid praporom Zhovtnia . . . 1921–1928. . . . Lviv, 1964.
"Plenums des IKKI: Ausschlus der Opposition aus der KP der Westukraine." *Internationale Presse-Korrespondenz* 2, no. 21 (1928).
Postanovleniia III Konferentsii Kommunisticheskoi partii Zapadnoi Belorussii. Izdanie TsK KPZB, N.p., 1926.
"Postanovy IV Plenumu TsK KPZU 9–11 XI 1924." *Nasha pravda,* no. 9–12 (1924).
Postanovy II Zizdu Komunistychnoi partii Zakhidnoi Ukrainy. Vydannia TsK KPZU. Lviv, 1925.
Postanovy piatoi Konferentsii Komunistychnoi partii Zakhidnoi Ukrainy. Vydannia Tsentralnoho Komitetu KPZU. Lviv, 1924.
Postanovy VIII Konferentsii KPZU. Vydannia TsK KPZU. Lviv, 1928.
Prohrama i orhanizatsiinyi statut Ukrainskoho seliansko-robitnychoho sotsiialistychnoho Obiednannia. "Sel-Rob." Lviv, 1927.
Przeciw rozbijaczom i zdrajcom—za Międzynarodôwką Komunistyczną. Dokumenty i materiały w sprawie prôby rozbicia KPZU. Lviv, 1928.
"Rezoliutsiia X Plenumu [KPZU]." *Nasha pravda,* no. 3–8 (1928).
"Rezoliutsiia plenumu TsK KPZU 3 II 1926." *Nasha pravda,* no. 1–4 (1926).
"Rezoliutsiia Zizdu Selrobu [pravytsi]." *Nashe slovo,* no. 32 (1928).
Shestoi rasshirennyi plenum Ispolkoma Kominterna. Stenograficheskii otchet. Moscow, 1927.
"VI Plenum TsK KPZU. Orhanizatsiina rezoliutsiia." *Nasha pravda,* no. 1–3 (1924).
VII Konferentsiia KPZU (rezoliutsiia). Vydannia TsK KPZU. Lviv, 1927.
Sotsialnyi i natsionalnyi sostav VKPb. Itogi vsesoiuznoi partiinoi perepisi. Moscow, 1927.
III Zjazd KPP. Sprawozdanie z obrad. N.p., [1925].
Uchwały IV Konferencji KPP. Nakładem KC KPP. Warsaw, 1926.
Uchwały III Zjazdu KPP. Nakładem KC KPP. Warsaw, 1925.
Uchwały III Zjazdu KPZU. Lviv, 1929.
Ukraina. Statystychnyi spravochnyk. TsSU USSR. Kharkiv, 1925.
"Wybory komunalne w województwie wołyńskim w roku 1927."

Supplement to *Dziennik Urzędowy Województwa Wołyńskiego*, no. 2 (1928).
"Wybory samorządowe." *Sprawy Narodowościowe* 7–9, no. 4 (1927).
Z istorii revoliutsiinoho rukhu v Lvovi. Dokumenty i materialy 1917–1939. Lviv, 1957.

Contemporary Periodical Press

Bilshovyk Ukrainy. 1921–8.
Biuleten A[git]propa TsK KPZU. 1924.
Biuleten TsK KPZU. 1925.
Biuletyn WAP. Seria Historyczna. 1958.
Bolshevik. 1926–7.
Droga. 1926.
Die Fahne des Kommunismus. 1928.
Informatsiinyi biuleten hrupy b. KPZU-bilshosty. 1929.
Internationale Presse-Korrespondenz. 1928.
Kommunisticheskii Internatsional. 1927.
Kultura. 1924–30.
Kultura i pobut. 1926.
Kurier Warszawski. 1933.
Nasha pravda. 1923–30.
Nashe slovo. 1927.
Nashe zhyttia. 1923–7.
Nash stiah. 1922.
Nova kultura. 1923.
Nowy Przegląd. 1925–7.
Prapor marksyzmu. 1928.
Pravda. 1929.
Selrob. 1928.
Sprawy Narodowościowe. 1927.
Svitlo. 1925.
Trybuna. 1921.
Volia naroda. 1924–7.
Walka Klas. 1928.
Zemlia i volia. 1929.

Reference Works

Entsyklopediia Ukrainoznavstva. Edited by V. Kubijovyč and

Z. Kuzelia. Volume 1. Part 2. Munich-New York, 1949.
Parlament Rzeczypospolitej Polskiej 1919–1927. Edited by H. Mościcki and W. Dzwonkowski. Warsaw, 1928.
Rzepecki, K., and T. Rzepecki. *Sejm i Senat 1928–1933*. Poznań, 1928.
Ukrainska Zahalna Entsyklopediia. 3 volumes. Lviv-Stanyslaviv-Kolomyia, n.d.

Other Literature

Andrusiak, M. *Narysy z istorii moskvofilstva*. Lviv, 1935.
Arsenych, P. "K. Savrych." *Ukrainskyi istorychnyi zhurnal*, no. 1 (1969).
Baczyński, M. *Kwestia mniejszościowa*. Lviv, 1935.
Bachynsky, P. "U borotbi za zdiisnennia leninskoi natsionalnoi polityky." *Ukrainskyi istorychnyi zhurnal*, no. 6 (1968).
Bocheński, A. "Położyć kres szaleństwu." *Polityka* (formerly *Bunt Młodych*), no. 23 (1937).
Bratun, A. "Natsionalnyi front." *Nashe zhyttia*, no. 10 (1926).
Bukshovany, O. [O. Ivanovych]. "Vid sabotazhu do sotsiialnoi revoliutsii." *Nasha pravda*, no. 2–3 (1924).
Chernetsky, A. *Spomyny z moho zhyttia*. London, 1964.
"Chy ie potribni rizni politychni partii?" *Volia naroda*, no. 294 (1926).
Czeszejko-Sochacki, J. [J. Bratkowski]. *Na drogach nacjonalizmu, oportunizmu i zdrady*. Lviv, 1928.
Danieluk, A. [E. Stefański]. "Od komunizma do bagna drobnomieszczańskiego nacjonalizmu." *Walka Klas*, no. 1–3 (1928).
Durdella, M. *Za iednist Selroba*. Leaflet. Lviv, 23 January 1928.
"Dva kroky." *Nashe zhyttia*, no. 47 (1924).
Feliński, M. "Klub Ukraiński." In *Parlament Rzeczypospolitej Polskiej 1919–1927*. Warsaw, 1928.
Feliński, M. "Ukraińskie Robitnycze Socjalistyczne Objednannie (Selrob)." *Sprawy Narodowościowe*, no. 5–6 (1927).
Głąbiński, S. *Wspomnienia polityczne*. Part 1. Pelpin, 1939.
Gorin, P. Review of: M. Iavorsky, *Istoriia Ukrainy v styslomu narysi*. In *Pravda*, no. 34 (1929).
"Lyst do redaktsii." *Prapor marksyzmu*, no. 5 (1929).
Grudowa, H. "Sprawa polska na V Kongresie Międzynarodówki Komunistycznej." *Z pola walki*, no. 4 (1962).

Halushko, Ie. "H. Ivanenko (Baraba)." *Ukrainskyi istorychnyi zhurnal*, no. 6 (1963).

Narysy istorii ideolohichnoi ta orhanizatsiinoi diialnosti KPZU v 1919–1928. Lviv, 1965.

Hirchak, Ie. *Shumskizm i rozlam v KPZU*. Kharkiv, 1928.

Hołówko, T. "Emigracja ukraińska w Czechach." *Robotnik*, no. 60 (1925).

"Metody i drogi sanacji stosunków we Wschodniej Galicji." *Droga*, no. 7–8 (1926).

"Mniejszoście narodowe." *Trybuna*, no. 43, 48, 49 (1921).

Holubnychy, Vsevolod. "Outline History of the Communist Party of Ukraine." In *Soviet Regional Economics: Selected Works of Vsevolod Holubnychy*. Edited by Iwan S. Koropeckyj. Edmonton, 1982.

Horwitz, M. [H. Walecki]. *Wybôr pism*. Volume 2. Warsaw, 1967.

Hoshovsky, A. "Ni slova pro spokii." *Ukrainskyi kalendar* (Warsaw), 1967.

"Pamiati zasnovnyka KPSH—Karla Maksymovycha." *Nasha kultura* (supplement to *Nashe slovo*), no. 1 (1967).

"Zasnovnyky i diiachi KPZU." *Ukrainskyi kalendar* (Warsaw), 1965.

Humaniuk, M. *Nash Kuzma. Za voliu narodnu*. Lviv, 1956.

"Iak povstaly natsionalni rukhy." *Volia naroda*, no. 286 (1926).

"Iak povstav kapitalizm." *Volia naroda*, no. 289 (1926).

Iavosky, M. "Donkikhotstvo chy rusotiapstvo." *Prapor marksyzmu*, no. 2 (1929).

Ievdokymenko, V. *Krytyka ideinykh osnov ukrainskoho burzhuaznoho natsionalizmu*. Second edition. Kiev, 1968.

Ilnytzkyj, R. *Deutschland und die Ukraine 1934–1945*. Volume 1. Munich, 1955.

Iwański, G. "Z dziejów Komunistycznej Partii Galicji Wschodniej." *Z pola walki*, no. 4 (1967).

Jabłoński, H. "Druga Rzeczpospolita a Galicja Wschodnia." *Wiedza i Życie*, no. 10 (1948).

Kaganovich, L. "Rozlam v KPZU i natsionalna polityka KPbU." *Nasha pravda*, no. 4–5 (1928).

Karpenko, O. "Do pytannia pro vynyknennia i orhanizatsiine oformlennia Komunistychnoi partii Skhidnoi Halychyny." *Z istorii zakhidnoukrainskykh zemel*. Volume 2. Kiev, 1957.

Kaufman, A. [Adam]. "V spravi orhanizatsiinoi polityky KPZU." *Nasha pravda*, no. 4–5 (1928).

"Kholmskyi povitovyi Zizd Selianskoho soiuzu." *Nashe zhyttia*, no. 35 (1924).

"Khruniada." *Nashe zhyttia*, no. 10 (1926).

Khrutsky, S. "Posly USDP v roli prorokiv." *Nashe zhyttia*, no. 29 (1924).

Khvylia, A. *Proty ukrainskoho i rosiiskoho natsionalizmu.* [Kharkiv,] 1926.

Vid ukhylu u prirvu. Kharkiv, 1928.

"Zradnyky." *Bilshovyk Ukrainy*, no. 7 (1928).

Khvyliovy, M. "Apolohety pysaryzmu. (Do problemy kulturnoi revoliutsii)." *Kultura i pobut*, no. 9–13 (1926).

Korolivsky, S., M. Rubach and N. Suprunenko. *Pobeda sovetskoi vlasti na Ukraine.* Moscow, 1967.

Kos. "Proty nastroiv." *Nasha pravda*, no. 1 (1924).

Kotovich-Klenovich, L. [K. Viniarsky]. "Z pryvodu pevnoi pomylkovoi kontseptsii." *Nasha pravda*, no. 1–2 (1930).

Kowalski, J. "Rozwój sytuacji wewnętrznej w KPP po przewrocie majowym 1926 (o sporze między 'większością' a 'mniejszością')." *Z pola walki*, no. 4 (1963).

Zarys historii polskiego ruchu robotniczego. Warsaw, 1962.

"Krasnoie znamia v Lunyntsi." (Editorial.) *Nashe zhyttia*, no. 5 (1926).

Kravets, M. *Narysy robitnychoho rukhu v Zakhidnii Ukraini 1921–1939.* Kiev, 1959.

Krilyk, O. [O. Vasylkiv]. "Do Biura Politychnoho TsK KPZU. (Zaiava)." *Zemlia i volia*, no. 1 (1929). Second expanded edition.

"KPRP na V-mu Kongresi Kominternu." *Nasha pravda*, no. 9–12 (1924).

"KPZU i druhyi Zizd KPRP." *Nasha pravda*, no. 1 (1923).

"Na pravylnyi shliakh." *Nasha pravda*, no 4–8 (1924).

"Natsionalne vyzvolennia a ukrainske dribnomishchanstvo." *Nasha pravda*, no. 1 (1924).

Kulichenko, M. "Taktika bolshevistskoi partii v sviazi s osobennostiami razvitiia sotsialisticheskoi revoliutsii na Ukraine." *Voprosy istorii*, no. 10 (1967).

"Kulturna sviaz." *Svitlo*, no. 1–2 (1925).

Kulykovsky, P. "Revoliutsiia, horozhanska viina i zbroine povstannia (na pidstavi tvoriv Lenina)." *Nasha pravda*, no. 2–3 (1924).

Kuzma, R. [N. Lazarkevych]. "Apolohiia i apolohety moskvofilstva." *Kultura*, no. 8–9 (1925).

[S...ki]. "Brief aus Polen." *Die Fahne des Kommunismus*, no. 16 (1928).

[N. Lazarkevych]. "Cherez pryzmu marksivskoi krytyky." *Kultura*, no. 7–8 (1928).

[Komar]. "Do dyskusii z pryvodu pytannia avtonomii." *Nasha pravda*, no. 5 (1926).

[Karpatsky]. "Do pytannia istorychnoi henezy KPZU." *Nasha pravda*, no. 3–8 (1928).

[R. Turiansky]. "Metody kahanovychivskoi borotby proty 'shumskivskoi' KPZU." *Nasha pravda*, no. 3–8 (1928).

[T...i]. "Na manivtsiakh ultra-livoho oportunizmu." *Nasha pravda*, no. 11–12 (1926).

[N. Lazarkevych]. "Pro ukhyly v ukrainskim natsionalnim pytanni." *Kultura*, no. 7–11 (1929).

[N. Lazarkevych]. "U vidpovid 'Voli naroda'. *Kultura*, no. 10–12 (1925).

[N. Lazarkevych]. "Vasylkivshchyna iak zakhidnoukrainska modyfikatsiia ukapizmu." *Kultura*, no. 7–12 (1930).

[N. Lazarkevych]. "Vid obiednannia do uhody." *Kultura*, no. 6–7 (1925).

Kuzmin, M. *Shkola i obrazovanie v Chekhoslovakii*. Moscow, 1971.

Ladan, P. [P. Netiaha]. "Vid porazky do orhanizatsiinoi peremohy (V lavakh Komunistychnoi partii Nimechchyny." *Nasha pravda*, no. 1 (1924).

"Landau, Z., and J. Tomaszewski. *Zarys historii gospodarczej Polski 1918–1939*. Warsaw, 1962.

Larin, Iu. "Ob izvrashcheniiakh pri provedenii natsionalnoi politiki." *Bolshevik*, no. 22–4 (1926); no. 1 (1927).

Lebed, D. *Sovetskaia Ukraina i natsionalnyi vopros za piat let*. Kharkiv, 1924.

Lenin, V. *Collected Works*. 45 volumes. Moscow, 1960–70.

Liubotets, S. "Shevchenko—patron natsionalnykh i sotsiialnykh zmahan ukrainskoho narodu." *Nashe zhyttia*, no. 11 (1926).

Lozynsky, M. *Halychyna 1918–1920*. Vienna, 1922.

Za derzhavnu nezalezhnist Halychyny. Vienna, 1921.

Luxemburg, R. *The Russian Revolution and Leninism or Marxism?* Ann Arbor, 1961.

Madajczyk, Cz. *Burżuazyjno-obszarnicza reforma rolna w Polsce. 1918–1939*. Warsaw, 1956.

Majstrenko, Iwan. *Borotbism: A Chapter in the History of Ukrainian Communism*. Research Program on the U.S.S.R. New York, 1954.

Makarewicz, J. *Mniejszości narodowe*. Lviv, 1924.

Makivka, S. "Iednaimosia, ale iak?" *Nashe zhyttia*, no. 5 (1926).

"Krainia pora." *Nashe zhyttia*, no. 36 (1926).

"Zemelna reforma." *Nashe zhyttia*, no. 3 (1926).

Mauersberg, S. *Szkolnictwo powszechne dla mniejszości narodowych w Polsce 1918–1939*. Wrocław-Cracow-Warsaw, 1968.

Mazlakh, S., and V. Shakhrai. *On the Current Situation in the Ukraine*. Ann Arbor, 1970.

Mikulicz, S. *Prometeizm w polityce II Rzeczypospolitej*. Warsaw, 1971.

Minc, P. [A]. "Zhydivske seredovyshche i zavdannia KPZU." *Nasha pravda*, no. 8 (1926).

Mniejszości narodowe w wyborach do Sejmu i Senatu w 1928 r. Wydział Narodowościowy Ministerstwa Spraw Wewnętrznych. Warsaw, 1928.

Mysłek, H. *Kościół katolicki w Polsce 1918–1939*. Warsaw, 1966.

"Nashe stanovyshche v natsionalnomu pytanni." *Volia naroda*, no. 295 (1926).

"Nauka nimetskykh podii." *Nasha pravda*, no. 2–3 (1924).

Nazarenko, I., *et al. Ocherki istorii Kommunisticheskoi partii Ukrainy*. Kiev, 1964.

Pavlyk, M. *Moskvofilstvo ta ukrainofilstvo sered avstro-ruskoho narodu*. Lviv, 1906.

"Pershyi kraievyi Zizd Partii Narodnoi voli." *Volia naroda*, no. 286 (1926).

P. K. "Novyi kurs u vnutrishniomu zhytti RKP." *Nasha pravda*, no. 1 (1924).

Pobóg-Malinowski, W. *Najnowsza historia polityczna Polski. 1914–1945*. Volume 2. Part 1. London, 1956.

Popov, M. [N. Łowicki]. "Co to jest szumskizm?" *Walka Klas*, no. 1–3 (1928).

"Dovesty borotbu do kintsia." *Nasha pravda*, no. 4–5 (1928).

Ocherk istorii Kommunisticheskoi partii (bolshevikov) Ukrainy. Kharkiv, 1929.

Ocherk istorii vsesoiuznoi kommunisticheskoi partii bolshevikov. Moscow-Leningrad, 1927.

Posłowie rewolucyjni w Sejmie. Wybór przemowień, interpelacji i wniosków. Warsaw, 1961.

"Proch z kyrynnykamy i intryganamy." *Nashe slovo*, 25 January 1927.

"Pro natsionalnu-terytoriialnu avtonomiiu." *Nasha pravda*, no. 6–7 (1926).

Pryideshyn, A. "Hnat Mykhailychenko." *Nova kultura*, no. 6 (1923).

"Radisna Pakhota." *Volia naroda*, no. 300 (1926).

Radziejowski, J. "Kwestia narodowa w partii komunistycznej na Ukrainie Radzieckiej." *Przegląd Historyczny*, no. 3 (1971).

Review of: Halushko, Ie. *Narysy istorii ideolohichnoi ta*

orhanizatsiinoi diialnosti KPZU v 1919–1928. In *Z pola walki*, no. 4 (1966).

"Roman Rosdolsky: Man, Activist and Scholar." *Science and Society*, no. 2 (1978).

"R. Rozdolsky—'Prokopovych'." *Nashe slovo*, 4 February 1968.

"Ruch narodowy i rewolucyjny na Ukrainie w okresie działalności Centralnej Rady (marzec 1917-kwiecień 1918)." *Studia z dziejów ZSRR i Europy Środkowej* 9 (1973).

Rafes, M. *Dva goda revoliutsii na Ukraine (Evoliutsiia i raskol Bunda)*. Moscow, 1920.

Ravich-Cherkassky, M. *Istoriia Kommunisticheskoi partii (bolshevikov) Ukrainy*. Kharkiv, 1923.

Rosdolsky, R. [V. S.]. "Do istorii ukrainskoho livo-sotsiialistychnoho rukhu v Halychyni (Pidchasvoienni 'Drahomanivky' 1916–18)." *Vpered*, no. 3–4 (1951).

[A. Tenet]. "Halytskyi vulkan." *Nash stiah*, no. 4 (1922).

[T. Prokopovych]. "Halytskyi vyborchyi konflikt i nashe stanovyshche." *Nash stiah*, no. 4 (1922).

[T. Prokopovych]. "V. Shakh-Rai contra Lienin. (Krytyka ukapistychnoi krytyky)." *Nash stiah*, no. 4 (1922).

"Rozbyvachi seliansko-robitnychoi iednosty." *Nashe zhyttia*, no. 38 (1927).

Savrych, K. [K. Maksymovych]. "Istoriia KPZU v natsionalistychnomu osvitlenni M. Levytskoho." *Nasha pravda*, no. 1–2 (1928).

Savrych, K. [K. Hak]. "Naiblyzhchi zavdannia nashoi partii." *Nasha pravda*, no. 9–12 (1924).

[K. Maksymovych]. "Zaiava." *Nasha pravda*, no. 1–2 (1928).

Seniuk, A. "Zaiava." *Selrob*, no. 63 (1928).

"Shche na vyborchomu fronti." *Nove zhyttia*, no. 32 (1927).

Shygymata, P. "Fakty do biohrafii M. Khvyliovoho." *Vpered*, no. 2 (1955).

Skrypnyk, M. "Do teorii borotby dvokh kultur." *Nasha pravda*, no. 6–7 (1926).

"Natsionalistychnyi ukhyl v KPZU. Dopovid na plenumi TsK KPbU 7 VI 1927." In *Dzherela ta prychyny rozlamu v KPZU*. Kharkiv, 1928.

"Pidsumky borotby z natsionalistychnoiu zradoiu." In *Statti i promovy*. Volume 2. Kharkiv, 1928.

"Smert natsionalizmu." *Nova kultura*, no. 2–3 (1929).

Solchanyk, R. "The Comintern and the Communist Party of Western Ukraine, 1919–1928." *Canadian Slavonic Papers*, no. 2 (1981).

"The Communist Party of Western Ukraine, 1919–1938." Ph.D.

dissertation: University of Michigan, 1973.
"The Foundation of the Communist Movement in Eastern Galicia, 1919–1921." *Slavic Review*, no. 4 (1970).
"Revolutionary Marxism in Galicia before 1918." *East European Quarterly*, no. 1 (1976).
Srokowski, K. *Sprawa narodowościowa na Kresach Wschodnich.* Cracow, 1924.
Stalin, J. *Works*. 13 volumes. Moscow, 1952–5.
Tesliuk, M. "Na shliakhu bilshovyzatsii KPZU (II Zizd KPZU)." In *Na choli vyzvolnoi borotby. Spohady kolyshnikh aktyvnykh diiachiv KPZU.* Kiev, 1965.
Tomaszewski, J. *Z dziejôw Polesia.* Warsaw, 1963.
Tymieniecka, A. *Polityka Polskiej Partii Socjalistycznej w latach 1924–1928.* Warsaw, 1969.
Die ukrainische Nationalfrage. Selbstverlag des ZK KPZU. Lviv, 1928.
Valnytsky, K. *Do istorii livo- i pravo-selrobivskykh ukhyliv.* [Lviv,] 1928.
"Po dyskusii." *Volia naroda*, no. 255 (1925).
"U vidpovid 'Kulturi'." *Volia naroda*, no. 250 and 254 (1925).
"V dobryi chas." *Nashe zhyttia*, no. 42 (1926).
Vikul, S. "Do korinnia natsionalizmu ta oportunizmu v KPZU." In *KPbU pro rozbyvachiv KPZU.* Vydannia TsK KPZU. Lviv, 1928.
[I. Pavlyshyn]. "Lenin i selianstvo." *Nasha pravda*, no. 2–3 (1924).
[I. Pavlyshyn]. "Pidsumky vyborchoi borotby." *Nasha pravda*, no. 6–7 (1927).
"V natsionalnii spravi." *Volia naroda*, no. 287 (1926).
Volobuev, M. "Do problemy ukrainskoi ekonomiky." *Bilshovyk Ukrainy*, no. 2–3 (1928).
Volynets, S. "SS striletska dyviziia Halychyna." *Kalendar. Za narod.* 1944.
"Voprosy diskussi v KPZU." *Kommunisticheskii Internatsional*, no. 43 (1927).
Warszawski, A. [A. Warski]. *Wybôr pism i przemowień.* Volume 2. Warsaw, 1958.
Witos, W. *Moje wspomnienia.* Volume 3. Paris, 1965.
Zabolotny, Z. *Neskorena Volyn. Narysy z istorii revoliutsiinoho rukhu na Volyni.* Lviv, 1964.
"Za pravilnoe osveshchenie istorii Kommunisticheskoi partii Zapadnoi Ukrainy." *Kommunist*, no. 10 (1963).
Zatonsky, V. "Materiialy do ukrainskoho natsionalnoho pytannia."

Bilshovyk Ukrainy, no. 6 (1927).
"Pershi kroky radianskoi vlady Zakhidnoi Ukrainy." In *KPZU: orhanizator revoliutsiinoi borotby. Spohady kolyshnikh chleniv KPZU*. Lviv, 1958.
"Pro pidsumky ukrainizatsii. Z dopovidi na chervnevomu plenumi TsK KPbU 1926." In *Budivnytstvo Radianskoi Ukrainy. Zbirnyk*. Volume 1: *Za leninsku natsionalnu polityku*. Kharkiv, n.d.
"Źdźbło w cudzym oku. Parę słów odpowiedzi t. Warskiemu." *Nowy Przegląd* (1924–5; reprint: Warsaw, 1959).
"Zizd Selianskoho soiuzu v Bresti." *Nashe zhyttia*, no. 41 (1924).
"Zizd Selianskoho soiuzu v Volodymyri." *Nashe zhyttia*, no. 50 (1924).
"Z temriavy narodnykh relihiinykh viruvan." *Volia naroda*, no. 286 (1926).

Index

8.50